# COLDITZ
The German Story

# COLDITZ
## The German Story

By Reinhold Eggers

Translated and edited by Howard Gee

NEW ENGLISH LIBRARY

TIMES MIRROR

First published in Great Britain by Robert Hale Ltd, in 1961
Reprinted March 1961
Reprinted April 1961
© Reinhold Eggers 1961
© English Translation Robert Hale Ltd.

❋

FIRST NEL PAPERBACK EDITION OCTOBER 1972
Reprinted November 1972
Reprinted June 1973
Reprinted April 1974

❋

*NEL Books are published by*
*New English Library Limited from Barnard's Inn, Holborn, London E.C.1.*
*Made and printed in Great Britain by Hunt Barnard Printing Ltd., Aylesbury, Bucks.*

45001296 4

# CONTENTS

# Preface

COLDITZ IS the most famous of the German prisoner-of-war camps, in the main as a result of the appearance of a number of books and a film about the exploits – which were indeed remarkable and unique – of its inmates. All these books have been written from the prisoner's point of view, and until this present volume no one has told the story of Colditz as seen from the other side.

I was on the Colditz staff for a longer period than any other member – from November 1940 until the castle was engulfed in the Allied advance a few days before the end of the war. First I was a Duty Officer and later the Security Officer. This, together with a knowledge of English and French, gave me as good a chance as anyone on the German staff of knowing what was going on. How little this sometimes was will become evident from this story. In fact it was not until I read some of the accounts of events in Colditz published in Britain and France that I discovered the secrets and results of some of the escape attempts. I think this account may be equally revealing to those who were prisoners in Colditz.

This is a mainly chronological narrative of events in Colditz as I and my colleagues was them. Only occasionally do the general course of the war and outside events in Germany come into the story. At times some mention must be made of them as they had a bearing on the relationship between the staff and guards and the prisoners. So on occasion did political ideology; the prisoners were both anti-German and anti-Nazi, and in the latter respect some of the staff were on common ground with them. My own outlook derived from experiences going back to the First World War.

One unshakeable conviction with which I came home after that struggle was – that the peoples of Europe *must* get away from the self-destruction of successive wars, and learn some-how to co-operate for the sake of their own survival. Towards this end, therefore, I sought, as soon as it became possible, and made, friends in England, France and Switzerland between the wars. So we were able to invite them home and I went abroad on return visits. In particular, I stayed at Cheltenham with some of my pupils, and boys from the grammar school there came over on exchange visits to where I was teaching. Travel was cheap in those days, only 120 marks for a month's stay including the journey, barely ten pounds in sterling. These visits were a great success. Obviously more must follow.

Then came 1933. I was denounced by six of my colleagues at school. The matter went to the Nazi Kommissar in charge of cleaning up the Civil Service and getting rid of anti-party men. I was accused of being leftist, pacifist and an internationalist. There followed questionnaires, difficult interviews – but as I belonged to no political party, my fate was only (though it was severe enough) down-grading from grammar school teacher to council school, and a ban on further promotion. The open doors of our house were closed by higher authority against our friends, and so we shut ourselves up in it too. Visits from abroad came to an end. But I would not be driven against my will into the Partei, or any part of it. If the worst came and I lost my job, I would live and work on the land, of which I owned about five acres.

In 1939 – the Second World War. Those who had de-nounced me stayed at home. My sons were called up. The Old World started on a further plunge downwards. How could we acclaim the Partei and its Leader, we who had come through one fruitless war and still held to our sense of honour and duty and decency? Toll would be levied, we knew, but how much? Like other officers on the Army reserve list, I listened anxiously for my call-up.

It was in a way odd that having been accused of being an internationalist I should spend most of the war in so uniquely 'internationalist' a place as Colditz. There we had officer prisoners of all nations (excepting the Soviet Union). We were all Europeans.

Many incidents have had to be omitted but I have tried to

avoid any omission or perversion of material facts. Such comments as appear are, of course, my personal views. In Colditz itself, now in the East Zone of Germany, the town museum houses the (I might say 'my') collection of escape material, documents and photos which served to train our security personnel. I offer this book in the hope that it may be worthy of a place on the shelf alongside its English and French counterparts.

## CHAPTER I

## Learning the Soft Way

THE NEW arrivals meant more trouble. In the yard surrounded by the ancient walls of the castle we searched them and their kit. Sometimes we found money, keys, maps and civilian clothing – all the contraband of the skilled escaper – but much was probably missed.

The prisoners looked on, amused by our efforts; later when we had them shut in their quarters they watched sardonically through the bars and the wire.

The late gaolers of the newcomers had been happy at the prospect of seeing the last of these troublemakers, but they had feared to lose some of them *en route*. Would we take over at the earliest possible point – or would we at least send reinforcements for their escort, where they changed from the main-line train? The usual pattern was for a party of heavily-guarded prisoners to set out on a two- or three-day journey to the castle, ten, twenty strong, perhaps more. Guards to the same, or even a greater number, would accompany them. Yet again and again, men would disappear on the way in the confusion of travel.

Some would be quickly recaught, some would vanish into occupied territory for so long, some would get away to a neutral country. Some would carry right on and get home. Some on the other hand would disappear for ever, never to be heard of again – perhaps nameless victims of the war.

And so, while ready to do our duty at all times and places, we felt we should cross the bridge only when we came to it, unless the prisoners had, in a sense, dismantled it before we got there! Let Kriegsgefangenenlager So-and-So deliver its charges to our door, into our very yard for preference. Then, and not till then, would we formally take delivery.

A couple of us from the castle met the party at the station

and showed them up through the town, for form's sake. In any case, no one could miss the great mass of buildings high above the town on the east bank of the river. Everyone in the place, the whole district around, certainly every PW camp in Germany knew, that up there was Officer PW Special Camp No. 4C, the only one in the Second World War.

A quarter of an hour from the station, and the group was in the yard ready for searching. Our telephone was at the disposal of their escorting officer, to advise whoever it might be that this or that prisoner had dodged the column. We were sympathetic. These things must be expected.

For this was Colditz and these prisoners were the bad types, undesirables in the eyes of the German High Command. Many of them had already established reputations as disturbers of the peace with their frequent attempts to get out of captivity. That was why they were sent to us.

Well fed and clothed from their parcels from home, men of brains and energy, we gave them in Colditz what they needed above all to synthesise these last in escape planning – time. Not subject to compulsory work, being officer PWs, they had all the time, and not much else, in the world to occupy themselves as they would. The obsession of the escapologist became the profession of the escaper.

We kept them in formally with rifles and bayonets and machineguns, with searchlights to spot them, and microphones to pick them up. We searched them by day and by night, individually and in groups. We censored their mail and their books and their parcels. We checked them with roll-calls, photos and fingerprints. And yet they got out.

We had more than enough on our hands in Colditz, where a hard core of such characters was built up over the war years from 1940 on. From these men we, representatives of the 'holding power', took lessons and instruction in escapology, lessons which we were in duty bound to interrupt. To these men we awarded the appropriate punishment, and our grudging admiration.

As often as not we had just got our current strength under control, or thought we had, when the OKW (the German High Command) threw a new handful of 'aces' into the prisoners' ranks. It took time to trump these men. We repeatedly thought that it was we who held all the cards in the escape game, but time and again the deal changed hands. Astute though we became, it was often the prisoner who was the sharper!

For over four years I was part and parcel of the first hurdle of authority that the Colditz escaper had to beat. But if some-one did not force a way through, someone else would more cleverly effect a move round or over the barrier. The safe, we thought, was locked and double-locked, and wired for sound, vision and shock, with a bare minimum of access, under the tightest control we could devise. At times I held one of the keys, for a while, all of the keys, yet so often it was the prisoner who made the safe get-away, leaving me with the keys and the combination, but neither swag nor swank for my pains.

Colditz was a tough proposition whichever way one looked at it. My introduction to prisoners-of-war was, however, rather a different affair.

In May 1940 I was called up to the reserve battalion of an infantry regiment, with the rank of Lieutenant. At that time, naturally enough, morale everywhere in Germany was sky-high. Two blitzkriegs had finished off Poland and France. Russia was our friend, by treaty. The USA was neutral and well out of it all. Was Hitler after all the genius he claimed to be?

Back in the army I found nothing much had changed in twenty years. Drill, shop, smoking, drink, and everlasting boredom. But officers' food nowadays came from the same kitchen as the men's. We all had the same rations. I noticed another remarkable thing, and was the happier for it, namely the coolness between the Wehrmacht (Armed Forces) and the Partei. We did our duty to, and by, the local bosses, but no more.

Meanwhile, leave was good that first summer of the war.

By the end of the summer we all got postings. Some officers went to 404 Division in Poland. Some went to France. I was over fifty now, and in a way a specialist, with my languages. And so Fate picked me for special treatment. In August I was sent on an interpreters' course at Dresden. In September I went to Hohnstein, in Saxony, as interpreter on the staff of Oflag (Officers' PW Camp) No. 4A.

So far, all right. Had I but known it, my time at Hohnstein was no true introduction to the underworld (there is no better word) of the prisoner-of-war life, with attacks on authority as its guiding theme, and counter-attacks by us, responsible for security, as its counterpoint. As a training course for Colditz, this first experience was a sorry let-down. Life may well be a game, with rules to be kept or broken at the dictates of duty, or with the evasions of expediency, but for life, as well as for sport, training must be hard if one is to stay the course, and even harder if one is to achieve honour on the way or at the finish.

In war, both bodies and minds should be as it were beaten into the one mould, from which come the physical and intellectual weapons of success. The forging of these weapons is the job of the experts in physical training, technical training, and the training of morale, three separates in one singleness of purpose. But at Hohnstein, we were far too truly in clover. The place was, anglice, a cushy billet. There was no conflict, physical or mental, between the Kommandantur or staff side, and the prisoners. There seemed, indeed, to be no problem at all in their handling. So none of us felt we had, or even could possibly need, anything to learn.

Hohnstein lies in the 'little Switzerland' of Saxony, where the streams drain through the sandstone cliffs to the Elbe. The whole area seemed to me so quiet and delightful that I felt the God of War had overlooked it completely. Every prospect pleased, and even my colleagues too!

Our Kommandantur, or Headquarters, was in a post office hostel on the edge of the woods. The town was like any other summer resort, clean and tidy, and mostly made up of guest houses and small 'pensions'. Not very far off, within walking distance, was the 'Brand' inn, up the Polenz valley, and a little further off lay Rathe, on the Elbe, famous for the Karl May Festivals.

The staff in charge of the prison camp was well, though fortuitously, chosen. The camp itself spread over quite a large space on the Hohe Stein, high up above the town, on a plateau surrounded by cliffs and approachable only one way – by a single road.

Our Kommandant was a seventy-two-year-old Lieut-General. During the First World War he had had command of a Württemberg regiment. In the late thirties he had retired to Württemberg as a professor of military science, in which he took an interest still. He used to type out theses and articles far into the night, keeping himself and his staff well up-to-date in his pet subject. The General had seen it all, the military and political rise and fall of the Kaisers, the Republic, and of soldiers and politicians without number, from the end of the nineteenth to well on into the twentieth century. This present war, and all the political background to it within and without our frontiers, were to him but another phase, which to his detached eye might turn out good or bad. But better or worse, he had known both and was prepared accordingly. Through all his life, duty had been his guiding star, and on that he set and held his course, however the winds might shift.

The General's address, when his staff was completed by my arrival, was something as follows: 'I am very happy to have again a staff under me, for the first time since 1918, that has known the rough winds of both peace and war around their ears. I want you, in carrying out your duties in this camp, to keep to that independence of thought and action you must have learnt for yourselves in life. My part I wish to restrict to serious matters only. The adjutant will see that you get as much leave as you are entitled to. No shop at meals, please. We'll have a party in the Mess once a week, and you can play cards and drink. But no gambling. And to keep your minds occupied, each one of you will write an appreciation of some phase of the Napoleonic Wars, as they affected the Kingdom of Saxony. You'll find all the books in Dresden. The camp is yours to control. I'm not going up there on duty matters. When I do visit the place, it'll be treated as an event.'

The prisoners at Hohnstein were in the main French officers, a hundred in number up to the rank of colonel, plus 28 generals. In addition, there were seven Dutch and 27 Polish generals, and orderlies of the different nationalities. They appreciated our General's attitude. Everything was very correct. There was practically no trouble of any kind. The prisoners laid on an entertainment every fortnight, and it was on the occasion of these shows that the Kommandant marked the event with his own visit, accepting regularly an invitation to attend. We laid on wine for all on these afternoons, as our contribution to the amiable atmosphere.

There had only once been an escape attempt from Hohnstein. Two Dutch officers got down the cliff with a fire hose, but were soon retaken. The senior French officer, senior under our regulations by length of service, was a colonel. We lent him a typewriter on parole, and he used to work away at 'The Causes of the Defeat of France'. He put it all down to Marxist Communism, and the consequent failure of French Parliamentary authority, with subsequent deficiencies in Service training and equipment. I remember from those days just one little incident with a hint of unpleasantness in it, absolutely nothing, though, compared with what was to come at Colditz.

The Dutch escapers were transferred to another camp, and at the search before they went, we found a list of all the PWs at Hohnstein, with name, rank, home address and military record. The Kommandant ordered the list to be confiscated, but with some hesitation. We in Security were quite sure of finding a second list concealed on their persons, but the General flatly refused to allow a personal search. 'I will not have any exaggerated interpretation of our duties to search,' he insisted.

We were a bit shocked by his point of view. Later, at Colditz, I wondered how long this state of mind would have lasted! I doubt if there the General could have kept the prisoners under control simply by standing on his rank and on the respect he would have laid claim to as an old soldier. That was naturally all right among Germans, who have a natural awe of the '*alter Soldat*', and with most foreigners of his own age and profession. But there were not many such among the Colditz 'types'.

The General was a great family man, too, with sons ranking high in the Luftwaffe. He was a keen gardener as well and spoke very house-proudly of his family home, and of the other homes he had made for his children and grandchildren. He had a tremendous respect for the common man, and was always ready to learn something from anyone, a gardening tip, a home hint, or some new way of getting interests into children's heads. To me he was unique, for all my eleven years in the army, and in all my civilian life, with his approach to, his quickness of understanding and so his control of, men. I have never known any man, and I must say it again, so respected by all he met casually, or dealt with authoritatively. He was one of the best of our German 'old school'.

There were no politics in our Mess. The Party was in power and the army found itself rehabilitated. We looked no further than that.

Life went on that autumn very pleasantly. The Kommandant picked out for my particular study, as ordered, the siege of Dresden in 1813 and the battle of Kulm and Nollendorf. Here the French and the Prussians under General von Kleist fought so fiercely that only night stopped the battle, and no one knew who had won! It was impossible to see who had most men left on the field. So they spent the night together round great fires, agreeing to fight no more till daylight which showed the French in full retreat, and who now was prisoner of whom!

Nothing disturbed our peaceful routine – we had no 'trouble' at all. We ran the camp at Hohnstein as close to the Geneva Convention as its not very detailed provisions required. This agreement had been initialled in July 1929, and ratified by Hitler in 1934. It placed prisoners-of-war under the discipline and control of the same arm of the service of their captors. It regulated visits by a so-called Protecting Power, who did what they could to see that the Convention and the humanities were observed. In this capacity, the Swiss looked after the British and De-Gaullists, and later the Americans. The Pétain Government looked after the French. The Dutch were under the care of the Swedish Government. But the Poles came under the care of the International Red Cross because, we argued, there was no longer any Polish State.

Personal relations between us Germans and the prisoners at

Hohnstein were in 1940 rather more than just correct. There was quite a degree of what I shortly was to recall as 'old-fashioned' politeness in our dealings. I had, for example, an hour's lesson daily in French from one of their colonels. A Dutch general taught me Dutch, which I found easy, as I speak *plattdeutsch* dialect.

I found the Polish officers difficult of approach, though we got on correctly enough in official matters. One day, an order came authorising a walk outside the camp area for two hours a day, for all prisoners excepting the Poles. This exceptional treatment was given to the Poles because the campaign in Poland had not been fought according to the rules of war by the civilians who had played a part, and therefore Polish prisoners should not receive favours of any kind. Although our Kommandant took pains to give them these reasons as passed down to him, in person, the Poles were naturally enraged at this victimisation, as they saw it. The suggestion that they, the Polish Army, must suffer for the deeds of the Polish people, they rejected as *quatsch* or nonsense, or whatever their own equivalent is. In other respects, they were on the same footing as the other prisoners.

It was all too good to last, but the end came most unexpectedly. In October 1940 I escorted two French officers to Strasbourg for release. One was a diabetes case. The other was a schoolmaster, wanted back by Paris. We left greetings from our General at the Hecht Hotel in Konstanz on the way, where he had stayed a good deal. Strasbourg looked nearly normal. The Rhine bridges, though, were still down. I noticed a synagogue burnt out, and a lot of property marked 'confiscated', but there was no general damage.

The two officers left me with thanks for their good treatment, and on my way back I stopped off at Halle for a couple of days' leave. There was an air-raid alarm that evening over the town, no trains were running and I had to walk home, over an hour, in a snowstorm with a minus temperature.

When I got back to Hohnstein on the last day of the month, the camp was empty. The prisoners had all been transferred and the Hitler Jugend was taking over the place for bombed-out children from Hamburg and Berlin. It was rumoured that the older officers among us would be released from service. The Kommandant went to the general reserve.

One by one the staff was posted. And still I awaited the next turn of Fate. On November 22nd, 1940, my orders came, for Kriegsgefangenenoffizierssonderlager 4C, at Colditz, a small town between Leipzig and Dresden. This sounded interesting – 'Officer PW Special Camp'. What kind of a place was this? What was special about it? I knew what prisoners were like. I knew how to handle them. I knew about prisoner–staff relationships, for I had done a stint of PW life. I thought I knew it all. I knew – as you say – 'd—— all'.

## CHAPTER II

## Learning the Hard Way

ON CHRISTMAS EVE 1940, the frost broke and it snowed heavily all night. Next morning in the courtyard of Colditz Castle, the circling prisoners packed the snow solid under foot. There were then about sixty Polish officers in this camp, a dozen Belgian, fifty French and thirty British, plus, of course, their orderlies – a total strength of not more than two hundred. All had been classified 'undesirable' by our authorities, some for their politics, some for their hatred of all things German, most for escape attempts from other camps. Against this 'international' was a German staff consisting of a Commandant and about ten to fifteen other officers, plus half a dozen NCOs and a Guard Company of about a hundred and fifty at a time, with, naturally, their own NCOs and officer in command. So far, although I had only been there a month, I had found nothing very unusual about this so-called 'sonderlager' or special camp. There had been no escape attempts up to then. The prisoners seemed a bit undisciplined, perhaps, by contrast with Hohnstein, where I had been before, but no doubt these too would soon all settle down to while away their time while the war ran its course.

Colditz Castle itself was an unattractive building, dominating four-square the small town of Colditz, which lies astride the River Mulde in Upper Saxony. Very roughly, the buildings consisted of two courtyards backing on to each other. The prisoners' courtyard contained buildings going back to the very earliest days of the castle, which had been built, rebuilt and added to repeatedly, ever since its first appearance in recorded history, in the year 1014. It had been a hunting lodge for the kings of Saxony. It had belonged in the sixteenth century to the Danish princess, Anne, who in 1583 married the Kurfuerst of Saxony. She it was who planted the small vineyard on the slopes across the valley north of the castle, overlooking the river. From 1603 to 1622 the daughter of the Kurfuerst of Brandenburg lived in the Schloss, and gave her name to the Sophienplatz in the town. In the Thirty Years War, Saxony was on the Protestant side. First the Imperialists sacked Colditz, in 1634, then the Swedes retook it and set up in the castle for several years. Swedish troops were there again in 1706 during the war with Russia.

As a residence for the Dukes of Saxony, Colditz ceased to be used after 1753. The castle became a prison as from 1800. From 1828 the place was a lunatic asylum, and the same, I often felt, between 1940 and 1945! A concentration camp was its next fate in 1933, and for a year after that became an Arbeitsdienst camp, for Hitler Youth.*

From October 1939 the castle had operated as a PW camp for Polish officers. In the summer of 1940 these had been largely replaced by Belgian officers. They in turn had mostly been released after the Blitzkrieg on signing a general parole. Finding it had a nearly empty camp on its hands, the OKW decided to set up a Sonderlager, or – '*Lager mit besonderer Bewachung*' – a special camp, with strict surveillance of the inmates, as permitted under Article 48 of the Geneva Convention, though without loss of any other prisoners' rights as provided by this agreement. In effect, this camp had a greater number of searches, roll-calls and so on than in normal camps, and much less room to move around in – just a forty-yards-square courtyard, and no open space except the park outside, which might only be visited for short and fixed periods daily under some restriction and much surveillance.

You might think at first sight that the place was impregnable. It probably was, but apart from putting bars on the windows it

*Today the castle is part hospital, part home for the aged. The town museum holds what is labelled a most remarkable collection of items and photographs of escape material, used by Allied officer PWs in World War II. This collection was brought down from the castle after the war from our "escape museum", which we used to allow the public to visit on Armed Forces Day, and where we also used to train newcomers of all ranks in the difficult job of countering this kind of ingenuity.

had never really been built for the purpose of keeping people in. As time went on I realised that while Colditz, like so many other castles, might be impregnable from without, it certainly was not 'impregnable' from within. Breaking out was shown to be much easier than breaking in!

The German administrative buildings were in the newer eighteenth-century yard, comprising Kommandantur offices, storerooms and so on. There were two ways into the German yard, one through the main gate and one from the park side. There was only one gateway into the prisoners' yard, with the guardroom adjacent. Access between the two yards was out of the north-west corner of our yard under what was known as the archway up along an approach yard to the guardroom and there sharp right through a door in a large double gate, to what I have called throughout the prisoners' yard, as opposed to the German yard. In both yards the buildings ran up three floors high with double attics above them. All round the entire castle the ground fell away in terraces, on the west towards the town and on the north and east sides down towards the park. The south side of the prisoners' yard was the north side of ours. We occupied the ground floors on our side – they had kitchens and so on, on theirs. But this stretch of building was only as it were one room thick above the ground floor. The rooms were all in our occupation – but at the south-east corner the prisoners' rooms backed on to ours, and at the other end of this 'seam' the Saalhaus rooms, which housed the allied senior officers, overlooked the German yard. The prisoners repeatedly exploited these points of junction and overlap for their own purposes – escape. A more unsuitable place to hold prisoners will probably never again be chosen. Escape attempts were made, and many succeeded, over the roofs, under the foundations, through the walls, through the bars, in disguises, in concealment, on an average of, I should say, once in ten days during the more than four years that I was in this camp. Details of some escapes I never discovered until ten years after the war was over, when I read about them in one or other of the books which were written by French or British ex-prisoners. Even today the methods followed in some of these escapes are still not completely known to me.

That Christmas of 1940 was one of suspense. Germany had won the first two rounds of the war against Poland and France with knock-out blows. She had drawn with England. In the west was now a stalemate. It seemed odd to me that with this situation the current propaganda on our side called for 'no capitulation' notices already – hardly victory talk. There was one of these up on a local factory. Bombs were being exchanged between Germany and England. The home fronts were part of the battlefield now, almost the only battlefield, excepting perhaps the Atlantic. Our National Socialists had things well in hand. No one dreamt of a war on two fronts. We were getting millions of tons of grain from Russia, so no one was hungry, and she was also letting through supplies of all kinds from Japan and America.

As my leave was over the New Year, I was on duty for this, my first Christmas among prisoners. I was interested to see how they would spend it. The French and Poles, of course, had long established letter and parcel-post contact with home. The British channels were still rather unorganised, but their first food parcels arrived at the beginning of December, from the British Red Cross. There was no shortage of food in the prisoners' yard that Christmas or in our German yard adjoining. There was wine and beer in both – though we rationed this among the prisoners and gave them no strong drink at all.

Entertainment was provided by the Poles. They put on a magnificent marionette show with musical accompaniments and a translated commentary. 'Snow White and the Seven Dwarfs' was the main piece. After that came a sort of allegory of Polish history, the finale showing these men returning to Poland after the ultimate victory, just as they had done in 1918, to re-establish their independence. Their national hymn, the Dombrowska March, tells that story.

I think the Polish officers were top in 'morale' at the end of that year 1940, although they had been in our hands for over fifteen months. The French were still solemn after their defeat. The British were digging themselves in, so I thought. Under the canteen floor, had we but known it, and not digging themselves in, but digging themselves out! It wasn't only to their national success that they were drinking on Boxing Day –

in one bottle of wine between three – from that very canteen. It was a local victory they were hoping for, also from the canteen where they had started a tunnel, by then well under way.

We had our own Christmas celebration in the Waldschänke, the inn in the forest. We all had a pound of real coffee beans in our extra rations, the last of it I saw for years. So quiet was Oflag 4C that I remember nothing of equal importance that Christmas!

After I got back from leave, Russian officer prisoners quartered in the town celebrated their orthodox Christmas on January 11th. Their Pope, or priest, came from Dresden, where there had been a White Russian community for years. He used to bring a choir with him for their Sunday Masses. These Russians were all from Wrangel's army – White Russians, who had settled mainly in France in the twenties, or in Yugoslavia, and had taken the appropriate nationality. The choir had some beautiful women singers and a Russian officer of French nationality professed to fall in love with one of them. They became officially betrothed. She helped him to escape; and there the acquaintance ended. He got safely to France, while she landed safe in gaol. This was my first lesson in PW duplicity!

Looking back now, I can hardly recognise myself as I was at Colditz at New Year 1941. It is difficult enough to make out anything at all of my own personality at the other side of the shattering events of that fatal year and all that followed, after Adolf Hitler finally brought in Russia, Japan and the United States and got the total war he had so long preached. I was then still judging events with the wordly wisdom of the 14–18 War and the international viewpoint that I had built up for myself in the years between. It was not long before I had to bring my nose rapidly down to earth, and on to the escape trails that I was to follow from then on for the next four years without a moment's break.

My records show that more than 300 would-be escapers were caught in the act, often the same people trying again and again. On about 130 occasions escapers actually got out of the castle or got away when in transit locally. The number who got clear away over the frontier and were never retaken was thirty, breaking down into six Dutch, fourteen French, nine British and one Polish, as near as I can remember. I was not in complete charge of security until 1944, but until then had, of course, to contribute what I knew or could find out or could work out, to our camp security office.

We held security conferences whenever an escape took place and at least every week as a matter of routine. Practically every routine occasion was an escape occasion, and one way and another every escape was an occasion in itself. In fact I claim some honour for having been part of a team, a very amateur team I admit, of a German 'holding' force whose clumsy efforts were nonetheless so successful that the experts had to lay on absolute masterpieces of escape to beat us.

The stage for this battle between the two security systems, German and Allied, was in some way set to the advantage of the prisoners. The PWs were, first of all, experienced in the job. In addition, our hands were somewhat tied by our not very practical superiors at Army Command HQ in Dresden and, above them, in Berlin. We made things better for the prisoners by cramming Colditz with new escape material week after week. Each new arrival brought with him knowledge of new methods of escape, acquaintance with fresh routes, knowledge of extra documents required, checks likely to be made at railway junctions and on trains, and so on. In this castle, the prisoners had the interior lines of communication and the initiative as well. Our effectives, real effectives, were hardly a dozen, while their team ran into hundreds.

No sooner did Twelfth Night bring down the decorations in the British quarters than the battle began, on the cold front. Our commandant decided on a New Year visit to the prisoners' quarters. It was January 9th, and still extremely cold. The sun did not get over the roofs into the prisoners' yard until a good ten o'clock in the shorter days of winter, but even then many were glad to be living in a stone building and not a wooden barracks, which is always damp and cold. There weren't many people walking in the yard that morning. I went in with the Kommandant and called out 'Achtung!' The circulation stopped for a moment. That was the drill. Everyone looked towards our Colonel for a second, he saluted, the circle moved round again.

We went into the kitchen. There was the British kitchen officer, Captain Barry. He did his official job there very well – his unofficial one (the use of the kitchen for escape purposes) he did even better. It was through the windows on the outer side of the kitchen looking to the German courtyard that four British officers got away in 1942 (as I learnt nearly fifteen years afterwards).*

From there we went out into the yard again, and up the circular staircase in the south-east corner. On the first floor were the Polish officers. 'Achtung!' I shouted. Most of the officers were lying on their beds reading, smoking, thinking. They all got up slowly, unwillingly, all except Lieut Siewert, who stayed on his bed. I took his name. On the evening parade I read out the Kommandant's sentence of five days' arrest, for failing to acknowledge a superior officer. This punishment was normal for officers in the German Army, and military prisoners were all subject to our own *Militärstrafgesetzbuch* (corresponding to Queen's Regulations). The sentence was read out also to the French, Belgian and British companies in their own language. We were all very formal in those days. The prisoners remained unimpressed by this disciplinary action – sometimes it was warmer in the cells!

Later on, to jump ahead a few months, when the camp got crowded, people actually asked to go in the cells to 'get away from it all'. I told them we really could not arrange rest cures for them, there was a war on. However, it wasn't difficult for them to 'swing' a few days in arrest. They only had to write abusive things about us in their letters home or turn up late for parade. That was always worth a few days' punishment. Of course, arrest became rather a farce in the end. I did not mind putting people away who had committed disciplinary offences. Sometimes it was a good thing for them – their psychology required that they should get on their own for a short while. Prisoners get obsessions. We didn't want them to go mad. But cells began to be used as a means of bribery and corruption

*See The *Colditz Story* by P. R. Reid

of the guards, as a means of escape, and people even began to feign insanity in the hope of escaping during trips for medical treatment. All the time we were balancing between security and humanity – though some would roll their eyes to heaven that I should write this.

So five days' arrest meant nothing to any Pole, and when I dismissed the parade, his compatriots rushed to their comrade, shook his hand, embraced him, and then, gathering round, threw him again and again into the air, catching him as he fell, as the Poles do with those they approve of.

I argued a moment with the Polish captain, 'If you want us to treat you correctly under the Geneva Convention you must behave correctly too.'

He destroyed my argument: 'You Germans don't apply the Geneva Convention to us. You say Poland as a country no longer exists. You don't even allow us a Protecting Power to look after our interests as prisoners. The Swiss visit the British every three months. The French have their Scapini Committee to look after them, and they have a Government you recognise, even though it's Pétain. The Dutch are looked after by the Swedish Government. But we, the Poles, are no one's children.'

I saw they had it all thought out, and were going to make a thing of it. Sure enough, a week later, the same incident occurred again. Again Siewert got 'arrest'. The third time it happened he got a court-martial in Leipzig. We allowed him a local lawyer, a man from the town, who was a prisoner-of-war in England during the first war. He claimed to have been well treated, and was always willing to do something in return for this.

In due course the prosecution at Leipzig demanded a heavy penalty. Here was a Pole, a member of an undisciplined and savage race, so they said, deliberately insulting a superior officer. An example must be made. The defence was that the prisoner did not understand the meaning of the word 'Achtung!' He got a year's imprisonment, and appealed. Colonel-General Von Beck, commanding our Reserve Army, allowed the appeal and Lieut Siewert returned to Colditz a free man. Tremendous enthusiasm among all the prisoners in the camp!

The Polish Senior Officer, Admiral Unrug, who in the First World War was a U-boat commander in the German Navy, protested against the insults to the Polish people uttered in Court. Our Kommandant tried in vain to get the appeal verdict upset. His failure made things worse, for the result was that saluting practically died out in Colditz, as between the Germans and prisoners, until our famous doctor tried to revive the practice a year later. The only occasions when we got a salute were when we took the parades, or roll-calls, each day. At the most, on other occasions, officers would stand up slowly when we entered quarters or reluctantly take their hands out of their pockets or their pipes out of their mouths when we spoke to them. We did not go into their quarters very often, and we tried to speak, as far as possible, only to the senior officers of the different companies, and through their official interpreters. But over this incident we lost face.

This Court decision in 1941 made things very difficult for us in Colditz. Not only was it a rebuff for the Kommandant, who had previously given orders that offenders in the matter of saluting were to be reported and punished, but it showed up differences of opinion among the four of us Germans who, as Lager Officers (Camp Officers or Duty Officers) were in constant contact with the prisoners, taking daily parades, attending searches, sorting out innumerable requests, inspecting the quarters and so on. The standard of discipline was ours to shape – the Kommandant's to set.

Unfortunately, we had two standards among the four of us. I was then LO3 (Lager Officer 3). LO 1 was a lively character, fond of battle, fond of life, very much of a joker, fond of the bottle too, and the only one who the English agreed had a sense of humour. Sometimes he would refer to them as 'the etceteras'. He would give out notices on parade as applying to the French, the Belgians, the Dutch, the Poles *und so weiter* ('and so on'). The British put on a variety show in the theatre once by the *'und so weiter'* group. This officer didn't worry much about discipline, in the strict military sense. He had been a schoolmaster like myself, and thought he knew how to handle the 'bad boys' camp.

LO 2 was a cavalry captain. He would blow up at the least

provocation, as the prisoners very soon discovered, and go literally blue in the face in a moment. He suffered from mortally high blood pressure, and was all for violence against his charges.

As for me, LO 3, I was not for peace at any price, but rather felt again in the position that I knew so well, of a teacher dealing with a lot of naughty boys. I knew that the first aim of an unruly class is to make the person in charge angry, whatever the consequences, and I also knew that if I lost my temper in the position I held in Colditz I had lost the day and possibly the years to come as well. I told the British Senior Officer once, 'I will never allow you gentlemen the honour of getting me rattled. Correct behaviour under the Convention or under our own disciplinary code is my line. Anything your officers do to offend, I shall report the fact. What happens then is not my affair.' I was provoked beyond belief time and again for four years on end by the hotheads among hundreds of officers of all nationalities, ages, rank and background. Time and again, I would start to react and then control myself. It is not easy to put up with active insolence, but dumb insolence can sometimes be even harder to bear.

LO 4 was much of my opinion, but there was no doubt of it, we four were not a harmonious team.

At least in Colditz it was true to say that there was never a dull moment. As time went on, we could see the pattern, and it was one that we had imposed upon us, whereas it was we who should have been the ones to call the tune rather than follow it. The prisoners and we were engaged in an unending game of leapfrog. First we were ahead with our security barriers, then they were, scheming successfully round them. Everything the PWs did or said or thought was planned to give them an advantage, an advantage either immediate, or several jumps ahead.

If, as a result of an escape or an attempt to escape, we altered our arrangements or introduced some new plan, they would catch on quicker than our own people who had, after all, other things to think about than their hours of duty up at the castle. Most of the prisoners were 'on duty' the whole time; they had no other life.

Another major security difficulty concerned our regular camp staff, particularly NCOs. The longer these stayed in the castle, the better they got to know the prisoners and their methods. But they became all the more subject to bribery with cigarettes, chocolate or coffee, and to the softening effect of familiarity and simple politeness between themselves and the prisoners. Another weakness was the disadvantage that any German of lower rank feels in dealing with officers, of whatever nationality. And if we replaced these NCOs it took the new arrivals months to learn the tricks of the trade, during which time the prisoners took full advantage of their ignorance.

All our NCOs at Colditz had nicknames, knew it and were rather amused by it. There was Cheese – he was a little man, what we call 'three cheeses high' (*Dreikäsehoch*); the Policeman; Hiawatha, who rather fancied himself until he disdiscovered that his mate was known as Minnehaha; Big Bum; Auntie, the Quartermaster – he was in Colditz right to the end; Fouine (the French word for a ferret) – known to the English as Dixon Hawke, very clever at smelling out tunnels; Mussolini, our staff sergeant in charge of the orderlies, an old soldier from the first war who disliked all officers, even his own!

These men, and of course the general mass of the guards, could not fail to be impressed by the active life of the castle, and more so by the tricks the prisoners got up to, but most of all by the escape successes they managed to register. All this reflected on us, their own officers, who were shown up as that much incompetent and helpless.

In February 1941 we began to fill up. A couple of hundred French officers arrived under General Le Bleu, who made no secret of his dislike of all things 'boche'. In March we were presented with sixty Dutch officers, many from the East Indies of mixed blood. They were model prisoners. They had no orderlies of their own, but kept their quarters clean themselves. Their discipline was faultless, their behaviour on parade exemplary, by which, as we shall see, they were able to profit. They dressed smartly at all times, too. The Poles behaved similarly, though they had not the uniforms for a smart appearance.

But the French and the British! On parade in pyjamas, unshaven, slopping about in clogs and slippers, smoking, reading books, wearing the first assortment of garments that came to hand when they got out of bed, just asking to be ridiculed. They insisted on distinguishing between 'parades' as on the King's birthday, when they turned out unrecognisably smart, and the daily 'roll-calls' we held to count them. Very quickly we saw through what was only superficially slipshod, though sometimes they all behaved wholeheartedly like urchins.

One day that spring, four British were missing from parade. We suspected that they hadn't really escaped. We did not warn the local security authorities but held our hands. In the afternoon we played a trick. We let off a round or two in the park below the castle. LO 1 and I went into the prisoners' yard and were asked what the shooting was about. We told them we had just shot one of the four, who had attempted to escape in the castle grounds. I watched their faces – they all broke into grins. Later that day, a solemn procession took place in the courtyard. I had a call from the guardroom that something was up, and went in to see. It was a mock funeral procession. Four officers carried the coffin – a clothes cupboard. It was covered with the Union Jack. The priest followed. Medals were carried on a pillow. Relatives followed in deep mourning. The wife, of course, wore a kilt. Candlebearers were in attendance too.

'What's all this?' we asked.

'We're burying the officer you've just shot.'

We looked into the coffin and there was one of the missing four!

They all turned up at the next parade. They had been hidden in the roof on the off-chance of getting away, but gave up in the end. But we had the last laugh that evening when LO 1 announced that, in future, interments could take place only on receipt of twenty-four hours' notice!

Of course, we on the spot always got into the worst trouble over escapes from above, and the prisoners knew it. We have a phrase in German, 'It's the one at the bottom that gets bitten'. Anything that rattled us was a point in the prisoners' favour. My cap was stolen once during an interview in the prisoners' quarters. I sent an orderly to our Mess to bring another. I couldn't leave the yard without one. The jeers would have been too much, and as for my guardroom, what would they think! I put on the new cap, went out across the yard, looked up, and there was my cap up near a window. I got it back. But I was sure that someone had been taking measurements and copying the badge on the front while the cap was out of my hands.

Water bombs were another irritation to us. These were made out of newspapers folding into cocked hats. As they fell they sprang open and the water inside splashed on us below.

Snowballs were inevitable in the winter and fairly harmless, but I was narrowly missed once by a very large one with a piece of bottle-glass inside it. Razor blades in the pig-swill we also had to contend with. We could have cut the prisoners' meat ration down in retaliation for our pig casualties, but we argued them out of that trick. How far they would have gone, or perhaps did go, if given the opportunity, I cannot say. We found a guard one morning, dead, in the parcel office, his revolver in his hand, shot in the head. We had no option but to assume suicide. Tools, clothing, cement, wire, wood, lead, plaster of paris, nails, anything and everything of any use or even of no immediate use, or even of only speculative use, were stolen by the prisoners on sight. If they weren't stolen, then, as the war drew on, these things were bribed out of our sentries or off civilian workers who were always about the camp doing repairs. Any piece of metal was always useful. Strong wire can be used to open simple locks. When one of the first British parties arrived, from Laufen in November 1940, we found the attic door over their temporary quarters had been opened the very first night. Unoccupied rooms were obviously best for working at tunnels. They were rarely inspected those early days.

In the British senior quarters we found wet clothing one day. The lock into the showerbaths had been picked. We replaced it. A few days later we found the head of a broken-off home-made key in the lock. That was on February 19th, 1941.

From the clandestine to the evident – from the evidence to the first culprit. On March 18th our NCO, whom I shall call throughout by his British nickname 'Dixon Hawke' or by his French one, La Fouine (the Ferret), found two of the French officers, Lieuts Cazaumayou and Paille, at the bottom of a ten-foot hole they had dug with a piece of bed-frame, below the clock tower in the north-west corner of the yard. They had fixed up a hoist to haul the rubble part way up inside the tower for eventual disposal in the attic. The Security Officer ordered the doors into this tower to be bricked up. There was one access door on each of the three floors. We shall see what a tremendous asset the prisoners found this 'security' measure to be, nearly a year later.

In the same month two Polish officers were caught at night sawing through the bars of the British canteen window in the south-east corner of the yard. We suspected that canteen. We put an extra padlock on the door. We lifted up a cover in the floor and examined the drain underneath. It was dry and bricked up, with no signs of any 'workings'. We cemented this cover in. (The prisoners loosened it before the cement had set, as we discovered several months later.)

It looked to me, now that spring was approaching, as if the balloon was going up.

## CHAPTER III

# The First Successful Escape

AFTER THE afternoon parade on April 12th, 1941, a French officer was missing – the first prisoner had got right away from Colditz. We checked the faces of the whole camp with their identity cards – a long and difficult business. The photos on these were a year old at least. Many officers wore beards now, or just moustaches then. They were not all easily recognisable.

At last we got to the capital 'Ls', and Lieut Leray was the one who was not there. LO 1 made his report – even he could find nothing amusing to say about the "*Dicke Zigarre*" (thick cigar) or 'rocket', which he got from the Kommandant. Generalkommando Dresden came into the affair. Their Abwehrstelle 4 (Security 4) asked, 'When did the prisoner escape, how did he get out, what clothes did he wear?' We didn't know. We gave the Leipzig police a description, and said that as the man was French he would probably go south-west. The OKW in Berlin wanted to know: 'How did the officer escape? Who was responsible, had he been punished – how? What had we done to stop similar escapes in future?' We couldn't answer all of this. LO 1 was in sore disgrace.

We assumed that Leray had climbed up on the roof and down a lightning conductor on the outer walls of the buildings, out of sight of the sentries somewhere. We wired up parts of the roof and the chimneys. We rigged up more and stronger searchlights. Even then the prisoners profited by this, two years later.

On the last day of April we held our monthly party in the Mess. This time we had as guests Partei officials, plus the local Mayor, and some of his council from the town. The party was protracted. LO 1 was below par. He realised that the serious business of escaping was upon us.

Things everywhere were hotting up. The war was shifting

from the west front to the east – Greece, Crete, and then Russia were to be the sequence.

LO 1 failed to show up the morning after the party. The Kommandant didn't miss him at first, but he was still absent at lunch.

Next day the blow fell. 'All in the Mess at 12 o'clock' was the order. There, the Kommandant pulled out every stop. 'We've all been made fools of by one prisoner over this escape. Now some of you are making fools of yourselves. The prisoners are playing with us. We are responsible for them, and for keeping them confined, yet no one can say when, where or how this French officer got away. An escaped prisoner is a breach in our national security defences, as well as in our Colditz ones, a double danger to us all. Pay more attention to your duties. Then you may have something worth celebrating. From now on, no drinks after midnight in the Mess. Lights Out 1 a.m.'

We were still suspicious of the British canteen. One of our NCOs said he had gone into the yard at night and had seen a movement of some kind over in that corner. Unfortunately he was short-sighted. (The prisoners soon found that out too.) He couldn't be too sure what he'd seen, or whom.

Had the prisoners made keys to unlock the doors at the foot of their staircases, that we locked each night? It became more and more evident as time went on, that no lock at all in Colditz really served its purpose. We kept finding people in what should have been barred or locked-off rooms, from which bit by bit we noticed all the light fittings disappear. Blankets vanished from the attics. Nothing was safe. We did not know the expert lock-pickers at the time, but later we discovered that the chief 'burglars' were Lieut Surmanowicz, Lieut O'Hare, Lieut Guigues, and the Dutch officer Captain van Doorninck, one from each of the main national groups.

At that time, the spring of 1941, the castle was far from full. There were some whole floors empty of occupants – of all permanent occupants, that is. The prisoners then occupied three floors on each of two sides of their courtyard. On the third or north side was the chapel with the two floors above it empty that year. The fourth or south side had only ground floor buildings, and at the back of these rose the sheer wall of the north side of our four-storey German courtyard. As a counter-measure to these break-ins we decided to move all unused equipment and furniture out of the unused quarters in the prison yard, and deprive the prisoners of this source of raw escape material. Naturally they turned this operation to their own advantage.

It was May 8th, 1941. As from 10 a.m. straw mattresses were brought down in dozens from an attic store by the orderlies, loaded on to a cart, taken down to the town, and dumped in a skittle alley. Eleven-thirty to 1 o'clock was the lunch break. Then on with the job.

About 2 o'clock the German NCO supervising the transport stepped back against a mattress lying on the ground. He felt something hard. He tapped it with his foot and then open it up. Inside was Lieut Hyde-Thomson, in civilian clothes. The Security Officer was informed and ordered a *Sonderappell* (special roll-call). The bugler blew up our 'Close fighting' call, '*Kartoffelsupp*'* (Potato Soup), for an immediate fall-in! One British officer was missing, Lieut Peter Allan. We went down town to the skittle alley. There we found an empty palliasse and an open window. The bird had flown.

Some days later we had a telegram from the Vienna Police Headquarters. They were holding Allan. Allan spoke good German, having studied at Jena before the war. How he got to Vienna, we never really discovered. He got lifts apparently, as his German was so good, and walked a lot of the way as well. He arrived exhausted in Vienna after about ten days' going and went to see the US Consul. Some of the staff at the Consulate were German. Allan asked to see the Consul. His American accent wasn't as good as his German one. A German secretary seemed suspicious.

The Consul was in a spot. Was Allan a stool pigeon? Was he really an American? 'I am an escaped British officer. I want to get to Budapest, neutral territory. Put fifty marks on the desk and look the other way.' The Consul did look the other way, and said, 'I am afraid the United States is neutral too. We can't assist you in any way.' Allan had reached the end of his

*'*Kartoffelsupp*, '*Kartoffelsupp*, Den ganzen Tag, Kartoffelsupp*'
(Potato soup, potato soup, all ruddy day, potato soup!(.

35

tether – so near and yet so far. 'Goddam the man!'

He went out and was caught soon afterwards.

At Colditz, Lieut Allan's escape resulted in strict control of all vehicles entering and leaving the prisoners' courtyard. Any wagon with a load in bulk was to be probed with a bayonet – preferably a French one, which was extra long. As most of our Home Guard who did guard duty at the castle were armed with captured French rifles this requirement caused no difficulty, provided they did their job properly.

There still seemed little we could do about the false keys that were being made to fit any and every type of lock we used, even Zeiss Ikon four-way locks.

One day two British officers were caught in a room which was normally kept locked. It was still locked when we discovered them inside. Captain Reid and Flight-Lieut Wardle had been let in and then locked in by one of the others. 'What are you doing here?' 'Physical jerks, by numbers. We chose this place because it was quiet!'

We locked them in again and sent for the LO 1. When we got back the two were out in the yard and the door was off its hinges, being solemnly carried round to great cheers from all about.

'We protest,' ran the note presented to us, 'against our incarceration without charge or trial. This is a breach of the German military disciplinary code and therefore of the Geneva Convention.'

In the end we agreed that the door should be replaced and no more said, except what we knew to be the purely formal question from us, 'How did you open the door?' They gave us a piece of bent wire in reply – but we'd seen that before, and anyway it was only a blind. Any old piece of wire was always produced as evidence of how locks were picked!

A few days after the 'mattress' affair came an escape attempt that is by all accounts a mystery to this day. Two Polish officers were doing time in the courtyard cells. There were very few arrest cells actually in the castle – four stood in one corner of the prisoners' yard, close to the gate. One of these looked out on to the west terrace, the other three overlooked the yard on ground floor level, but a few steps up, as the yard sloped down to the gate. They had their windows painted over. All the cell doors gave on to a corridor and at the end of this was the main door out to the yard steps. All doors were locked and bolted day and night. Lieut Surmanowicz was in one cell, Lieut Chmiel in another. Somehow, during the night, Surmanowicz got out of his cell, released Chmiel from his and then opened the door from the cells to the yard. From the Polish quarters three floors up, a rope was lowered, and the two were hauled up one at a time on to a ledge. They sidled along the ledge to a gutter, got up on the roof of the guardhouse, hauling the rope after them, and here, through a window, they climbed down into an attic. They then hung the rope out of the front window and started to slide down. Surmanowicz wore rubber soles, but unfortunately Chmiel had nails in his boots which scraped down the wall. A guard heard them and they were caught in mid-air.

As a result of this attempt, we stationed a sentry permanently inside the prisoners' courtyard day and night. This western face of the castle had plainly been the object of much thought among the prisoners, for two days later came another attempt, from the Archway as it was called. This lay outside the prisoners' courtyard. You passed under it between our German yard and the small approach yard, below the PW Senior Officers' quarters. The approach was to the prisoners' gate and the guardroom just beside it. Prisoners got into the archway cells only when the four yard punishment cells were occupied. There were three cells under the archway and they looked on to the outer side of the castle. The ground beneath dropped down about forty feet to a terrace garden. From the edge of this garden, about fifty yards out, towards the valley, there was another drop down a steep bank to the backs of houses in the town at street level.

Lieut Hyde-Thomson was doing time for his 'mattress' attempt of May 8th. In the cell next door to him was the Polish Lieut Just. How he came to be there is a story of its own.

Two Polish lieutenants, Just and Bednarski, succeeded in convincing our camp doctor, with the backing of their own man, that they required operative treatment. He sent them to Königswartha, near Bautzen. On the night of April 5th, the day before they were to be operated upon, both got away. Lieut Just got on a goods train, but found it going the wrong way. He jumped off safely, and boarded one going back to Bautzen. Feeling he had been spotted he jumped off a second time, but on this occasion he hit his head on the ground and lay unconscious in the rain all night. He gave himself up next day and returned to Colditz and the archway cell next to Hyde-Thomson. In due course, these two opened a door between their cells, and on the night of May 13th got up to the window with a rope made of bed-sheets. It wasn't long enough. Hyde-Thomson held one end and Just slid as far as he could and then dropped to the ground. He crossed the garden, climbed through the wire fence and disappeared into the town. He was caught three days later at Stühlingen near Basel, following the railway line to the Swiss frontier. They took him to a hospital at Villingen, in the Black Forest. A month later he got away again, and was caught swimming the Rhine below Basel, at night. He came to a barbed wire barrier in the water and tried to dive under it. An alarm went off, searchlights came on, and a boat brought Just ashore, and so back to Colditz again, for three weeks' more cells. As a security measure, we put a kind of cat's cradle of wire under the window of the archway cell he got out of.

To follow up the fate of Lieut Bednarski who had got away with Lieut Just from Königswartha in April. This officer had much better luck. He got as far as Cracow, where he should certainly have been quite safe. Although our people could not discover all the underground network in that city, we were able to get our hands on part of it. And so the Gestapo picked up Bednarski and in due course returned him to us as an officer prisoner-of-war. Naturally he came back with the most valuable information of all kinds from which his fellow-prisoners were able to benefit.

Now back to the British canteen at Colditz, still the object of our suspicions, and still the month of May. The prisoners were indeed leading us a merry dance. A sentry reported that he'd been offered 700 marks (about £50) to keep his eyes shut some night to be specified, while on duty at guard post No. 9 outside the canteen. There was another terrace at this point, which went out about fifteen yards from the window, and the sentry's beat was below it. The ground, as I have said, was terraced all round the Schloss buildings. The top terraces were close up against the walls, and left a belt of dead ground outside our sentries' range of view all round the three sides of the prisoners' buildings. Sentry beats were everywhere at the foot of these first terrace projections. There was a small lawn on the terrace above post No. 9, lit at night by searchlights.

Seven hundred marks was a lot of money. How on earth had the PWs got hold of it?

We held a security meeting. The money was obviously being smuggled in. How, we found later. It came in in parcels, and also on the persons of new arrivals. A British officer once boasted to me that the British 'bank' held over 2,000 marks in real German money, hidden away. It took me nearly four years to find this treasure, but I got it in the end. This was 1941, however, when 'hot' money was still 'tight'.

We told this particular sentry to carry on with the game and keep us informed. In due course he got 100 marks as the first part of his bribe. Whitsun was coming. Staff were going on leave, and tension would be relaxed. The guard was due on duty again between 9 and 11 o'clock the Thursday evening before Whitsun, May 29th. It was then light till 8 o'clock. Two days before, the guard was told, 'From now on keep your head down when on duty.' He passed this on to us and we made our preparations.

The canteen. Somewhere near there they were going to break out, but where? From below? Impossible. The inside drain cover in the canteen floor was sealed. From above? Not in the searchlights. Would they fuse the lights and come down a rope in the dark? Would they get out of the canteen by one of the windows? The guard had been assured that there would be no traces after the escape, so he couldn't possibly be suspected. How 'Zum Donnerwetter' were they going to get out? We thought and talked and felt very foolish. That we should have to wait on the prisoners for a line of action!

All duty officers and a number of guards concentrated in a room in the Kommandantur building, where our north-east corner backed on to the canteen corner of the prisoners' yard.

The door on to the grass terrace outside this damned canteen was on our side of the join in the two yards. We unlocked it quietly. An NCO and ten men were held ready in the guard-room outside the prisoners' gate, at the end of the approach yard. A phone call on our internal exchange would rush them to any part of the castle we specified. We decided the break would definitely be attempted on the Thursday. That evening we must have been quite as keyed up as the prisoners. We took the evening parade under the strictest orders to give no hint that we knew or suspected anything. Everything seemed quite normal. Everyone was present. Were they perhaps more quiet than usual? The parade was dismissed. We left the yard and took up our positions at the danger spot. We checked back by phone to the guardroom. They knew their orders. The tension among us was terrific. It was at moments like these that the hotheads could make trouble.

'No firing without orders from an officer.' '*Ja wohl*, Herr Hauptmann.'

Twilight fell and the lights came on. The stage was set, we waited in the wings for the actors. Sentry No. 9 was pacing up and down. We couldn't see him as he was in dead ground below the level of the terrace. He was an absolute mass of nerves, and so the one most likely to start shooting. We were the ones most likely to catch it, too. We waited and watched. But what should we watch? Where to focus? We blinked at every sound. Our eyes watered with the strain. We watched. Suddenly came a movement on the grass. Was it a moth over the searchlight that flicked a shadow over the lawn? Now we could focus. A line appeared – a break. A patch of grass started to move, upward. LO 1 made a sign, 'Wait!' A square of turf rose straight up out of the ground, held in a wooden frame, with legs, which now showed themselves. Then a man's hands and arms followed, pushing up the turf and frame by the legs. Then the frame was stood aside, and up came the British Captain Reid!

'*Heraus*' – and we were on him! One man to the phone told the guard to occupy the canteen at once. Anyone in there to remain there. '*Los!*' We caught ten British and two Polish officers in the canteen tunnel, including the British Senior

Officer, Colonel German. All were in civilian clothes, all had passes; 85 marks in real money was found on the party, and 150 lb. weight of provisions, all Red Cross food, mostly in tins, plus chocolate and biscuits. What a haul for us!

The prisoners had loosened the drain cover in the canteen and picked their way along the drain through the side wall. For night working this involved picking the locks of two doors, from their own staircase into the yard, and from the yard into the canteen.

Security counter-measures followed. We began to change the sentries at irregular times. We saw to it that the same men did not return each time to the same post. We aimed to break any rhythm in guard postings that might give the prisoners a fixed person or fixed timing of any kind on which they could work.

And the guard? He kept his 100 marks. He got extra leave, promotion, and the War Service Cross. It was worth it.

This was our first big success, and due solely to the loyalty of one of our men.

## CHAPTER IV

# Skirmishings and Exchanges

THE YEAR was 1941, and the Russian campaign had not yet started. A year later, I began to wonder if our guard company was 100 per cent reliable any more. By then, 1942, the tables had begun to turn. Belts were tightening, bombs were falling and spirits and hopes along with them; German speakers among the prisoners spread propaganda unceasingly among the guards, and the tighter we sought to draw the net of supervision, the closer came the contacts on whom they could work. Lieut Allan was always busy this way, and so were Howard Gee and Giles Romilly, two civilians whom the OKW had ordered to Colditz in 1942.* Romilly was for a long time in a class of his own. He was the first of the *'Prominente'* or hostages as they were intended to be. He came at the end of 1941, from a civilian internment camp. As a nephew of Sir Winston Churchill he was a valuable prize. The OKW thought that Colditz was the safest place for him. Both he and Gee had set a very bad example to their fellow-internees. Many were of Anglo-German birth, or of Anglo-French descent. All had British passports, but on some occasions their loyalties were rather divided. These two had both escaped at different times

---

*I was in Colditz on two separate occasions, arriving first in 1940 as orderly to a group of British officers who had escaped by tunnel from a camp at Laufen near Salzburg. At the time I was rated as an other rank prisoner, having been picked up in Oslo with several other Englishmen. The Germans did not believe that we were returning from Finland where we had been volunteers for the Finnish International Brigade. They thought that we were British troops in civilian clothes, waiting for the British invasion of Norway, which they had just forestalled. There were some sharp exchanges as to the fate we might deserve. I left Colditz at the beginning of 1941, on being recognised as a civilian, and spent a year in internment camps, returning to Colditz in 1942 (classed now as a civilian with officer status), with an escape and nuisance record. I remained in the castle until the end.—ED.

from Wülzburg Castle in Bavaria, and on recapture were removed to Colditz via Silesia before the infection spread. Both spoke good German.

Three days after we had foiled the mass escape from the canteen tunnel, a French officer was missing, Lieut Colin. How he got out, we again did not know, any more than in the case of Lieut Leray who had vanished in April.

We suspected the park.

The afternoon exercise at Colditz, the walk in the park, was the weakest point in all our arrangements. We had the prisoners, as it were, bricked into their yard, barred in as well, with bars on all the windows. Since Surmanowicz' and Chmiel's attempt, there was now a sentry on duty day and night in the yard itself, and there were searchlights and sentries and naturally barbed wire aprons seven feet high all round the outside of the building. Yet we were compelled by our own High Command, in spite of our Kommandant's protests, to let these men out of this security ring every afternoon for two hours, so that they might have some fresh air and exercise, under the provisions of the Geneva Convention. It took nearly fifteen minutes to walk down into the ravine behind the castle, on the east side, where we had wired up an enclosure about 200 yards by 50, adjoining a smaller fenced and wired 'sheep pen', as the French called it, where the prisoners played football among the trees. All round the full perimeter of sheep pen and larger extension we posted sentries during the exercise period. We had a couple of dogs there as well. Yet the escape incidents that arose during these walks were hair-raising, in number illustrating (by contrast) the first principle that prisoners should at all costs be kept static. The second principle unfortunately is that they should always be kept on the move (before they have time to break their tunnels, and so that they lose all their dumps of material and money). The time lapse between the application of these contrary principles is the vital factor. Unfortunately at Colditz the paradox was never resolved. We kept the prisoners static in their courtyard, occasionally moving them to another floor or side of the yard, and yet every day we let them right out of this built-in prison, under guard, and time and again someone slipped the leash and got away.

The drill for the walk was as follows. If thirty officers could be found to make up that minimum number, we let them out of their yard and formed up in the approach yard between the guardroom and the archway. They were counted, and the figure entered in the book. Guards formed up each side of the party, with an NCO of ours at one end, and perhaps an officer at the other, and sometimes a police dog as well. Right turn, quick march, under the archway, then half left across the German yard. Turn right, through the gate out of our yard on to a roadway and then left, off the road in 150 yards, right down a steep path, with a hairpin back to the stream at the bottom of the little valley, right, over the bridge into the wired enclosure and halt! Between the roadway above, and the stream fifty feet below, the path ran close by some buildings. There were two gates on this path, one where you started down on it in a fence on the left of the roadway, the other a little way down at the end of the buildings. Sentries were unsighted at one or two spots.

The column of walkers always trailed and slopped along. Some walked fast, some slow. No one kept step with anyone else. Certainly no one ever marched!

In the small pen at one end of the main enclosure down in the park, there was a summer-house, open-sided. The far end of this pen was bounded by the park wall, about ten feet high. It ran down the side of the valley, across the stream and forty yards of flat, and then up the other slope.

On arrival in the park the party halted. A second count was then taken. The guards next marched to positions outside the wire all round the enclosed area, at thirty-yard intervals, and then the prisoners could move round as they wished, inside the six-foot barbed wire fence and inside the warning wire about a yard in from this, a foot or so from the ground. It was forbidden to step over this wire and approach the main fence on a threat of being shot.

After an hour or so, the whistle called all together. The count was taken a third time. Then the guards were brought in from outside the wire, and the party marched or shambled back up to the castle. The dogs meanwhile had a sniff around the enclosures in case the count had been faked. Back up outside the yard gate a fourth count took place, and if all was correct the prisoners were let back into their cage.

Was this confounded walk necessary?

The Geneva Convention prescribes fresh air every day for the prisoners. Well, it could be said that they had fresh air in their courtyard, which was about 45 by 35 yards in size. How fresh? – there's nothing in the Convention on that point. Nor does the Convention say how much space for exercise must be allowed per head. It says nothing about grass or trees, as the Kommandant pointed out to protesting senior officers when he succeeded in stopping the walk. The Convention says nothing as to the sun having to shine either – it just says 'fresh air must be available'. We contended that the prisoners, therefore, were getting something as an extra, a concession, when, that first winter, we let them go down to the park for exercise. And when there was trouble we stopped this concession, as a punishment. The prisoners then complained: (*a*) they had lost their access to fresh air; (*b*) they were being collectively punished – both breaches of the Convention. The protecting power for the British, that is the Swiss Government, took the matter to our High Command. Our Kommandant stated when asked to report that as it was difficult to get even 20 per cent of the prisoners on occasion to attend for the walk, and usually only about 5 per cent could be found willing to go, there was no great demand shown for this 'right'. Officers used to beg their friends to come out and make up the number. But the OKW decided that the walk was a right which must continue, and was not a concession. We lost a point there and so found ourselves with a problem on our hands that needed as much attention for two hours daily, involving at the most 40 per cent of the prisoners, as the whole camp required for the twenty-four hours day and night together, for anything up to 600 of them.

I have described the drill for the park walk as we laid it down for our charges, but these devils disposed otherwise. The assembly before the march down resembled on occasions a crowd going on an excursion to the Black Forest. They dribbled out of the yard through the gate one by one, they went back in to call to a comrade to join them. There was always a last-minute rush before the gate closed. The babble and Babel of tongues reminded one of a parrot house. The variety of uniforms and undress was certainly distracting – some would go down in shorts to play football, some to run, some to swing on the bar which we kindly provided. Some went to read quietly in a corner, some to walk, some to talk, some to sleep, some to keep their eyes very much open, some to plant seeds in a small garden bed, some to plant small tins of contraband there. They wore any combination of uniform or clothing that suited them.

Everyone had his different intention, as individual as his style of dress, and yet everyone agreed that he shared a common interest, namely to upset us in every possible way, during the escape opportunity that these walks presented. First the assembly, stage one, getting the party out of the yard. Then stage two, falling them in, in five ranks, for the count outside the guardroom. No one was ever in a hurry. People stood around chatting. '*Zu fünf, meine Herren,*' bawled our NCO in charge. No one moved. 'Guard turn out.'

Those on duty for the walk eventually started to line up, in fives. Gradually the prisoners drifted into ranks, 'close up here', 'cover off there', and then the count. Someone moved, someone shuffled, someone dropped his football, someone had to be shouted out of his book. Perhaps a recount was necessary, and then another one, and finally the total was written down and off they went, not in quick time, but in broken time, crocodiling round the corners, concertinaing on the straight bits, jostling in the gateway, pointing, calling back, calling forward, dropping things, causing the whole time some kind of diversion. And all the same again on the way back.

We felt that behind all this organised disorder the two French lieutenants must somehow have escaped. We had some confirmation of this, we thought, on June 18th, when a man rang up from the asylum at Zschadrass to say he had seen a man in the Tiergarten. This was the upper part of the valley in which the park lay, beyond the main wall that bounded the far end of the sheep pen. We held an immediate parade and to our horror again a French officer was missing, Lieut Odry.

We sent out a search party, and we sent a truck to the bridge at Gross Sermuth. They overtook the escaper on the way. Obviously he must have used the walk as a getaway. We sounded him for his way out, but he would not talk.

A week later took place another very neat attempt to escape during the walk. The work behind this escape attempt must have gone on for weeks. The column straggled down to the park, swelled through this door and that door. It double jinked left-right off the roadway on to the path down the steep slope. It eddied a moment at the gate there, to let a woman come through. Oddly enough, for men so long in captivity, not many of those at the gate paid much attention to this woman, but as she walked back up the roadway along the approaching line, someone's sharp eyes noticed she had dropped a watch just by the gate. Instead of quietly pocketing it, as most prisoners would have done, chivalrous feelings supervened.

'Hey, Fräulein, your watch!' The woman didn't hear. The NCO in charge saw what had happened and sent a man after the woman with her watch. . . . Bad luck – Lieut Boulay's disguise was good. He had concealed it well under blankets and an overcoat, whipped off at the right moment. But for the broken watch strap he might have escaped.

Security measures – in future the Duty Officer must personally count the prisoners for the walk as they come out through the yard gate. They must have their overcoats undone. Only one blanket allowed for each person going down to the walk, to stop any concealment. All counts on the walk to be taken simultaneously by the NCO and Duty Officer, one in front and one at the rear of the files.

Then came July 20th. At last we thought we had found the gap the French had made in our defences. The ground down to the park fell very steeply once you left the road by that little gate on the left-hand side. There was a house with its ground floor on the level of the road and its basement level with the path below, along which the walk straggled down the slope. The house was built as it were up the side of a cliff and above it. By distracting the guards on the inner or house side of the path, by weaving out or in, or by speaking to them or

47

causing a diversion to make the inside guards look across the line of march away from the house, it was possible to create a blind spot for a few seconds. In these few moments one man or even two could whip round a corner or projection and dive into concealment behind a blast wall at one point, provided, of course, there was no one on the roadway above watching the crowd amble up or down the steep path.

One afternoon in the middle of June the walk was two short on its return. Much argument followed. The guardroom demanded the same number back as had left, according to their record in the book. The Security Officer ordered a special parade for everyone. Two officers were definitely missing. We went back step by step to the park, and back up again. The dogs came with us. Meanwhile all our telephone lines were in action outward. We phoned the code word 'mousetrap' to all police stations within three miles – 'prisoner escaped'. At Leipzig, fifteen miles off, they had duplicate photos and the numbers of all our prisoners. We just said who was missing and gave a brief description. We phoned the local foresters and railway stations. Parties were sent out on bicycles and on foot to beat around the woods and watch crossroads and scan the open country. But on the way back from the park that day we suddenly thought of an air-raid shelter in the basement of that projecting house overlooking the zigzag path. We tried the door. It was unlocked. The two missing prisoners were inside: Captains Elliot and Lados.

They went down for twenty-one days, Lados in a cell under the archway between the two yards. He had the far cell, with a window looking down the side of that building and not straight out towards town. Since Lieut Just's escape we had put bars on this window. He got hold of a hacksaw somehow, cut the bars we had installed, swung down the length of his bed-sheet one night and dropped to the ground twenty feet below. He was undetected, and accomplished the amazing feat of reaching the Swiss frontier in spite of immense pain from a broken bone in his ankle. He was caught and brought back a week later.

For sheer mad yet calculated daring, the successful escape of the French cavalry lieutenant, Pierre Mairesse-Lebrun will not, I think, ever be beaten. Lebrun had been out twice

48

before he came to Colditz, and had been retaken each time near the Swiss frontier.

At the beginning of June 1941, the 9th to be exact, we had had a call one evening from Grossbothen station, a few miles away. They asked if anyone was missing. No. Why should there be? 'We have a man here under guard. Might be one of your PWs. He asked for a ticket to Leipzig just now and offered us out-of-date money for it – an old blue 100-mark note. He can't be German.'

At that time we still had a car and petrol. We fetched the man in; it was Lieut Mairesse-Lebrun. He was dressed in the smartest civilian clothes, complete with monocle. But we didn't know how he had got out and naturally he refused to tell us. There was plainly an exit from the camp, and the prisoners were using it sparingly and successfully. It seemed the French alone had the right of way, as well. When, ten days later, we caught those two officers, Elliot and Lados, in the air-raid shelter, we thought we had closed the gap. Perhaps now we could spend a little time studying the maps of our new front – the Russian one, just opened up.

Mairesse-Lebrun got twenty-one days' cells, the usual punishment. It was what we call *Stubenarrest*, confinement to quarters, the German military punishment for officers. We couldn't 'confine' officer prisoners under *Stubenarrest* to their already confined quarters which they shared with dozens of others, so we gave them 'rooms' on their own. These had, in the circumstances, to be cells.

Those in arrest had all their normal German rations but nothing extra by way of Red Cross food. They also had two hours' exercise daily, which in those days was taken down in the park under guard, in the small enclosure with the summer-house. At one end of this was the cross wall down and up the sides of the ravine, with the deer garden or zoo (Tiergarten) beyond it – so called because three hundred years ago the Dukes of Saxony used to keep deer for the table there. It was handier to have them on the doorstep than going out all day shooting for the pot. This enclosure the French called the sheep pen – *parc à moutons*.

Mairesse-Lebrun and several others also in arrest were

down there at exercise one day – July 2nd – playing leap-frog. The sentries were rather bored, standing up the sides of the valley, overlooking the small enclosure, and counting the minutes until they should go back to the guardroom. Everything was peaceful on a warm sunny morning.

Lebrun and his comrade were frogging along the fence which ran out from the cross wall. The ground rose steeply from the other side of the fence and was fairly thick with trees. The two sentries along that side were twenty yards up the slope, spread out on a path parallel to, but well above, that side of the sheep pen. The two French officers stopped for a breather. Lebrun took a few steps out from the fence. His friend stood with his back to it. It was about eight feet high, a sort of palisade. Suddenly Lebrun ran. The other officer clasped his hands together and made a step just below waist level. Lebrun put his foot in the stirrup, as it were, and with a heave he was up and over the fence. Everyone woke up. The sentries unslung their rifles and began firing. Lebrun ran along to the right in the dead ground at the foot of the slope and got over the park wall untouched. He was wearing gloves to help him with the barbed wire at the angle of the fence and the cross wall. Wearing only shorts and a singlet and shoes, he dashed away up the Tiergarten, the sentries firing at him in vain.

The NCO in charge immediately took the party back to the guardroom and reported. He might have done better to climb the wall and go off in pursuit himself. We turned out the whole countryside, police, Home Guard, Hitler Youth, and every dog we had. The dogs lost the trail in the deer park stream, but as there were still several hours of daylight we thought we could catch the fugitive in that time. Apparently Lebrun found a hide in a cornfield; anyway we failed to catch him.

In his cell he had left his kit tied up and addressed to himself in France, with a note: '*Au cas ou je réussirai je serai reconnaissant que l'on me fasse parvenir mes affaires à l'addresse suivante – Lieut Pierre Mairesse-Lebrun – Orange (Vaucluse). Que Deiu m'aide !*'* A few weeks later he wrote for it from his

*'Should I succeed, I should be obliged by the dispatch of my effects to me at the following address – Lieut. Pierre Mairesse-Lebrun, Orange (Vaucluse). May God help me!'

home in then unoccupied France and we sent it on.

Once again, after the horse had gone, we took belated steps. We put a door in the park wall so that our men could get through it quickly if necessary. We heightened the palisade fence of the sheep pen with two feet of barbed wire. Those in arrest were in future to exercise morning and afternoon, not in the park, but on a terrace along the west face of the castle at the back of the guardroom, with a sentry each end of this terrace to watch them. Later an escape similar to Lebrun's was tried even from here.

As a special camp, or rather a specialist's camp, we could get authorisation for any material we liked from the OKW, yet by the summer of 1941 we had not even sunk microphones as a warning against tunnelling, nor had we installed any other electrical warning system where our buildings backed on to those of the prisoners. All the OKW had given us, all we had indeed scratched out of our brains as worth asking for, were four police dogs and their keepers and one old pensioned-off Kriminalkommissar. The latter was quickly nicknamed 'Tiger' by the British. They alleged that he admitted to being so old that he had fought against Napoleon. And they even claimed that when they asked him which Napoleon, Napoleon III in 1870 or Napoleon the Great, he had replied that he was so old he could not remember! The dogs did sniff out one or two escapers in the park, but I don't think Tiger ever caught anybody at all. We put him in charge of the cells in the end, and the prisoners used to go and ask: how full are the cells? when will there be an empty one for me? and would you see that I have a cell looking out on to the terrace? (there was only one of these – over the west terrace). And Tiger would oblige.

Every month we ran a big search on one floor or another of the castle. Unfortunately the prisoners very often could not fail to notice our preparations, or found out through their 'agents' and so were forewarned.

We had no regular stool pigeons of our own at any time in the whole five years of Colditz, but we did get two tips from informers that were useful to us, of which I shall tell later. One prisoner who came to the camp did volunteer to inform, but he was discovered as pro-German from his past record within twenty-four hours of his arrival by the prisoners' own 'security service', and removed by us upon advice from the Senior Officer concerned. He was no good to us at all.

Our two German NCOs, Mussolini and Dixon Hawke, the Ferret, knew as much as anyone of the goings-on in the camp, and certainly knew practically all the prisoners by sight. But they were far too busy on routine jobs to keep more than a fleeting eye on their own suspicions.

We did think up one useful move about this time – the Roll-kommando, or Fire Brigade, or Riot Squad. This consisted of an NCO and six men, some of whom would now and again just dash into the yard and up these or those stairs, perhaps on spec. or perhaps following up something spotted as suspicious through the spy-hole in the yard gate or from one of our windows overlooking the prisoners' yard. But the moment the Riot Squad appeared through the gate a yell would go up from all present in the yard, which served to warn that any clandestine activity must stop or be covered up. As the Riot Squad thundered up the circular staircases in the corner of the yard they would be shepherded along with cries of 'Les Schleus!' from the French, 'Skopy!' from the Poles, or 'Goons up!' from the British, according to whose quarters they were storming. However, they did have some successes to their credit.

The Dutch took their advent more quietly on these occasions and thereby once lost a great horde of material, their warning system having failed. Basic activities like tunnels never succeeded in Colditz although we found over twenty in various stages of construction over the five years.

Disguises were surprisingly successful, in spite of our frantic efforts to stop them. The success of an impersonation depends on the watchfulness of the first of the enemy you meet, and decreases proportionately as you move away from the centre.

We could and did eventually take mechanical measures against tunnels, but disguises required a rather better human element than we had at our disposal for duty all through the war.

Every week we used to receive a publication called *Das Abwehrblatt* (Security News) from the OKW, telling of escape methods in all the different camps. Alas that our own reports should have appeared in it so often! It was fascinating reading. Prisoners seemed to find it best to be conspicuous in a normal way, rather than try to be nervously inconspicuous. One man, apparently, had gone all the way to Switzerland disguised as a chimney-sweep. During the first war, I heard, a prisoner had pushed a wheelbarrow all the way to freedom.

To show the detail with which the prisoners planned their different schemes, during one search we picked up a notebook containing details of the new variations in our guard changings, introduced after the canteen tunnel episode, as well as lighting-up time for the searchlights, and personal details of our officers and NCOs, even to the appearance and state of joviality on Sunday mornings of our LO 1. They didn't miss much!

For the rest of July, after Mairesse-Lebrun's escape, we had a quiet time, and thought it safe to undertake repainting in the French quarters. Three painters were put on the job and we gave them a guard to stop what might be two-way traffic in contraband.

One evening two of them turned up at the gate on their own to be let out, at the end of the day. To the question where was their mate and the sentry, they replied '*Kommt gleich*' ('He's coming') and wandered off down the approach yard towards the archway. The gate man was more concerned about the missing painter and sentry, but the guardroom NCO was on the *qui vive* and yelled out to the two workmen, by now almost at the archway, to bring back their brass tallies. As they did not seem to hear his shouts, he sent a man out to chase them. They had no brass discs at all, because they were two prisoners (not painters) in first-rate 'painters' disguise but quite unaware that every civilian or sentry going into the prisoners' yard nowadays had to have a brass disc with a number stamped on it. These were issued before entry into the prisoners' yard, and the name and number of the recipient were entered in a book in the guardroom, and checked when he came out of the yard. And that was the end of that escape.

After this attempt, as an additional precautionary measure, all civilians working in the camp now had to wear a yellow arm-band with a swastika stamped on it, which they had to hand in with their number plates when they had finished their work. A day or two later two Dutchmen disguised this time as German soldiers tried to walk out of the gate. Again – no check numbers. However, the prisoners at last realised that not only civilians but military personnel, too, had to have these tags. And that, of course, meant that the prisoners must have the things as well!

The painting was still going on in the prison quarters, and the next thing was that one of the painters, an oldish man, reported the loss of his disc, No. 26. We warned all NCOs on the gate to look out for it.

A fortnight later, in the first week in August, the sentries all left the yard together after manning the staircases as usual, during evening parade. Some had rifles, some not. There wasn't too much light at the gate, as the searchlights shone only on the walls above it, and not on the gate itself. There was quite a scramble to get back to the guardroom. The NCO on the gate glanced only casually at the number plates thrust into his hand. A junior NCO handed one in and said, 'I've got a message to the Kommandant from the Duty Officer', and turned off sharply left towards the archway, and not right, to the guardroom, like all the others. The NCO looked after him a moment, not quite sure about his face, and then down at the disc. Number 26! He gave a yell. Number 26 walked on. Several guards started to shout, and Number 26 walked on quicker – and then one short, sharp address from in front of him, the sentry under the archway shouted, 'Halt, or I fire,' and he came to a stop. Number 26 was the British lieutenant Airey Neave.

We searched him thoroughly, more thoroughly than usual, and on his body we found a cellophane container, such as we used to sell toothbrushes in, stuffed with money.

The next day LO 1 excelled himself. 'Gefreiter (Corporal) Neave,' he announced, 'is posted to the Russian front.' There was an almighty roar of laughter. Lieut Neave looked very rueful. Six months later, though, he had the last laugh. But for the moment we were top dog.

In the stable again, knee-deep in posthumous precautions.

All escapers and new arrivals now to be submitted to mouth and body inspection when checked into the yard. All military personnel to carry a printed pass, stamped and signed by the Adjutant. This to be shown to all sentries. A fine rule on paper, but what newly-arrived fifty-five-year-old grandfather is going to make a nuisance of himself demanding passes from captains and majors and colonels and showing his ignorance of the identity, perhaps, of even the Kommandant's deputy? The Kommandant himself was not included in this rule; sentries did not have to demand a pass from him. But this rule was never 100 per cent observed.

We also extended the system of a simultaneous count fore and aft of the ranks, hitherto used only for checking the walk to the parades in the yard itself. These parades, or roll-calls as they really were, took place two, later four, times a day. Each nationality formed up separately in five ranks, and our Duty Officer took the count himself, walking slowly along the front rank counting the files. We soon caught the French out with their 'rabbit run' method of faking the count. When anyone was missing they would leave an empty file towards, but not at, the left-hand end of their third rank. The officers in the second and fourth ranks would be taller on the whole than those in the third. When the count started, with Germans checking the dressing of the files, and counting, in front as well as behind, as soon as his file had been counted a man three or four files from the right-hand end in the third rank would run quickly and quietly to the empty file at the far or left-hand end – arriving before our people, who naturally took their time checking along the ranks. This trick was employed by the British also with success. Flying Officer Dominic Bruce was their chief actor, being small and active.

The Dutch covered up gaps in their ranks in a most original way. I said before that their parade discipline as well as their general behaviour was exemplary. They stood motionless on parade. So motionless as to look like dummies. So they made two dummies, called Max and Moritz, who also stood on parade when necessary, filling in the gaps for Dutch officers who had escaped.

On July 28th, 1941, a new passage to freedom was discovered. As always, the point of junction, or what we call the *'Nahtstelle'*, or seam, is a weakness in any position or framework. In one part of the prison yard, the Saalhaus, the building rose to four storeys with two attics on the top. Here were quartered the senior officers, with the theatre above them, and baths below. Down through the building ran an air shaft. This was about twenty feet square. The prisoners had access to the theatre on the top floor and so to the top of the air shaft. The windows into this shaft on the other floors were bricked up.

Now, the ground floor at the bottom of the shaft was the German kitchen quarters. The shaft came down to a tiled floor with a door one way to our kitchen and out into our courtyard. Two doors also gave off this lowest floor level to a refrigerator room and a large storeroom. A careful watch from the air shaft windows at theatre level told the prisoners that at certain times the frequent visits from the kitchen to one or other of these two rooms by the German kitchen staff ceased altogether. At a guess the kitchen would then be empty. These times were usually after a meal had been served and the kitchen cleaned up.

On the day in question, two French officers sawed through the ornamental ironwork over the windows at the theatre level and lowered themselves down a forty-foot rope to the ground floor. They were dressed in civilian clothes with yellow arm-bands as required. Several people were standing about the German yard as these two left the kitchen and turned left towards the gate out towards the park. There was a sentry at this point, but his post did not carry a check list of passes in and out, and no brass disc was required here either. Quite a lot of coming and going went on through what we called the park gate, as the married quarters were just down the roadway outside.

The sentry opened the gate to a knock, saw a couple of workmen with their arm-bands on, satisfied himself just by that that everything was all right, and let them through. But among the odd people around in the German yard was the man who controlled the laundry for the whole castle. He was standing in the doorway of his store. Officer prisoners were not entitled to separate sheets on their beds; instead they had sleeping bags of blue and white check material made up in one piece like a sack about six feet by three. There were hundreds of these in use, not only officially as bed sheets, but unofficially as bags for carting rubbish in tunnels, as ropes, or as dress material for ladies in disguise. The laundry man wondered idly, who are these two? He knew all the comers and goers among the workmen; they were friends of his from the town. He thought again slowly, who are they? In the end, after a good hour, when his job was finished, he was still asking who those two fellows were. In the end he went to the Security Officer and asked him. The Security Officer had no idea, so we set the dogs on the trail. They went so fast that our men could follow on bicycles. We caught up with the escapers about six miles away, near Leisnig. Who were these two, anyway? Lieuts Thibaud and Perrin.

On the last day of July we foiled a second mass outbreak. This was to have taken place from the British quarters above the canteen, out of their so-called Long Room.

This was a real cat-and-mouse act, more so than with the other attempted British mass break through the canteen tunnel. In that case we were ignorant of the exit until the tunnel actually broke. This time we knew where they were coming out and organised a proper reception committee.

The guard quarters in the Kommandantur were in the north-east corner of our yard at the far end of a corridor on the first floor. Right at the end were our lavatories. The wall behind the lavatories was the wall of the British Long Room. One night while the guard was doing duty the prisoners started to work at their side of the wall. They assumed our quarters were empty, but our telephone switchboard was up that way, and day and night a telephonist was on duty. He went out to the lavatory during the night. He heard a noise, a scratching in the wall. It stopped and started again. Our man called up Security. The Security Officer came along with the Duty Officer, and they listened. Someone was working behind the wall there, level with the second lavatory. They decided to do nothing.

'Let them tunnel. It will keep them busy and happy,' said

LO 1. 'And go on using the lavatories normally.'

Next day the Riot Squad kept a check on the noises; they went on at intervals night and day. The wall was not more than eighteen inches thick. Any break-out would happen very soon. The prisoners must have known they couldn't hope to hide the working end of their hole for long.

We reckoned the break would be over the week-end at meal-time. Our officers would then be in their mess, the guard would be on duty or having their meal too. The Kommandantur buildings would be practically empty. They were going to break into that building obviously, but how did they think they were going to get out of it?

To get in through the lavatory was only the first step. They had then to get out of the Kommandantur somehow, without being seen. Perhaps they thought they could get out of one of our windows, unbarred on the east side of our part of the castle.

Anyway, once again the mouse would not have the chance to wander further than the cat would let him. We set to work too. We bored a hole through the door of the guards' sleeping quarters so as to keep a watch on the door coming out of the lavatories. We kept this door closed. For two days the Riot Squad listened and watched. Finally they noticed a minute spy-hole in the plaster of the lavatory back wall on our side. Action stations. It was Sunday.

Tiger was there with six men, plus the Duty Officer LO 1. In due course out of the lavatories came the first pair. They closed the door and started off on their adventure.

We whipped our door open – 'This way, please, gentlemen!'

Astounded, they followed us in, so astounded that they did not even shout to warn the others behind them.

It was now our turn to be funny at the prisoners' expense. The NCO in charge of the parcel office, known to the French as the Beaux Max, and to the British as Nichtwahr ('Ain't it'), suggested that we should strip these first two escapers, and send two of our men down to the park in their civvies. No sooner said than done, and the British Padre, Platt, in his diary which came to us every now and again for censoring, recorded the delight with which his comrades observed the apparent success of the undertaking – there were Allen and Flynn, out of the Kommandantur, going down happily towards the park! – 'Audacity – that's it!' was the comment back there in the Long Room – hastily translated from the Napoleonic French of the Belgian officers in the escape party – *'L'audace – L'audace – Toujours l'audace !'*

No fewer than five pairs came out in all at five-minute intervals. Then there was a long wait. Tiger, worried perhaps about the impending rush on his cell accommodation, got permission to go and have a look inside the lavatory – and the game was up. We rang the guardroom, and the Riot Squad stormed across the yard up to the British Long Room. Everyone there was in uniform, the rest of the escape queue had done a quick change. We found one of the stoves crammed with civilian clothes, and the haul of passes and money and food from the ten we did catch was impressive. Those concerned were Lieuts Elliott, Allen, Cheetham (RNAS) and Hyde-Thomson, Flight Lieuts Middleton and Flynn, the Belgian Lieuts Gaston, Arcque and Verkest, and the Polish Cadet-Officer Karpf.

## CHAPTER V

# Sniping and Sapping

THE 'WALK', as it was called, meaning the park exercise party, was coming back up the zigzag path more slowly than ever in the August heat. No one was very much awake. Suddenly down the line came two *Hitlerjugend* in shorts and vests with a swastika on the front. Our NCO bringing up the rear of the column got the Hitler salute from these two but '*Herrgott* – what do they think that is meant to be? – Hitler salute? Hitler salute, Fascist salute, Communist salute?' Alas, it was more like an English Boy Scouts' greeting! Lieuts Thom and Boustead had not worked out quite the right angle for this escape attempt, though their disguise was first-class.

For an officer to take the place of an orderly in a group going out of the castle on a job was not a very safe method of escape, due to the close knowledge of the orderlies that our two NCOs, Mussolini and Dixon Hawke, had acquired. They knew all the orderlies, French, British and Polish, who were under their control, by name and by sight and by characteristics. The orderlies were housed in one block in the prisoners' yard and were detailed for regular or staff jobs inside and also for occasional outside work.

Thinking perhaps we were beginning to drown in the depths of our own thoughts on complicated possibilities of escape, a prisoner tried one of those so simple methods that we had almost forgotten. His escape nearly came off. Captain Lawton got in with a group of British orderlies going to work in the park (always the park!) and got away over the wall. But he was seen near Zschirla by farmworkers, reported and caught near Scoplau by our cycle patrol. It was Mussolini who got the '*Zigarre*' for this one.

Then, a week later, Lieut Durant did the same thing in a group of French orderlies. He switched with one of them before they went out to work, and likewise got over the park wall. But he was stopped by an old Home Guard man in charge of an outlying Arbeitskommando, a working party on a farm, who was bringing a man to Colditz for medical treatment. The *Zigarre* this time went to Fouine, the Ferret.

Between these two 'passing-off' escapes there occurred the first of a series of escapes in the park which quite shattered our morale. I suppose we had been growing careless through over-confidence but these events made us adopt almost panic security measures. These increased our own duties to such an extent that we almost fell over each other with the constant watching and endless checking of our own prisoners and each other.

The head of the Dutch escape organisation was the inventive and active Captain van den Heuvel. We could never tell if anything was 'going on' among the Dutch. Their behaviour was always the same – perfect discipline, quiet in their manner, naturally and easily dropping into and out of a conversation whenever they wished. They never made themselves conspicuous in any way. Hence their success in springing surprises. Then only would they approach the bounds of familiarity, with the broadest of grins among themselves and occasionally shared with us. They rejoiced in the exercise ground in the park as a field for escape manœuvres, and profited by it more than anyone else.

On this particular day, five Dutch officers were missing after the walk. '*Sonderappell!* – Five missing! – Good God!' We had thwarted several minor and one major escape during July and August and we had really felt we were getting the place properly bottled up. We were, in a sense, always thinking this. And every time, the prisoners popped out like corks from unexpected places.

The officers missing this day were Captains Larive and Steinmetz and Lieuts Kruimink, van der Krap, and van Lynden (Royal Netherlands Navy). We ran a snap search in the Dutch quarters and found various articles of civilian clothing and, most interesting of all, a map with detailed instructions how to get from Tuttlingen, in south-west Germany, to the Swiss frontier and over it. A few days later,

Captains Larive and Steinmetz got across the Swiss border, presumably by this very route. Captains Dufour and Smit, who escaped later in the same mysterious way, were caught near Singen on what appeared to be the regular route.

The three others were found ten days later concealed in an empty space in the Schloss to which they had access through a camouflaged hole in their rooms.

Once more we were faced with an unknown breach in our defences. We cancelled the walk for a while, and tightened up every part of our patrol system. We also arranged for a halt on the way back from the park now and again, to make an extra count when the 'walk' was not expecting one. But the moment the walk started up again, two more Dutch disappeared, Major Giebel and Lieut Trijbar. We thought that perhaps during some diversion, perhaps during the football or handball games in the sheep pen they might have dug under the palisade fence and got down unobserved into the stream and perhaps hidden up under the bridge until the 'walk' had gone. In due course we learned that these two also had made a successful crossing to Switzerland. That meant that four out of sixty Dutch officers had got right away in six weeks. We could work out on paper how long it would be at this rate before the lot were gone! The French had got three right away. The British, Poles and Belgians none up to now.

Some weeks later, one of our more observant sentries on park duty noticed quite a crowd of prisoners concentrated, for no obvious purpose, round a manhole cover in the sheep pen. He kept his eye on the group and then noticed two of them lift up the cover and disappear below ground. He made a report – and there were Lieuts Wardle and Wojchieckowski down inside. I felt, however, that this must really be the Dutch escape route, and wondered what bargaining had induced them to lend it to the British and Poles. We had looked at that cover so many times. It had a great bolt on the top, which we tried again and again. We had looked inside as well. Nothing ever there. Perhaps it would have been better had we left the cover off altogether. There was a water conduit underneath, about eight feet down. We worked out how this could have been exploited.

Thinking back, a few Dutch officers often used to gather round this manhole, standing and talking, or sitting and talking. They often wore long black cloaks, part of their uniform. After a while the small gathering at this spot was nothing unusual. Then, on three occasions, they must have slipped two of their number down the drain under cover of the group, and in the concealment of their cloaks. It must have been nerve-racking for the two concerned, who may well have had to wait day after day until the few moments came when the two or three of our own NCOs were looking or walking the other way in the main enclosure and the two sentries up the slope either side were unsighted by trees as they moved about, or were distracted by some incident – a football over the fence perhaps at the other end of the pen, or a faked dispute between players and a referee.

Getting their men under the cover was only one third of the whole show. First a bolt had to be taken off the cover and then, after the men were inside, it had to be replaced. The replacement bolt, however, was not made of iron. It was identical to look at, but it was made of glass with a wooden nut at one end. When the glass bolt was pushed from underneath it broke. A third bolt, or possibly the original one, was put in place by the two escapers after they had got out and before they left. They collected all the glass splinters of the second bolt and took them with them.

Again we had the paradox – doors and covers should be kept locked for safety! But doors and covers should be kept open for inspections! And again, as the pendulum swung between these two rules, the prisoners dodged it, and away.

It was about this time that we began to take considerable interest in a mysterious escape occupation of which we found clues over a period of several months, before discovering the cause of the evidence. We found a cracked beam up in the French quarters. It had given way, we discovered, due to the weight above it, which weight came *du Lieber Himmel!* from tons of dirt and rubble under the inner eaves of the double attics. These were heavy enough by themselves, but now at least 25 per cent heavier with masses of accumulated debris. We examined the stuff – bricks, dressed stone, mortar, even

63

pieces of virgin porphyry rock! We sat back and thought. A tunnel obviously, somewhere in the French quarters. The volume of the rubbish showed not only a long tunnel, but a tunnel a long time building. That meant a perfected warning and working organisation, since till then we had not had the slightest hint of any large-scale activity at all. Did this mean a vast mass escape in the offing? Was that why September and October had been so quiet? Had all the experts got together to finish off an almighty tunnel and so get everyone out in one fell swoop? Were they all just digging, disposing of the waste, distracting our attention? There must be at least a dozen men on the prisoners' warning system for this tunnel.

We laid on three roll-calls a day, to shorten the time available for the miners on shift work. But we couldn't really lay on night roll-calls too. We would never have got the prisoners down into the yard. If they could fake accounts by day they could fake them in the weak light in the yard at night. And our own people would not have been very much up to the mark on night shift in any case. Sentries, after two hours in the snow (it began on November 3rd that 1941 winter, as well we all remember) liked to keep warm in the guardroom and not spend their time off sentry duty being made frozen monkeys of by prisoners in the yard.

But we did think up one quite useful trick. The last parade of the day was now to be any time between seven and nine, with only half an hour's notice on the yard bell. But that still left twelve hours at night for the tunnel work to go on. We put two NCOs into the yard semi-permanently day and night, just wandering about to no fixed plan, just looking for this tunnel. But they were followed, even preceded, a lot of the time, by a sort of herald to announce their progress, particularly when they started up this or that staircase. They were not very successful. Dresden and Berlin, that is Ast. 4 and OKW Security, showered us with advice, all quite useless since they knew absolutely nothing of the circumstances or of the people concerned. The whole burden of Colditz security fell on barely ten of us, officers in the Kommandantur and NCOs on the staff.

'Now when, can you tell us, will your tourists be starting off

64

on their holiday ?' 'Is this the Channel tunnel ? The Führer's secret weapon ?' These questions came up in various forms in our Mess, or in the town. 'Can't find the hole, eh ?' was the question bandied round the guardroom. Something must be done.

Berlin and Dresden sent down a small army of searchers, police officials, security personnel from neighbouring camps, and so on, to help us out, as they thought.

So it was that after one morning parade we left the sentries on the staircase entrances, kept the prisoners in the yard and let one of these mobs in through the gate for an all-time record search. No one was very surprised in the yard, for the comings and goings in the Kommandantur, the cars, the busy air of the place, had all been spotted by our 'guests', and the welcome to the incoming 'tourists' was impressive. The welkin resounded. God will the French attics don't collapse, I thought. A pity this crowd of useless helpers couldn't carry away a sack of rubbish each! The search went on till the afternoon. All floors on both sides of the yard and the two empty floors above the chapel were gone over. The kitchen and theatre were searched; and the Saalhaus in the south-west corner of the yard where the senior officers had their separate rooms – that was searched too. We of the regular staff just showed these visiting characters where the doors were and left them to it. Heaven knows, it was even necessary to show them the right doors, because a good many of the normally placed ones had been bricked up. The sum total of all this was a haul such as we would expect to get in a normal month's work, but '*Gott verdammt*', no tunnel entry!

Among the booty of this search we were shaken to find brand-new German tools. It seemed that bribery and corruption were beginning to work. The home front was weakening.

On November 8th we heard an outbreak of firing in that ever condemnable park. In due course the deputy Kommandant rang up and told me to go with him into the yard and into the British quarters, on the first floor, overlooking the park. We took a few of the Riot Squad, and went into the yard and up the cricular staircase in the right-hand or south-east corner by the canteen. Up in the British quarters bullets were flying around from the window, where the British flag hung out on a broomstick.

'Take it in,' roared our Major. No one seemed to understand. I repeated the command in English.

From the floor, where all those prisoners present were lying prone, came the query, 'Why don't you take it in yourself?' In the end the senior prisoner present – an Australian squadron-leader – hauled the thing in. But the firing still went on. We looked out carefully, but from the noise above us it was plain that the sentries were now firing up at the French quarters on the next floor. Up the staircase we went.

The French had hung a tin hat made of cardboard out of one of their windows. This was now the target for our marksmen. The shooting was good and one bullet had struck the top of the window embrasure. Later the French wrote round it, '*Il nous faut des victimes*', quoting one of our officers who once had said, 'A few dead men in this castle would soon stop these riots.' But now they hauled in the tin hat and the battle ceased. Masses of prisoners, meanwhile, had assembled down in the yard. The French were giving tongue. '*Où sont les Allemandes – Dans la m . . . Qu'ils y restent – jusqu'au cou . . . !*'*

We left the yard crestfallen, to discover the cause of the disturbance. Two Belgian officers, Lieuts Leroy and le Jeune, had got away in the park, and these diversions in the castle were laid on to distract the sentries firing at them. The Belgians gave up when they discovered they could not cross the park wall. When we conducted an inquiry, some five of our sentries swore that they were actually fired on from the castle! And two swore on their Diensteid (Service oath) that they had seen the smoke from the shots! This was really too much, but presumably you could crack two bedboards together and blow out a concentration of smoke or tooth powder from a paper bag or football bladder. These five were absolutely certain that they were firing in self-defence. Thank God they killed no one. It would have been a nice question for the Leipzig court-martial,

*This is an old *récitatif* from the First World War special camp, known as Kavalier Scharnhorst. General de Gaulle was there for some months, and Marshal Tuchaschevsky, then both young lieutenants.—ED.

or even later, for Nuremberg!

It was about this time that we got our first political prisoner, Mr Giles Romilly, a nephew of Sir Winston Churchill. He had been captured in Narvik in 1940 as a civilian – reporting for the *Daily Express*. He had escaped earlier that year from an internment camp in Bavaria, dressed as a woman. He ranked as a *Prominente* – a social prize (so our OKW considered) of some standing – maybe useful as a hostage. For us in Colditz he was just another security headache. Our instructions were as follows, and they came from the very highest source:

1. Kommandant and Security Officer answer for Romilly's security with their heads.
2. His security is to be assured by any and every exceptional measure you care to take.

Kommandant and Security Officer worked this out as follows:

1. Romilly's code name was to be Emil.
2. All members of the Kommandantur and guard companies must familiarise themselves with Emil's appearance.

Photos were posted up in the guardroom, the Kommandantur, the office, etc.

3. Anyone finding this man outside the prisoners' yard would take him at once to the Kommandantur.
4. The Rollkommando was to search him out every hour and note in a book where he was at that time.
5. By day he might move around the castle where he wished.
6. No park walk. At every walk a special check to be made that Romilly was not with the group.
7. He was to be locked in his own room immediately after evening parades. A spy-hole to be put in the door, and a guard outside and the light burning all night (later just a blue light). The bed to be within range of the spy-hole.
8. His presence to be checked at night at irregular intervals.

Mr Romilly was a short, dark man in his thirties. He liked boxing, but in camp stage shows he played women's roles. For some months he reacted to our special measures, especially the disturbance of his sleep. He used to fling his boots against the door and put paper over the spy-hole, but in the end he accepted these inconveniences. On one occasion we caught him disguised as an orderly on a coal cart due to leave the yard. He spoke good German and certainly played his part in undermining the morale of the guards with whom he could converse easily at his door, at any time of the evening and night.

Apart from the undiscoverable tunnel and the Dutch escapes from the park and the discovery of their exit, the ball was kept rolling in November by several more escape attempts. On the 23rd, after the teatime parade, our sentry in the prisoners' yard was under covert observation. He walked back and forth across the yard regularly, as was his known custom. He stopped every three or four turns for just so long. The prisoners knew his timings well. He never stopped halfway across and went back again to the wall he started from. It must have been known that this particular 'goon', as the British so kindly called us, would be on duty – and everything, and those concerned, was ready. As this man moved out from the kitchen again, towards the other side of the yard (the north or chapel side), he had about forty yards to go before stopping and turning. It was getting dark. The light in the yard was due to go on any minute. When the sentry got well away from the kitchen, two British officers whipped up on to the roof of this single-storey building, backing on to the high four-storey back wall of the German yard, and with the help of a lightning conductor pulled themselves up on the roof. They then worked their way to the foot of a smoke stack, braced with iron bands every three or four feet of its height. Unfortunately the searchlights came on just too soon and they were seen. To get at them we had to go up into the orderlies' quarters in the south-west block. There we found four other British officers. Their story was that they were collecting their washing. We gaoled the lot. The last four protested they had nothing to do with this escape. We replied, 'You had no right in the orderlies' quarters anyway, as you know. You will do cells for that, then.'

By now rehearsals were under way for the great British Christmas production 'Ballet Nonsense'. The stage on the third floor of the Saalhaus block (in the south-west corner) rocked with the 'horsepower' of the chorus. The prima ballerina, known as 'Old Horse', was Captain Rogers, about the hairiest 'girl' that could be found among the prisoners, but best known to us as a mining engineer, responsible for the great tunnel built in 1941 at Laufen, near Salzburg, which resulted in all Royal Engineer officers at that camp being sent to Colditz. Laufen,* or Oflag 7A, was a camp for Dunkirk and St Valery prisoners taken in the summer of 1940.

This theatre, I felt, was another possible weak spot of ours. To us, it had one, but only one, slight advantage. It was a privilege. We could stop this privilege as a disciplinary measure, for what that was worth! It was about the only general punishment that we could inflict, although we didn't call it a general punishment; we simply called it the withdrawal of a privilege. Privileges could be withdrawn at any time, for no particular admitted reason. We had done the same with the park walk in the early days, but the OKW had not backed us up, declaring this walk to be a right and not a favour to the prisoners.

Two weeks before Christmas we had a good day taking two tricks in one, but still no tunnel! That day the party for the park was rather large and more than usually unruly, particularly when being counted before the march back. The NCOs in charge were suspicious and checked very, very carefully.

The officer in charge, LO 1 that day, suddenly spotted the reason. 'All from here to the right, move to the right. All from here to the left, move to the left.'

That left one file standing, plus an extra man to the right, in a file of his own. Why hadn't he moved? LO 1 soon found out. This Dutch officer was a dummy! So that was how it was done! We counted again but there were still two missing. We put the dogs on immediately and under a patch of leaves were Lieut

---

*The practice of escaping began among British military personnel on the march from France to Germany. Oflag 7C, Laufen, was the scene of the first attempts from enclosed camps – the first three away being a Gunner Doherty (sent later to Colditz), with two civilians, volunteers from the Finnish war against the Soviets, Messrs. G. Stephenson and A. Hunderson. They were recaught a few miles short of the Yugoslavian border.—ED.

Kruimink and Captain van der Krap. The 'leaves' were a camouflage net.

The Dutch were masters at this sort of thing. Their covering-up of hidey-holes in their rooms was absolutely first-rate. They were thorough and they were stickers.

Only four days later two German officers presented themselves at the yard gate. The guard let them out and saluted. They went off left towards the archway. The guard was a bit slow. He locked the door first of all, and then – the passes? Orders were to demand all passes at all gates from all military personnel. He didn't want to leave his post. Still, he was suspicious and ran after the officers and asked for their '*Ausweise*'.

'That's all right, we're coming straight back,' was the answer, in good German. But not good enough. The guard was called out, and stopped Lieut van Lynden and Captain Steenhover in borrowed, but home-made, plumage.

Two days later leave postings went up. Half of us had the 22nd to the 28th, but my leave was again over the New Year. I had been in Colditz for just over twelve months now and had indeed something to look back on,

Our Kommandant, sixty-nine years old, was on a month's sick leave. His deputy was the third we'd had, an officer we all got on with very well. He had lost an arm in the first war and was no stickler for discipline. We looked forward to our Christmas party that night.

Our Quartermaster officer did us proud, even though belts were tightening. The Ukraine might well be all that our propaganda claimed, but nothing much had arrived from that 'granary' yet. No transport, probably. But in the illustrated papers it was becoming a joke.

That evening, after dinner, we had a show put on by the troops. The guard company provided music and song, and a series of sketches, poking fun at their officers or 'dragging us through the cocoa' as we say in Germany.

Unfortunately the proceedings were somewhat damped by a phone call which put 'a hair in the soup', just as it was coming up – a Christmas present from the prisoners!

The guard NCO hurried in – 'Three French officers have

just escaped from the dentist's.'

'Man all telephones. Mousetrap's the word,' and we called up the local alarm network.

These visits to dentists and hospitals were another gift to the prisoners, putting them outside the normal restrictions of Colditz Castle. They provided a splendid start to possible escaping enterprises. That evening, a party of seven were sent down to the town dentist, under a guard, because up in the Schloss the French officer dentist hadn't the material for more than simple fillings. The patients all came out of our dentist's house together after treatment. Their guard came last. It was very foggy and it was raining too that evening. Three of the party just bolted down the street: Lieuts Durand-Hornus, de Frondeville and Trot. There was nothing the guard could do about it. He couldn't run three ways at once. He daren't fire blindly into the fog. We could do nothing more either once we had warned everyone. So back we went to our Christmas festivities, but the soup was cold and the spirit of the feast was much watered down. The three in due course got right back to France.

We had a lot on our minds that Christmas of 1941. The miners in the castle, whoever they were and wherever they were digging, had got their tunnel through our foundations. We found plain earth now on the dumps up in the attics – no more bricks and stones. We laid on another *Grossrazzia*, or class-one search; but no sign of the tunnel.

A week before Christmas, the prisoners' Theatre Committee wanted a new grand piano. They paid up in camp money, and in due course the thing arrived on a lorry. I knew there would be trouble – there was. Three men took the piano up the narrow stairs to the theatre in sections. They were civilian workers from Leipzig. It was a long, heavy and awkward job, so they took their coats and caps off. They never saw them again. The prisoners refused to return their clothes. They didn't care that clothes cost not only money but clothing coupons as well. So we closed the theatre. The prisoners, anxious for their 'Ballet Nonsense', offered a lump sum. The Kommandant was still away on his cure, so his deputy accepted the offer and the theatre reopened. After this curtain-raiser, the pantomime was a great success!

The year before, the best of the sketches had caricatured a Conservative Member of Parliament making a speech to his constituents. This year, the cream of the show was a German schoolteacher's address to his pupils on the subject of Nazism.

The prisoners' food supply was in some way better than ours, this third Christmas of the war. Red Cross parcels arrived now not only from England, but from New Zealand and the USA as well. They contained butter, biscuits, tins of meat, coffee, sugar, chocolate, cigarettes and so on – good for bribery! Cigarettes also arrived in bulk – tens of thousands at a time. The prisoners had so much sugar that the Poles started making wine from raisins and prunes. Then they began distilling the wine! Where did they get the yeast? From our sentries obviously.

Books began to arrive in large quantities. We provided a room for a library. Gramophone records came in, gramophones, musical instruments. Though everything looked as innocent as it could be, appearances were sometimes deceptive. Our censorship was hard at work.

At New Year the prisoners had their lights on until 1 a.m. At 12.30 each group sang its National Anthem in the yard and then retired to its quarters. I was on duty that New Year's Eve. What had they all got to sing about? I was beginning to see, but at least a year was to go by before I even thought to agree with them. At the same time, I wondered if perhaps they mightn't have some secret source of news to cheer them up. They had maps, of course, all over the camp. There was a big map of Africa on the wall in room No. 406 of the French quarters. I had noticed that – and later was to examine it much more closely.

Meanwhile, we German officers were put on rations too and got food points, just like our civilians. All our rations were reduced by this new grading. For us, it meant only half our old military quota of meat. In fact we were now worse off than the men. We pooled half our points and had one good meal in the mess, at midday. For breakfast and evening meals we looked out for ourselves. Our Kommandment protested over this to

Area Headquarters at Dresden. He got no satisfaction there at all, and, anyway, we noticed on our visits to Ast. 4 there that they didn't eat much better than we did. So we started keeping rabbits and poultry to improve our menu. There were still over three more years of war – war with the Allies, who now included the United States, and, for us at Colditz, war with these prisoners in our gates. Our prisoners didn't really go short of food until the end of 1944, and then the Allied bombing was mainly responsible.

Our German doctor, a Bavarian, sparked off a stupid row about this time, over saluting. He insisted on his salute, or tried to. He insisted that Poland didn't exist and that therefore he was entitled to a salute not only from officers of equal and lower ranks but even from the Polish General Piskor himself. This was too much even for our Kommandant, now back from leave. He refused to back up the *Tierarzt* (or horse-doctor, as they called him in the yard). The French called him the '*Mèdecin Imaginaire*'.

He was responsible, they said, for several 'Malades' – their own General Le Bleu, the English Colonel German, and other high-ranking officers, who were given cells for not saluting the Stabsarzt (of the rank of Captain).

The French were making themselves very conspicuous these days. They were being extremely cocky. Were they creating a diversion? Had they a guilty secret (a tunnel) to hide? Certainly they were the most active company as far as we could see, at the turn of the year 1941–42.

For example, they asked to have the chapel open daily from 6 a.m. to 6 p.m. on religious grounds – they needed, so they said, the spiritual consolation of choir practice and choral recitals and religious instruction to improve the cultural life of the camp in general. We couldn't see why they shouldn't have this and we agreed, occasionally checking the chapel. The spiritual and cultural life of the camp seemed to be going very well in there and, as we discovered very shortly, so indeed was the French tunnel along with it, or rather underneath it! Anticipating what transpired, I cannot agree that this deception was anything other than the very grossest abuse of our concession to culture and religious worship. I feel these

73

prisoners would have stolen the lead out of each other's coffins if they'd had the chance – and during the funeral service, too! There seemed to be no occasion, however sacred, that some of them would not exploit.

The *Tierarzt* was made a complete fool of, over apparently genuine medical cases which the prisoners brought to his notice for operational treatment, through their own doctors. He learned to be more careful when he found his patients had started a tunnel under one of the beds in our sick bay. As for sending operation cases away, whose was the final responsibility? Medically, it was his, but if the 'serious case' escaped from the hospital, Security got the 'cigar'. I have put 'hospital' escapes together in a later chapter, but they were, and to me still are, a very sore point. But we made our greatest error ever, over the Parcel Office. The French General le Brigant asked for one of his officers to be allowed to check the sacks containing private parcels when they arrived from France at Colditz station. He also asked for his Parcel Officer to be allowed to make up a list of the addressees from the labels. This double request was allegedly made because (a) sacks had been found broken into when they got to the castle and (b) the Germans were not very clever at making out names in French. A parole was accepted that the officer concerned 'would not while so occupied escape or make any escape preparations or do anything to the injury of the German Reich'. The officer concerned, who spoke good French and German (being from Lothringen) held this office permanently, as we agreed he kept strictly to his parole.*

The escape figures for the year 1941 are interesting. Altogether 104 prisoners took part in 49 attempts. The English who tried to get away numbered 35, of whom 33 were caught during the attempt, 2 were caught outside the camp, and 0 made the home run. The corresponding figures for other nationalities were: French, 30, 6, 14, 10; Belgian, 6, 6, 0, 0; Polish, 19, 10, 8, 1; Dutch 14, 8, 2, 4.

*Years later, on reading the French story of Colditz, I discovered how wrong we were. See *Les Indomptables* by General Le Brigant.

CHAPTER VI

# Private Enterprise

THE TURN of the year is perhaps a good point in this story to take a breather from the uninterrupted chronicle of escape and attempts to escape that had gone on without a break in one sense, yet with too many breakaways in another, ever since I arrived at Colditz way back in November 1940.

One aspect of our relationship with the prisoners was the matter of 'correctness'. The prisoners took every possible opportunity to nag us about this, but never once in five years did any of their senior officers call for proper behaviour towards us on the part of their own men (so far as we knew). Indiscipline, I can truly say, was the unspoken order of the day on their side; indiscipline often amounting to plain personal insolence, or at least studied offhandedness.

The Dutch officers offended least of all in this respect, and as their escape record was the best, having regard to their numbers, I cannot see that this kind of attitude to us served any purpose, beyond allowing prisoners to work off their repressions.

On the other hand, there were occasions when they would dance on the other foot. I remember one request for a book which I did not wish to issue to one of the British. His note began, 'As this book refers to the battle of Waterloo, the last occasion your troops had the honour to serve under British command . . .'(!) I issued the book.

Another began, 'I should be glad if you would permit me to have this book. It is largely a satire on the stupidness, emptyheadedness and incompetence of the British landed gentry.' I issued this one too.

One day I was searching an English officer, a newcomer to the camp, when he said, 'I am the guest of the Third Reich, and I hope you will value this honour!'

The OKW required a propaganda officer on every PW camp staff. We battled for a long time against this appointment at Colditz. What an utter waste of time! These people were the stoniest possible ground for such airy-fairy seed. We did distribute the weekly propaganda papers in different languages that we had from Berlin – the *Trait d'Union* and the *Camp*, but they were harmless anyway and this was the best way to be rid of them! At first, the British Senior Officer at Colditz confiscated all copies of this latter weekly, refusing to let his officers read it on the grounds that it might be subversive. He soon realised how harmless the publication was, and it circulated freely till finally ending up as fuel.

Most French officers in Colditz abhorred the collaboration of the Pétain-Laval Government in France and thought it their duty more than ever to show their disapproval by hostility to us both in word and deed. Politically, we had no approach at all to the British.

Anti-Semitism didn't get us very far either. We had a number of French-Jewish officers in Colditz. They were put in a separate room, which became known as 'The Ghetto'. There was a little sympathy for them at being so singled out, but I think they preferred to all be together. Certainly they played as active a part proportionately in escape matters as any of the others. No hostility to them among the PWs was ever openly expressed. Some of the French, to tell the truth, were hostile to the British, but we got nothing out of such undercurrents as showed themselves, for instance, during a reading in French of *Joan of Arc* in the courtyard.

The Poles used to court-martial each other, it was said, but kept all these dissensions very much to themselves. We heard that duels were due to be fought out after the war, but we never discovered the identity of the disputants, and so had no opening here to divide and rule!

The Dutch disciplined their officers with 'Room Arrest', which was much the same punishment, basically, as '*Stuben-arrest*' in the German Army, but, again, this was quite normal procedure, and we had no chance whatever of exploiting a disgruntled subaltern.

The British, in 1944, suffered a migration of their more

undisciplined younger officers to what had been once the Ghetto, and later the Belgian quarters. This last company had by then long left the camp but their name remained. This group of British 'activists' was in fact known as 'The Belgians' and prided itself thereon. They issued challenges of every kind to the rest of the British company and at one time seemed to be a thorn in the side of their own senior officer. But never did we profit as 'tertius gaudens' from these subdivisions inside the five national groups in the camp, which differences indeed we barely suspected.

There were only two possible common factors between us and the Allied prisoners. One was hostility to Bolshevism; the other was common achievements in broadly cultural or technical matters. We did have one or two volunteers for the anti-Bolshevist front, but as hardened escapers those concerned were not to be trusted, being plainly out for a free ride over the first obstacle to freedom – the ring around the Schloss.

Eventually being entrusted by the OKW with the hopeless task of Propaganda Officer, near the end of the war I got a meagre attendance at lectures on the historical background of Germany with especial reference to the Reformation, literature, science, and so on. I once asked one of the British officers why he attended, and received the reply, 'Well, I think I'd like a job in the Army of Occupation, and your lectures make a very good German lesson.' I also gave them copies of *Research and Progress*, a very good technical publication which we issued in English and French. And as long as this line wasn't sledge-hammered in, it could be considered a hopeful way of gaining the prisoners' attention – the first step in propaganda.

Through the years I showed films in the castle theatre, but yells of 'propaganda' arose at the slightest excuse. Once or twice we sent groups down to the town cinema, after everyone going had signed the usual parole 'not to escape, make preparations for escape, or in any way injure the German Reich', but some sort of row blew up each time and in the end the cinema manager said, 'No more of that lot, thanks.'

The British, a few times, were allowed out to use the town football ground under guard. Oh, what a smart crowd marched down – yes, marched – through the town! Nothing like the rabble that each afternoon slopped down to our park and back. First-class turnout – boots polished – free chocolate for the kids – boisterous, healthy enthusiasm while playing rugby. These football excursions did not last, for we found ourselves the victims of a magnificent piece of counter-propaganda, largely staged by us. My success as Propaganda Officer, therefore, and I admit it, was 100 per cent nil.

The Christmas and New Year spirit of 1941-2 ebbed slowly away. Thick heads both sides of the wire profited by the sun and snow. LO 1 went off on leave to recover. I took his place. Maybe that tunnel, ever on our minds, was going to break under my nose? Obviously, until it did, there could be no close season for escaping. In fact, there never was any let-up whatsoever right up to the end, over four long years.

The first event of any note for the New Year 1942 was the transfer of a group of thirty-one French officers to Oflag 4D Elsterhorst. Insignificant though this transfer seemed to be, a fortnight later it raised Cain in the ranks of the French company at Colditz. Only one incident marred the operation.

Between Döbeln and Riesa Lieut Bykhowetz got out of the carriage window and along the running-board to a safe place between the carriages. However, he was seen climbing along the train, and two guards followed him outside along the icy steps in the freezing cold. Bykhowetz retreated as they advanced and all three finished up on the buffers at the very end of the train. Bykhowetz was making up his mind to jump. The guards were simply waiting for the train to stop before they could grab him. Realising that if he jumped the guards would jump as well, and there would be no getting away, Bykhowetz stayed where he was and, when the train drew to a stop, he was a prisoner once more.

On January 7th we found four officers had gone – 'spurlo. verschwunden' – vanished without trace! Those missing were two Dutch lieutenants, Luteyn and Donkers, and two British Neave and Hyde-Thomson. Their senior officers gladly and most unexpectedly gave us their names, without putting us to the trouble of finding out exactly who had got away. How very suspicious! How very damnably sure they must have been of themselves and their mysterious bolt-hole! And not a breath of suspicion to be traced anywhere around our ring of guards.

We ran another of our special searches, from 10 a.m. to 2 in the afternoon of that day, keeping over 500 prisoners in the cold of the yard while we did it. The noise was so loud, unceasing and so threatening, that the Kreisleiter phoned from the town to ask what was up. He said the townspeople were getting upset! We found nothing. Tiger and his dogs went round the outside of the Schloss along the upper edge of the park, looking for a tunnel exit or traces in the snow. No luck at all.

By then the OKW was getting worried. They began to ask about the 'spoil' from an obvious tunnel which we had been reporting off and on for weeks. They bombarded us with questions and advice. One night they rang up, 'Is Romilly there? Is Emil there?' We sent the Riot Squad NCO to his cell. 'Yes, he's there. No, there's not somebody in his place. No, it's not a dummy. We've been in and woken him up.' Trying to catch us, eh?

Five days after the four vanished we clawed back a point. The railway police at Ulm had let two suspicious Dutch electrical workers carry on with their journey through, on the 8th, the day after the escape from Colditz. But when two more arrived by the same train at the same time the next day, going likewise to Tuttlingen, the police questioned them a little more closely, and finally phoned us that they had Lieuts Hyde-Thomson and Donkers, of our address, if we wished to collect them. Neave and Luteyn got over the Swiss frontier successfully.

A few days later I found our Emil trotting round the yard. I hadn't seen Romilly taking exercise like this before.

'What does this mean?' I asked jokingly. 'In training?'

'Aha!' he replied, 'when it's my turn to make the trip I must be fit.'

'Well,' I thought, 'that's a smart reaction. If Romilly has it in mind to be away too, the exit must be from inside the castle and not down in the park. Romilly never leaves the castle yard.'

This exit could really only be found by the Senior Duty Officer, who at this time was myself, co-operating with the staff NCOs, Mussolini and Dixon Hawke, who were in charge of the orderlies and daily jobs in the prisoners' quarters and yard. This was our world. We knew more about it than anybody else. Something just had to be done. The Kommandant and Security Officer were panicking.

So we three held a meeting and, unknown to the Kommandant and the Security Officer, made out the following Plan:

(1) To list every conceivable place where an exit could have been made.
(2) To concentrate on unoccupied rooms.
(3) To report any comments, however casual, made by the prisoners during conversation with us.
(4) To keep the search quiet from all our own people.

This last point arose for two reasons:

(a) Kommandant and Security were in a panic over these escapes by yet another unknown route. What would happen to them if Romilly should get away?
(b) There were one or two in our own Mess who would have been delighted at any further escapes, since these would show that our 'tame' policy towards the prisoners just did not pay.

We wanted no excitement over this job that we had set ourselves and certainly no more mass searches. We felt that just a few of us working in the spirit of private enterprise would do very much better.

Having made our plan to search all the parts of the castle not occupied in the normal way, Mussolini, Dixon Hawke and I started on our more or less private search.

First we looked into the big cellar under the French quarters in the west, or cellar, block. Nothing but potatoes here, the walls all solid stonework or natural rock. No suspicion of an indication of any digging here. Next we searched the former wine cellar, long since empty of bottles. Often I had examined the walls, which were also partly cut into the natural rock. We found nothing. How near we were had we but known it! But we were looking for one escape route – in reality there were two.

We left the potato cellar and next day we searched the chapel. We moved the altar aside – nothing underneath. We went through the sacristy pretty thoroughly – nothing there. We inspected the organ and the deep window niches – everything in order, even to the layers of dust.

By the 13th we had discovered nothing. On parade that morning no one was missing, so we felt safe for another days On the other hand, we had felt just the same the previous week when four officers had been found missing and, furthermore, must have been missing and somehow covered up for more than one roll-call.

That morning the theatre was down on our list for search. This was on the third floor of the Saalhaus. It was used for plays, concerts, PT, boxing, fencing, lectures, and so on. We occupied some of the ground floor of that block, so there wasn't much prospect of finding a tunnel. The south end of the upper floors, occupied by the prisoners, had window. looking out over our own yard, or else was walled off from our north wing. The west front of this building looked out over the approach yard between the archway and the guardroom, the back adjoined the orderlies' quarters, which looked out over the prisoners' yard.

We went over the theatre floor, tapped the walls, looked up at the ceiling, examined the window bars, and inspected the small greenrooms each side of the stage. Then we came to the stage itself. There it was – just a stage. I ran my eye over it, and my mind around it. Was there a trapdoor in this stage, I wondered? How deep was it underneath? And then – had we ever looked under the stage? The Ferret said we never had, as far as he could remember. So I told him to get down into the prompter's box and shine his torch around.

Fouine prised a board out of the prompter's steps and did what I said. I told him to climb in and search around under the boards. He couldn't get through the hole, being too fat, and I was on the point of giving up the idea. However, we had made a rule, and that demanded that we inspect every single surface, even the most unlikely ones. Seeking a further reason for the extra mental effort on my part, and the extra physical one on the Ferret's, or someone else's, I thought we might find a hide under the stage. So I went down to the guardroom and told them to send the smallest man they had up to the theatre, to force a way through and have a look at this slightly suspected space under the stage. I was still in the guardroom ten minutes later when the man came hurrying down again – 'Herr Hauptmann – we have found a hole under the stage.'

I rushed back upstairs, to find they had broken away all the prompter's steps, crawled to the back and found a hole about two feet square in the flooring. Fouine had pulled out a plaster-covered framework which covered the hole, fixed with turn-buckles to the joists each side. The floor under the stage was, at the back, the ceiling of an unused cul-de-sac below, that came from the German quarters on the upper floor of the guardroom building. We had never taken measurements of all the floors as this passageway was never used, and it was behind a locked door on our side. So we had left the prisoners a very simple barrier, no more than a floor–ceiling between their quarters plus a door into a passage on our side to get through. What's more, the passage ran from the Saalhaus building, to the guardroom building, over the top of the yard gate! There was even a window in it above the gate. Never seeing anyone at this window, the PWs must have worked out that here was some more dead ground for them to work in! They did not have to break through a vertical wall – they simply had little more than to drop through a horizontal one of lath and plaster. I went down to the guardroom, up the stairs, along the passage over the gate, through a door and arrived at the dead end under the back of the stage. We had taken the framework out and there was the hole in the ceiling large enough to take a man through without brushing off the plaster each side. So confident had they been over this exit that no camouflage to speak of had been used to cover the frame-work on the top side, and close alongside, under the stage, we found a rope made of bed-sheets, for lowering the escapers to the floor underneath. This was obviously how the four of them had got out the week previously.

The corridor ran back over the yard gate to the top floor of the guardroom building, and from there a spiral staircase descended past our officers' Mess, or Casino as we called it, down past the guard quarters on the first floor, and so to a passage outside the guardroom on the ground floor.

We checked back, interviewing guards. Naturally no one remembered anything a week after the event, but some one or more of them must have let four prisoners past, two on each of two occasions, presumably in perfect disguise as German military personnel. That meant they had not been stopped for their passes. This was a breach of one of our most important orders, one which we could never get properly observed. We worked out all the possibilities, and in the end decided there was only one way the four could have taken, and that was straight past the guardroom at the foot of the staircase, out of the guardroom entrance into the approach yard and on under the archway into the German yard. Now from here we did find there was a possible way out, completely unguarded. At the south-west corner of our yard the way led again under an archway, and over a bridge, crossing the old moat or ditch, to the main gate. At the inner end of the bridge there was a wicket gate and a path leading down into the moat and along to the married quarters as a short cut. Officers going out for hospital treatment could have noticed this wide-open gap in our defences, and made a mental note of it for future use.

More precautionary measures were once again forced upon us. To begin with, we walled up the wicket gate, and made a new door in view of the gatehouse guard. Then we closed the theatre, which didn't hurt anybody really, and moved our officers' Mess from over the guardroom to the comparative safety of the German yard. Sarcastic comments from the 'opposition' in our Mess. The prisoners were driving us out of our own Casino! Who runs this joint? The door at the top of the guardroom stairs, which led to this dead-end passage, was doubly bolted. The horses, however, had gone. Two never came back. But I got a week's leave and a bottle of champagne from the Kommandant for my discovery up in the theatre.

The success of our trio, Mussolini, Dixon Hawke and myself, earned us the most vicious hatred of the French company. It also earned me the nickname of Tartuffe, due, no doubt, to my habit of suppressing all my hostile or unpleased reactions beneath a somewhat strained and wavering grin. I would not lose my temper to these tormentors whose insults were undoubtedly directed at me personally, as well as at me as a German officer. I may have made an unfavourable impression on the French company, but really it was better that way. Personally, I was naturally upset to have aroused so much hatred, but as this arose from my job I took it as the measure of my success.

However, while we had found an exit that we hadn't suspected, we still had to find the tunnel. On January 14th, the day after we found that theatre hole, we whipped the English down to a building outside the castle for the day, while we put their quarters, as it were, through a sieve. We did not find much, and they replaced something of what they lost by stripping the building we put them into temporarily of all available fittings. Two of them were found in hiding when it was time to come back to the castle, but I think they were just mere face-savers to show that the spirit was willing, although the weather was dreadful.

Still no tunnel. We did find one entry though, in the floor over the canteen below the British Long Room. This showed traces of tunnelling in the hollow space between the vaulting and the floor, but the workings were only on a small scale.

My private Search Committee met again. Had we really been over every single surface, up or down and sideways, in every single unoccupied space in the Schloss? We crossed off the attics, theatre, cellars – and our minds wandered round the rooms, floors, landings, corridors, buttresses and entrances that we knew so well.

Suddenly I thought of the clock tower in the north-west corner of the yard, at the corner where the north, or chapel, side of the yard met the west block, or Kellerhaus (Cellarhouse). On the ground floor of the Cellarhouse were the parcel office and stores, and the infirmary. Above, on 1st, 2nd, 3rd and top floors were the French company. Over a year previously we'd found two French officers digging at the very bottom of the tower. We had thereupon bricked up the doors giving access to the floorings inside this tower – one on each floor level. The clock weights used to hang down inside through holes in the tower floors, but the clock had never worked in our time, and the weights and cables had been removed by our Security Officer in 1940. We had never, now we thought it over, looked inside this vertical shaft. The top was sealed off with beams. We'd often stood on them in the attic. I arranged an inspection of the clock tower for January 15th. That morning, I sent Mussolini to the top of the tower to get a couple of beams off and shine a light down below. Mussolini moved two beams from the top of the shaft and saw a light and heard movement down below. He looked down the canvas pipe, down which the clock weights used to hang, passing through holes in the landings in the tower. He had a boy with him expressly to lower down this shaft. The boy went down the rope and immediately started to shout: 'There's someone here.'

Three French officers were down there, caught in the act, shifting rubble. Fifty feet above ground we'd found the way down into their tunnel. The French terrified the boy on his rope with threats, while they bashed their way out through a half brick side wall. Mussolini sent for help. He couldn't fire down the shaft because of the boy and we hadn't even put guards on each of the three floor exits from the tower landings which we had bricked up in 1941. There seemed no point in that. The French burst through into a bathroom, actually into a bath (occupied), and escaped.

I was told all this after I had hurried over from my quarters and had gone up to see what Mussolini had discovered. I had the lowest door into the shaft broken open. We climbed in and looked up through the holes in the floors. A vertical approach again, like the air shaft down to our kitchen – like the hole down from the stage! Stacks of treasure trove fell into our hands – tools, clothes, but only, alas, twenty-three marks in German money. Still, we had found the start of the tunnel. It began, of all places, right at the top of the building – hardly the place to look for an underground tunnel! But still we hadn't found the main run of the prisoners' tunnel – only the start of it. They got into this vertical shaft which we had, in effect, presented them with a year previously, by moving the beams at the top, and then what? They got down to the bottom of the shaft and into the cellar by this simple, unobserved way. But from somewhere in the cellar there must be a horizontal shaft. We went down and looked around. There was no hole anywhere in the floor or in the walls.

I left a sentry down in the cellar and went off to report and think. The sentry was a bright lad. He got a hammer and tapped away at every square foot of all the four walls of that cellar and the floor as well, and in the end he found a loose square of stonework and there, behind it, was the entrance to the tunnel.

But this horizontal shaft did not run north by the shortest route to outside the wire. It went due east under the chapel. Great iron-hard and centuries-old supporting beams under the chapel floor had been sawn right through. A single track line and trolley served to bring back the rubble from the working face to the foot of the tower up which it was hauled to the roof and disposed of under the attics, as we knew. An electric lighting and signalling system had been installed. This was run from the circuit in the sacristy and was controlled from there when necessary, under cover of the 'religious and cultural ceremonies' which we so foolishly had permitted six months previously. Why had they gone east under the chapel, and not the shortest way out – due north? We thought they had suspected a crypt.

At the end of the chapel, the tunnel went down vertically for more than twenty feet to get under the foundations, and then out again towards the steep slope of the park. I crawled to the end and right out to the working face. Over my head I could just hear, now and then, the sentries marching up and down. There were only about thirty more feet to go. The earth was soft and easy to work. We were only just in time.

The French were quite certain that the tunnel had been given away through injudicious talk by some of their number who had recently been transferred to Elsterhorst, but that was not true. The circumstances of the start of our inspection of the clock tower that morning showed that we had had absolutely no idea of what was waiting for us. We certainly never expected to find the entrance to a tunnel right up under the roof. If we had indeed had a tip-off about this, we certainly should at least have put sentries on each floor up against the bricked-up tower entrances. This find was one of those lucky chances that happen occasionally if one follows a sound principle long enough. In this case our rule was to close in slowly and methodically upon a suspected danger spot, ignoring lack of results until the job was finished, whether successfully or unsuccessfully. This was indeed a find – at least six months of work must have gone into this tunnel project. We were all cock-a-hoop – especially the Kommandant. He gave our Search Committee special leave as a reward, and in a fit of generosity included the man who'd actually found the entrance in the cellar among the beneficiaries!

## CHAPTER VII

# *Overconfidence Undermined*

IT MAY have been the general reaction of fury and helpless rage over the discovery of the chapel tunnel, particularly among the French officers, that provoked the incident involving Lieut Verkest of the Belgian company. This officer went just too far one morning, in his refusal to salute the Duty Officer, and to take his hands out of his pockets when ordered to. This occurred when all were lined up for parade and in the immediate presence of a number of other officers. A court-martial was ordered on a charge of disobeying an order. The local lawyer, the ex-prisoner-of-war from England, undertook the defence. The hearing was due in March, till when Verkest remained in arrest.

Meanwhile, we wrangled long and loud with the prisoners over the repairs to be done in the clock tower, under the chapel and in the attics. Who was going to pay for this and for the removal of several tons of rubble? A local contractor wanted twelve thousand marks – nearly a thousand pounds – for the clearance job! He had to fill up the holes with concrete as well, by the way. The Kommandant made a forced levy out of all prisoners' pay. Prisoners were entitled to half their home rate of pay at an exchange rate of so many marks to their own currency (15 marks to the English £). This was given them in camp marks – not legal tender. The Swiss Government held the real cash, which both we and the Allies paid up as backing for camp money issued on both sides. The OKW came into the tunnel dispute at the prisoners' request, and ruled against this collective fine. They ordered the repayment of these sums, arguing that this was a collective punishment and the Kommandant had no authority to inflict it. They said it was illegal under the Geneva Convention. We lost face at first, but regained it, and our money, by a happy interpretation of the same Convention, supported this time by the barrack-room lawyers of the OKW.

We used the canteen profits, which under the Convention, as we so happily noted, might be used 'for the benefit of the prisoners'. Obviously, we said, it was to the prisoners' advantage that the roof should not collapse upon them or the floor in their so valuable chapel should not subside beneath them! And there was no gainsaying that!

As to defence measures – we closed the chapel indefinitely. It had been misused. We also buried microphones every thirty feet all round the outside of the prisoners' buildings. More brand new tools found in the clock tower again showed that the bribery and corruption of our guard company was still rampant. The OKW ordered their replacement.

One might now have thought that the loss of two major hopes, the British exit under the stage and the French tunnel under the chapel, plus the frightful cold (20° below zero Centigrade), would have lowered the prisoners' will to active resistance. Far from it! A year or two under prison restraint does not necessarily break a man's spirit. Some, indeed, do go down. On the other hand, some undoubtedly profit by the experience, both at the time, and in later life as well.

In January we had an escape from an unexpected quarter. Medical and religious personnel were to some extent privileged under the Geneva Convention. We allowed doctors and ministers, as well as Red Cross orderlies, to go outside the limits of the park for exercise. They went out on walks in the Colditz Forest, more 'escorted' by one guard than guarded by several. We certainly didn't think that they would try to get away. On this occasion, the irrepressible French priest, Jean-Jean, and their doctor, Leguet, made a break while out in the woods. There was only one guard to the group of five, and he could not, of course, stop them. They got as far as Saarbrücken before recapture, in civilian clothes, with the usual false papers on them and German money. This escape we felt to be a breach of trust. In any case, privileged or not privileged, these two took their twenty-one days' cells without protest!

Still undeterred by nearly a month of defeat, the prisoners carried on undaunted with their regular business of attempting to escape. Hoping to profit by the distraction of all the recent excitement, a Dutch cadet officer, Linck, nearly got out in a cartload of sacks filled with empty cartons from the parcel office. The orderlies were in the know but, try as they could, Linck's weight required two of them for that particular sack, whereas all the others were light enough for one man. The NCO in the parcel office was on the alert and so Linck was discovered.

In view of the escape of three French officers at Christmas from the town dentist, we thought it safer for the latter to come up to the castle to give treatment. One day his hat and fur coat were stolen by the waiting 'patients'. After a long wrangle we took 320 marks out of the canteen profits in return. It was surely 'to their advantage' to have dental treatment available? LO 1 got his usual fun out of the event – 'This coat costs 320 marks,' he announced. 'The next one will cost 1,000.'

The indiscipline in the camp never ceased to have its effect in the cold war between staff and prisoners. LO 1 was held largely responsible for this. We had some argument about it. As senior Duty Officer, had he not started off, right back in 1940, on the wrong foot? This sort of life was no joke, and we felt it was he who had set the tone of our relations from the beginning, and that it was the wrong tone entirely. Besides, he liked his drink, and everyone, the prisoners and ourselves, knew it. There were some stand-up rows in the Mess about him, and in the end, although he was well in with the Kommandant, LO 1 was helped upstairs to the post of Deputy Kommandant which kept him out of the prisoners' yard pretty well altogether. At the same time, his sharpest critic, LO 4, was posted down in the town, in charge of the Indian prisoners in the Schützenhaus camp there.

It fell to me now to bear the maximum brunt of contact with the 'bad boys', with three roll-calls and several arguments per day to work from. I had been doing this work while LO 1 was on leave, and shortly after his return and promotion I found myself in his shoes as the new No. 1 Duty Officer.

When Mussolini and the Ferret got back from their special leave after our recent successes, there was still just one more place on the list of 'unoccupied quarters', that we had not visited. This was a kind of buttress on the eastern outer wall of the castle. It looked rather like a lift shaft or an outside staircase built up the side of a house. I asked a paymaster, who knew the place from before the war, as an asylum, whether this was a solid or a hollow construction. 'It's solid,' he said. 'I know this place from boyhood. I've been everywhere in this castle. You can't get in there.'

Before we made up our minds to search this last possible hole on our list, however, the prisoners showed that our list wasn't complete!

February 21st was a Saturday, time for a slight week-end relaxation, perhaps. But no!

The yard sentry reported a missing bar in the end inner window of the British Long Room, over the canteen. Our Duty Officer and Fouine came in to inspect the break. Several bars had, in fact, been removed from the window, which gave on to a narrow piece of flat roof, on top of the one-storey building on the south side of the prisoners' yard.

A tunnel had been dug in the deep snow on this roof, right out from the window and as close as possible along the back wall of our quarters which rose up sheer the full four floors on the north side of the German yard.

This piece of flat roof came to an end ten feet out from the Long Room window, against the side of a sloping slate roof which covered some sort of attic over the ceiling of the Conference Room below. This attic no one of us, till then, had ever entered or even noticed. The prisoners had beaten us to it into this penthouse, barely fifteen feet square, with two dormer windows which had never been opened, in our time, overlooking the prisoners' yard. Here was an unoccupied 'room', of whose very existence our special search squad was completely unaware!

As Fouine wriggled along the tunnel, one of the dormer windows opened and a shower of tools landed in the snow a dozen feet below. Willing hands snaffled them up and vanished. As our NCO wormed through a gap in the slate-hung side of the penthouse, a figure slipped down from the open window, following the tools to the ground below and, likewise, disappeared up the corner staircase into the British quarters.

Our yard sentry watched all this, pop-eyed, his rifle not even cocked. There were still two officers in the penthouse, and now the Ferret let fly with his revolver as a warning against whoever else might make for the window exit.

'*Sch — ssen Sie mir, bitte, nicht*,' observed one of them, tortuously but politely requesting that no harm might fall upon him. We found on these two, Lieuts Mackenzie and Orr-Ewing, thirty German marks, a pass and a compass. Who it was who had escaped out of the window, I never found out.*

An examination of the floor of the penthouse showed that while most of it corresponded with the ceiling of the Conference Room below, that part nearest the corner of the yard was over an empty space between the Evidenz Room and the canteen. This area was roughly in the shape of a slice of cheese, six feet wide up against the German back wall, and about two feet wide where it narrowed to the prisoners' yard. It had no window, but a trapdoor connected the attic with this empty place below.

We hit on the idea of making a passage through the main wall between the penthouse and our own quarters, with a door each end of it. The wall was six feet thick at this point. One door gave on to one of our rooms, the other into the penthouse. We could get through the doors and into the penthouse, and then drop down through the trapdoor into the empty room and, then, by putting in a small access door, we could slip sideways into the Evidenz Room. This access route might serve handy if we wished to get into the prisoners' yard quickly and entirely unobserved. I can't in point of fact recall that we ever did use this route, but more than once the PWs tried to use it, in our direction. In fact, only a few days after this new piece of work had been completed, we surprised two officers in the attic, fiddling with the lock on one of our new doors, the one on their side of the wall. They got away, but we put bolts on our side of that door as well for additional precautions.

*I learnt, many years after the war, on reading *The Colditz Story*, that the escaper on this occasion was the author of that book, Captain P. R. Reid.

Anxious to get to the end of our search list without further interruptions, we finally arranged to tap the suspected buttress on the outer side of the prisoners' east wall. A few days later we went into the yard (unannounced, of course) with a couple of men, and moved smartly up the staircase into the Dutch quarters, against which this buttress was built. Their warning system seemed to have let them down. Learning from our error with the French in the clock tower, we put guards on all the floors of this building before we started work. This time our surprise and our precautions were fully effective.

As we broke through into the hollow building (not solid as we had been advised), a rope ladder whipped up before our eyes. I left the sentries in place and sent for some iron pins, and using these as pitons in the side of the shaft we had holed into, I climbed up to the top at third-floor level. There waiting for me, were two Dutch officers, Captains Dames and Hagemann. They had been digging a tunnel at the foot of this buttress and had gone up the rope ladder as we came in. As we reached them they went out sideways through the wall. The wall, of course, opened to assist them, and we found the hinged door two foot square in the masonry to be at the back of their urinal. This was their entrance and exit to the buttress. On the urinal side it was camouflaged with the creosote we used to hand out so liberally at the earnest request of the Dutch 'in the interests of hygiene'! Also on the inside, fortunately, was a guard, who held these two officers until we followed them out.

The treasure was immense. Five whole boxes of clothing, containing items of German uniform and complete home-made civilian suits, two sacks of cement which we had been missing for some time, and best of all two lifesize dummies which must have been used to cover up the January theatre escapes on parades. We had found one dummy in a park attempt in December; they must have made these since then. At roll-calls – when the Dutch stood like dummies and the dummies stood like Dutch!

This Dutch tunnel was new, but it was only fifteen yards to an eventual exit in the park – almost as close as the French had got after what must have taken months of work under the chapel.

We put a window at the bottom of this shaft and a light inside it, and we checked it every day from outside.

Next on the list for some excitement came the *Stabsarzt*, the Horse Doctor as he was known to the prisoners. He was fairly lenient with his patients, and if anyone really looked ill (and saluted him smartly too) he let them into the Revier, or Infirmary, without too much questioning, where they could lie up for a few days. Imagine his fury when, one day, on receipt of certain information (the first and very nearly the only occasion that we ever got anything out of a stooge), we went straight to one of the beds and found underneath the tunnel which the informer had told us of. It hadn't much hope of success, but there it was, in a room full of sick prisoners! The *Tierarzt* reduced the number by half on the spot.

The Kommandant stopped the walk to the park as well. He knew he couldn't do it for long, but he would annoy the few ever going out for a walk that fearful winter for a few days, just until they could get an '*antrag*', or complaint, in to higher authorities and get his ruling reversed. And he also stopped the sale of beer. I don't think that had much effect either because, as we knew, the prisoners were now making their own wine from raisins and distilling was well on in the experimental stage.

The war in the Far East was going badly for the Allies. Singapore fell, Hong Kong, Java and all the Dutch islands. The *Scharnhorst* got through the Channel. In a British diary I found an entry under March 12th: 'Debate—the rot has set in? —motion carried.' Naval setbacks always hit the British hardest.

Two months after the discovery of the French tunnel, cartloads of rubble were still coming down from the attics. The orderlies loaded it into a cart (only one was available) and this trotted back and forth to the town rubbish dump.

It was only a matter of time before Lieut Desjobert got into the cart during the lunch break, while the driver and his horse were out of the yard for their meal. When the work started again the officer was covered by the French and British orderlies with the first few shovelfuls of rubble as intended, but unfortunately they put too much over him and he began to stifle when the load moved off. He managed to last as far as the main street of the town, but there he had to get out from under and breathe. Soldiers in the town brought him back to the castle. The 'zigarre' this time came to me first, as I was LO 1. I passed it on to Mussolini, as being in charge of the orderlies, and he shrugged it off on the guard who was actually supervising the loading. He passed it back to the guardroom, saying anyway the final check was theirs to carry out. We had, you may remember, told the NCOs in charge of the guard, whenever bulk loads came in or out they were to probe with their bayonets. They had omitted to do this and the escape nearly succeeded. At the same time, it showed how responsibility became scaled down as between orders at top level and performance at the bottom. No doubt the burden of responsibility passes as quickly upwards or downwards in the German Army as in any other!

At the end of that month of March, the prisoners showed that they had still not given up the idea of breaking through from their quarters into the Kommandantur side of the German yard where they joined. The attic approach by means of the snow tunnel had failed. Now Lieut van Lynden managed to get through the overlapping floor of the Dutch quarters into the guard quarters below, on our side, where at the time there was, or should have been, no one at all. It was a Sunday afternoon and all quiet. Van Lynden was disguised as a German officer. When he was safely down he took a broom and began to sweep away traces of the plaster knocked down from above, while his comrades fixed up a camouflage. But a sentry interrupted from behind a cupboard, saying, 'Please, Captain, would it not be better for me to do the sweeping?' It was one of our own men who had stayed behind that afternoon, had heard a noise above and had hidden while van Lynden came down through the ceiling.

The last event of March was the court-martial of the Belgian officer, Lieut Verkest, who had flatly refused recognition of our Duty Officer back in January. This was held by the Court to be disobedience and Verkest, for that, was sentenced to three years. At the same time, during the court-martial, Verkest revealed that the group of thirty-three Belgian officers in Colditz had agreed to disobey the Kommandant's orders about saluting – although, in our view, they were subject to his discipline under the Convention.

They had also passed a resolution concerning those members of the Belgian Armed Forces who had given their parole to us and returned to freedom. The Court held this, as well as the group refusal to salute, to be an 'agreement to disobey orders concerning duty matters', and therefore mutiny. Verkest was sentenced to death. Sentence was suspended for three months. The Head of State must confirm it. After a while the papers came back from the OKW with Hitler's marginal note 'Loss of freedom sufficient'. The Court sat again at Leipzig (on July 21st); Verkest was sentenced to two years. By the time he was out the Belgians had left Colditz.

This death sentence shook the prisoners, as I think nothing else ever did. The battle for salutes quietened down. A few weeks later, the *Tierarzt*, our great champion at the saluting base (although we could have done without his enthusiasm), left the camp. He was replaced by the doctor from the French generals' camp at Königstein.

The month of March chalked us up yet one more success, to make it the most favourable quarter we ever knew on that cold front between the prisoners and their freedom.

It so happened that about this time we had one of our periodic visits from members of the International Red Cross. They came to see that all was well with the supply, either directly, or as directed by them, of food parcels to the prisoners from the different Allied countries on the one hand, or from relatives on the other.

I should perhaps lead up to our discovery of the use to which some parcels were put by saying something about the system and the supplies which it passed through to prisoners-of-war in Germany. Food parcels were more or less standardised to weigh about 10 lb. each. They came from different countries and the British prisoners received them from England, Australia, Canada and United States, in bulk. In addition, four private parcels could be sent per annum to each prisoner, from families or friends, and we controlled the arrival of these parcels by an arrangement whereby they might only be sent against a special type of label which was issued in the permitted quantity to the person authorised. Private parcels usually contained clothing or books. Cigarette parcels were also allowed to individuals in unlimited quantity. Besides food, the Red Cross also sent bulk consignments of cigarettes and tobacco for distribution among the inmates of the camps. From 1941 onwards the supply of parcels of different kinds was regular enough to keep at least all the British prisoners decently clothed, and sufficient also to provide one food parcel per week for each prisoner in their ranks, as well as fifty cigarettes a week.

The French received food parcels mainly from private sources, but they did have a certain amount of bulk supply in the form of what they called 'Singe' or 'Monkey' which was tinned meat from their Army reserve. It came from Madagascar. I remember the name Antananarivo (Tanarive) on the tins. They also had large quantities of 'Biscuits Pétain', French army biscuits, which they exchanged with the British for cigarettes at the rate of one for one. The Poles and Dutch had private food parcels but in no such quantity as the British mass or private supplies, so that they were not particularly well off for food or clothes or cigarettes at any time during the war.

From 1942 onwards it would be true to say that most of the Colditz prisoners were better fed than the German civilians in the town, at least as regards calorie intake. They had chocolates, sugar, butter, tinned meat and dried fruit in quantities, and went so far as to make wine from their sugar and raisins and to distil from this wine a foully intoxicating alcoholic mixture. What they did lack, all of them, was, of course, fish and fresh fruit. All these parcels, together with the mail, were subjected to a strict censorship on our side. What we were after was contraband. I say here and now that we never on any occasion found any contraband, or anything that could be described as contraband, in the bulk supplies which came from, or through, the International Red Cross. We did, however, find a tremendous amount of forbidden goods in private clothing parcels and in private food parcels, in particular in those which came from France. We also found a lot of contraband in the 'Welfare' parcels which were sent out from England either individually or by under-cover organisations.

The Red Cross could not possibly connive at this game, as it was acting exclusively on humanitarian grounds, and indeed was also organising supplies from Germany to our own prisoners in Allied hands. Had there been instances of misuse of this authority, there is no doubt that both sides would have suffered and the International Red Cross's reputation would have been done irreparable harm.

We were a little late in the contraband stakes, and the prisoners were several jumps ahead before we discovered exactly what was going on in this line under our very noses.

One of our censors worked in the book trade in Leipzig. In the early part of 1942, he noticed that the covers on some of the books that he was handling seemed rather thicker than usual, especially as paper was in short supply all over the world. At his suggestion the covers of half a dozen books sent by the Prisoner's Leisure Hour Fund from Lisbon, were opened up. They were found to contain in every case either 100-mark notes, or maps on silk of, for example, the Swiss frontier, the Yugoslav frontier, the Dutch and Belgian frontiers, the layout of Danzig harbour, and so on. We even found tiny hacksaw blades in these covers as well. It then struck us that we had recently received and passed on to individual prisoners several other parcels from this same source in Lisbon. Something had to be done. At least these books must be taken back. That meant a visit from me to the British library.

The British librarian was now the Methodist minister Platt. I knew him well. He had heard of me from a mutual friend in England before the war. I went over to the prisoners' library and got him to give me back several of these Lisbon books. I said I wanted them for 'statistical purposes'. Some of these books were out on loan to readers, but Platt promised to get them back, and let me have them, by the afternoon.

Back in the censor's office we found that the books I had collected also had unusual covers with valuable contents.

But when I got the rest of the books that afternoon, I found that the covers had all been cut open and emptied, and the endpapers stuck back on again. The prisoners must have realised what I was after, and had removed the contraband from what till then had been a first-rate hiding place.

From then on, no book covers at all were allowed, and to save ourselves trouble we put it through to the OKW and they agreed with us, that the prisoners should be allowed to receive only books with paper backs. For once there was no argument in Colditz.

I admit I played a trick on the Padre with those books. I won half the trick and lost the other half. But did he really expect me to say we thought there was contraband in these books, and that was why I wanted them back?

We now began to take a very much closer interest in parcels from sources other than the International Red Cross. We installed an X-ray apparatus and subjected every incoming object without exception to its revealing gaze. We then found that the Licensed Victuallers Sports Association was also helping most effectively to replenish the prisoners' stocks of escape material. Hollow-handled tennis rackets contained tiny compasses and hacksaw blades. Gramophone records contained maps and yet more money in the centre. Playing cards had maps inside them.

When one new prisoner arrived we discovered in his chess set 1,000 Reichsmarks, three compasses and seven maps!

We felt that our X-ray machine would soon put a stop to all this, but while it blocked one smuggling route used by the British, I learnt (but only over ten years later!) that it merely served to open another and better one for the French.

At Easter 1942, the chapel was still closed for repairs and so the Catholics celebrated their Easter ceremonies in their yard. Their services were in Latin. The Protestants or sectarians here, and elsewhere, celebrated their Easter without saints and song, and much more simply. They had their own services, each in his own quarters and each in his own tongue. The Jews in Colditz had apparently no particular observance of the day of this Christian feast. There was no Rabbi among them anyway.

In the Schützenhaus camp in the town, the Indian prisoners worshipped Mahommed, turning their faces and kneeling towards the east every day. The group of White Russians from the old 1920 Wrangel Army, prisoners now from the French and Jugoslav Armies, cried to each other – '*Xpnctoc Bockpece! Bouctunno Bockpece!*' – 'Christ is risen – In truth he has risen' – on the occasion of Easter, their greatest orthodox feast.

Christ – Mahommed – Allah – Brahma – Buddha. We had in Colditz an 'International' of religion as well as of race. So had the Soviets, but their religion claimed no God but godlessness. I recalled Goethe's reply to the rigid immovable dogmatists – 'What religion do you confess?' – 'None of those that you name.' 'And why?' – 'On religious grounds.' The Soviets had broken the circle. For them godlessness was god. A White Russian officer told me how he once gave the story of Christ to Soviet prisoners in one of our hospitals. They listened to him open-mouthed, as to an unheard-of fairy story.

Four days from the end of April, no less than five 'serious medical cases' from Colditz escaped from a military hospital at Gnaschwitz, near Dresden, where the *Tierarzt* had sent them for treatment. He was wild with fury! Two were Polish officers, Lieuts Wychodzew and Niestrzeba. These two coolly sent our Kommandant a picture postcard from Hof. That meant they were going south-west. We warned Stuttgart Kriminal polizei, and they picked up the first-named at the station after two days at large. I went to collect him. Lieut Niestrzeba was caught in a train the next day at Singen near the Swiss frontier, disguised as a Belgian worker, with papers in the name of Carl Winterbeck. Unfortunately he also had on him his PW number plate, with Oflag 4C on it!

The other three 'sick' were the Polish lieutenant Just (yet again!), the Belgian lieutenant Remy, and the British squadron-leader Paddon. These three all posed as Belgian workers. In Leipzig they came under suspicion. Just and Remy were being watched when Remy suddenly dashed away. We never heard of him again. Paddon and Just, who had intended to travel separately, met again by chance, and were both picked up while casually talking. There was a bad error in their passports. These, of course, were faked. Paddon had exactly the same signature on two of his documents, although ostensibly issued at different centres, one in Leipzig, the other in Dresden. Identical handwriting with Paddon's appeared on Just's pass. Some time later we discovered among papers during a search, the Paddon Escape Rules – a memorandum written up after this escape. Born of experience, this is what they said:

(1) Travel in slow trains, not by expresses or specials, as no pass is required when buying tickets. No control of passes on slow trains under the first 100 kilometres.

(2) Express trains – Between Leipzig and Dresden the control is carried out by a German sergeant. He requires only our identity cards.

(3) Passes recognised by police as forged because
    (a) they had seen this type of phoney pass before;
    (b) there is no such thing as a Nebenbauamt (Branch Works Office) stamp;
    (c) no such thing as Bauinspektor (Buildings Inspector);
    (d) the signature on Lieut Just's identity card and mine were different, but in the same handwriting;
    (e) the stamp was poor – it was weak and hence illegible;
    (f) same handwriting in both my passes, although one was issued in Leipzig and one in Dresden.

(4) Brown pass O.K. for identification only. Not for travelling. For 24 hours the police thought I was a Belgian. The interpreter in French at Leipzig police station spoke worst French than Just and I together!

(5) Best of all is a leave pass. Everyone asks for it and it commands fare reductions. This is the key to everything, and it must be a pleasure to travel with a good one.

(6) Tuttlingen is in the frontier zone. Tickets to Stuttgart issued sometimes with and sometimes without identity cards being demanded.

(7) We went from Dresden to Stuttgart via Leipzig. Wish I had followed my own intention and not taken the advice of the train conductress.

(8) German civvies better clad than we had thought, especially on Sundays – a bad day therefore for travelling.

(9) It is always possible to get something to eat without having to produce coupons. I'll never again carry chocolate or Red Cross food.

(10) Remove all names from clothes, or sew false ones on if you have none. Lieut Just had his name and 'Oflag 4C' on his trousers! That's why they were so suspicious about my story of having just been shot down. Just and I

met in Leipzig quite by chance after our initial escape.

(11) Remy, who travelled with Just, made himself conspicuous. Both were watched in the train by a civilian (? Gestapo) after they had been checked by the sergeant. Remy disappeared suddenly when they got to Leipzig, while Just was left trying in vain to get rid of the overcoat that Remy had left behind in the compartment. Although he pretended not to see it, people pressed it on him as belonging to his friend. I was picked up half an hour later as I was speaking to Just, thinking he was by then clear of suspicion.

(12) He travels best who travels alone!

As I said, I went back to collect Lieut Wychodzew from Stuttgart as soon as the police rang up. On the way back we noticed tremendous security activity everywhere. The story soon leaked out. The French general Giraud had escaped from Königstein. One hundred thousand marks were offered for his capture.

This escape was followed by a general security check over the entire Reich. As it was thought that we at Colditz knew more about escape precautions than anyone else, our Kommandant, though now over seventy years old, together with our Security Officer, was ordered to Königstein to advise on security. Fame at last! The Colditz Escape Academy was now getting some recognition from the OKW. Either they agreed that we knew more than they did, or else they were passing the buck – probably both! After a week, these two officers returned, and I was posted there myself for a week. Plainly I had graduated! The buck was now mine.

This was at first a temporary move, but on May 26th I went again to Königstein indefinitely. At the same time the *Tierarzt* left Colditz for good. I took some leave before reporting to my new job, because the Kommandant at Königstein had said to me on my first brief visit there, 'I don't believe in too much leave. Take what you can get before you come back here!' I took his advice over Whitsun 1942.

## CHAPTER VIII

# A Reshuffle — The Game Goes On

I STAYED as Security Officer at Königstein until August 1942. It was quite a rest cure after Colditz, and I believe that was the last summer I enjoyed for the next fifteen years. The camp was situated in a castle up on a high plateau, rather like that at Hohnstein, the camp where two long years ago I had begun to learn the ways of prisoners, in a similar quiet and peaceful setting.

There were seventy French generals at Königstein, of whom I particularly remember Generals Flavigny, Musse, Muserey, Burquairt and Mesny. I searched the quarters pretty thoroughly over a period of weeks, looking for a clue to General Giraud's escape, but was convinced that if they had a hide, it would be in some unoccupied room. I was after a rope of some kind, being quite sure that this was the only way that the general could have got out of this fortress.

Sure enough, my Colditz methods yielded the desired result. In an attic I found a length of telephone cable. Now we began to fit the evidence together. We had found scratches on the rocks at the bottom of the cliff below the castle, and we had also found a pair of thick gloves down there. On these were fragments of insulating material. This was the same material as was round the telephone cable. Giraud must have worn the gloves while sliding down the cable. At least we now had some pretty genuine answer to the question from the OKW, 'How did the prisoner get out?'

As we learned later, from an interview which General Giraud gave to an American magazine before the war finished, he eventually escaped to Switzerland and then North Africa, where he joined the Free French forces. I spotted this article in a *Reader's Digest*\* and sent it up to the OKW as proof of

\*See *Reader's Digest* – October 1943.—ED.

the correctness of my theory at Königstein.

General Giraud had received the cable wire from his wife, concealed inside a side of ham!

The parcels at Königstein were given out uncensored, as security measures were very slack there. The general was able to lower himself by means of this telephone cable about 100 feet or more down the face of the cliff on which the castle was perched, in broad daylight after the morning roll-call. He had twelve hours' start in any case until the evening roll-call, when his absence was noticed. But for some reason the warning system failed that night. The Kommandant and Security Officer were both absent at Dresden, and the officer in charge did not seem to grasp the importance of this escape. So the general had twenty-four hours' start before his absence was noticed. Himmler and Hitler were furious and ordered security checks throughout Germany and France, with no result. The two senior officers who were ultimately responsible for the prisoners at Königstein, namely the Kommandant and his Security Officer, each got six months in the military prison at Gollnow in Pomerania. We thought they were lucky to get away with that, because Romilly, our civilian hostage, was a standing death sentence to the two officers in the same position at Colditz.

As I was away at Königstein until the last days of July, however, I can only report briefly, and from the record, the events that occurred on the escape front at Colditz in my absence. The park as usual figured a good deal in escape bids that summer of 1942.

After the walk one day a Dutch officer was found by the dogs under some leaves and loose earth. This concealment had been effected under the (literal) cover of a Bible study circle, attended by a group of officers wearing the long black cloaks that were part of the Dutch uniform.

On May 28th again the walk returned one short. When they checked, it was Lieut Girot, the youngest French officer, who was missing. They found a window bar sawn through in one of the French rooms, but I think this must have been a blind. They could not find any trace of the way he had gone, if he had gone from the park. Had there really been an empty file on return from the park? It was too late to check. They then wondered if the French had got hold of another secret goon-proof exit, for they found no clue whatever to this getaway. Girot was caught in a train going to Frankfurt and came back to Colditz.

Two new arrivals in my absence were first one of the best-known Battle of Britain fighter pilots, Wing Commander Douglas Bader, whom I remember so well later swinging round the yard on his artificial limbs, and Lieut Michael Sinclair of the Rifle Brigade, whose escape attempts were unbeaten, as to their number and as regards the risks he took to effect them. Sinclair had escaped from a camp at Posen, together with a Major Littledale. Sinclair was caught on the Bulgarian frontier and sent to Colditz via Vienna. He jumped the train on the way but was recaptured. Both officers ended up in Colditz. Sinclair suffered permanently from sinus trouble, and we used to send him out of the camp for treatment. On one such occasion, at Leipzig on June 2nd, he escaped from his guard. In Cologne, a few days later, there had been a heavy air-raid and the police were looking for pilots who had come down by parachute. Sinclair was stopped and questioned, and his disguise failed. Back he came to Colditz. This was the first of several tries.

Squadron-Leader Paddon, who had escaped with the other four 'patients' from hospital at the end of April, and had been retaken, was due for a court-martial at Thorn in Posen during June. The charge had followed him on from his previous camp, where he had accused a German NCO of theft.

We knew that these trips, even for courts-martial, which took the prisoners outside our castle security ring, were a godsend to would-be escapers, and knowing Paddon's record, we sent Dixon Hawke as his escort. They travelled overnight.

Next morning, in the prison at Thorn, when the Ferret went to collect his prisoner to bring him before the Court, the cell was empty. The Court was compelled to adjourn, *sine die*!

We never discovered how Paddon escaped. We suspected that he had somehow joined a party of British orderlies, working in the prison, and had gone out with them on some job.

Dogs followed a trail from one working party, having been given some of his clothing to sniff. The trail ended in a bog. Perhaps they thought that was the best place to report the last trace of this turbulent beast! Later, his comrades told us that he was home in England, having got there via Sweden.

On July 6th the Riot Squad again beat the Dutch to the touchdown, and found them just closing up a hole in one of their walls. They had sunk another shaft to make up for the buttress which we had discovered earlier.

Some time later two Dutch officers, Lieuts Winkenbosch and Verley, were caught in the kitchen scullery making a hole in the back of the camp boilerhouse, which was in our yard. On the same day, noises on the wall between our quarters and the prisoners' showed that the British were up to something. We sent the Riot Squad up to investigate on the third floor over the canteen (always trouble in that south-east corner, where the 'seam' was), and there they found Captain van Den Heuvel, Lieuts Kruimink and Storie-Pugh actually climbing out of an Anglo-Dutch hole they had made from their end mess-room into the attic on our side.

Only a few more days and a twelve-foot tunnel was found in the ground floor of the Senior Officer's quarters, with three prisoners working in it. At first sight the tunnel seemed pointless, until we realised it was probably aimed to link up with the drainage system. We also had a good haul from a hide there, which included a home-made typewriter! That explained these first-rate passes found on escapers!

But most serious of all, we found a message in code, a very simple code, which we worked out quite easily, warning prisoners against using Leipzig Central Station, and telling how to shortcircuit it by tram. A phone number contact in Leipzig was given as well. Working from this our Criminal Police discovered an electrical equipment tradesman, a German, who had been in the old Guard Company that we had moved from the castle as unreliable.

Before the war, this man's business partner in Leipzig had been one of the Polish officers now a prisoner in Colditz. It was between these two that the messages were passing as well as quite a number of tools. We even found a list – in fact it was a bill – for all the tools that had gone into the castle, with details, and the amounts of coffee and cigarettes that had been passed out in exchange through this man or through intermediaries after he'd left. The actual price seemed very small for the risk taken. The prisoner, of course, we couldn't touch, but the traitor was very severely punished.

I left Königstein on July 26th and, after a few days' leave, returned on duty at Colditz, to find that our Kommandant had just retired. He was over seventy. The new Kommandant was very much a new broom. He insisted on the greatest thoroughness in all our work, down to the last detail, and made frequent speeches of exhortation (i.e. pep talks). For instance, it was our duty, he said, to set an example to our own men. We must insist on the correct application of the Geneva Convention and all its rules, as regards the treatment of prisoners-of-war. We must demand that they behaved themselves correspondingly. He required 'watchfulness, circumspection, presence of mind, calm, and persistence' from us in our jobs. He, the Kommandant, would set an example. But he would not frequent the prisoners' yard overmuch. He must seem to be what he was – the symbol of ultimate authority!

It all sounded very fine, but this officer obviously had no idea of what he was letting himself in for, or the position he was trying to push us into! These words sounded very well as we listened in respectful silence in our 'Casino'. I don't think they would have had a similar reception in the prisoners' yard. One real change I remember was, that during his time in command, we expanded more than ever our relations with the Partei.

One good idea ( ?) that this second Colditz Kommandant did think up, was special parades at any time of the night. This really was asking for trouble. We could not get the prisoners out of their bunks for one thing. We couldn't tell whether they were in the right groups, naturally, since they did not dress properly for these parades (or indeed any parades, which they declared were only roll-calls). They simply came down in any old garment they could lay their hands on.

On one of these riotous occasions a rifle was missing for some time until we found it down a prisoner's trouser-leg.

We had sent guards up to get them down, either out of beds or out of cupboards, and in order to open a cupboard a sentry had to put his rifle down for a second, in which time it disappeared.

Another night there was a special parade for the French only. The rest of the prisoners stood at their windows yelling through the bars. The LO was quite beside himself. The entire guard was called into the yard, and lined up in a storm of jeers, facing the buildings on the east side.

'Back from the windows,' shouted our Duty Officer.

No one heeded him. The yelling continued.

'Take aim' – the guard pointed their rifles up at the windows.

Our LO, who was quite inaudible in the row that was going on, screamed, 'If that shouting up there doesn't stop, I shall order the guard to fire.'

One of the guards, more weary than the rest at that time of night, did not hold his muzzle high enough. In fact he let it droop so far that it was aimed at the head of a French officer standing close in front of him.

'*Höher*,' bawled the Frenchman – ('Higher').

His accent was wide of the mark, and so a guard down the line thought he heard the order '*Feuer*' ('Fire!').

He let go. They all did. Nineteen shots in all were fired at the windows. By some incredible miracle, no one was even touched.

This rioting, as one may call it, was something our new Kommandant just did not understand. Indiscipline, bribery, stealing – he wasn't used to it. He had come from the front, and this was a kind of behaviour with which he could not cope at all. The halo of his authority was quite simply ignored. Had we carried out his orders in detail, we should have required one cell between five prisoners, with probably four of them sharing it permanently, and hardly anyone in the quarters at all!

Early in August, some Russian prisoners were brought in for de-lousing rather unexpectedly. Two British officers were caught tunnelling in the de-lousing shed. This hole, too, was aiming to tie up with the drains that ran out from the yard, under the gate, down to the archway, and so I know not where.

By this time we had realised that the four courtyard cells,

which we used to accommodate prisoners under arrest, plus the three more under the archway between the German court-yard and the approach yard, really did not suffice to hold all those who at any one time were under a sentence of arrest. Not even when we doubled up those confined could we deal with the masses of prisoners coming in to our lists for prison accommodation. These cells averaged about ten by six feet and there were never less than a dozen prisoners in at any one time for a term of anything from five to twenty-one days.

We were therefore compelled to seek extra prison accom-modation and we had found it in the old town gaol – a 150-year-old building now out of use, which was properly fitted up on the first floor with ten old-fashioned cells and a guardroom, plus a small exercise yard. This was ten minutes' walk from the castle down in the town but it suited our purpose exactly and the Kommandant obtained authority from the ever-obliging OKW to rent this building. Our first prisoners moved in there at Easter 1942, and thereafter pretty well every cell was constantly occupied both in the castle and down in the local jug, or Hotel Stadt, or Town Hotel, as it became known.

For exercise there the prisoners filed out of their cells down the staircase to the ground floor and then out into the small yard for an hour, morning and afternoon. They were marched down the stairs with one sentry at the head of the line and one at the back. In the yard a sentry stood at each end and kept an eye on the prisoners as they walked up and down the inter-vening twenty-five–thirty yards.

Flight-Lieut Dickinson was a man of snap decisions, as befitted an Air Force pilot. On August 18th, 1942, after an hour standing in the hot afternoon sun at each end of the small gaol yard, the sentries were glad to call 'Time' to the small group of prisoners walking back and forth between them.

The first sentry turned and opened the door of the ground floor prison building and went in and up the stairs. The prisoners shuffled around the entrance, while the second sentry came up from his far end of the yard.

Suddenly Dickinson bolted to the side wall, put his foot on the lock of a door in it and swung up and over and down into an orchard on the other side. The sentry still in the yard was slow on the draw. In any case he couldn't let fly wildly because there were houses surrounding the yard and he might have hit some innocent civilian. He was no good at all at climbing over walls, and so Dickinson got away safely over the far orchard wall and picked up a bicycle which for some reason was standing in the town square unlocked. He made off at speed and finished up in Chemnitz that evening, where the police, warned by *'Mausefalle'*, picked him up. It was a splendid effort. Unfortunately for Dickinson he hadn't sufficient equipment with him in the form of clothing or passes or money. It was just another snap escape like Desjobert's in the previous October.

He told the police that he was an Air Force pilot shot down over Cologne. But he was back in Colditz later that night.

Two days later we again sent the painters into the prisoners' yard. A French officer saw his opportunity, and rigged himself up with a white jacket and trousers. He went on the walk one afternoon wearing this disguise under his greatcoat, carrying a blanket for further concealment, and where the walk left the roadway through the wicket gate for the zigzag path down to the park, his friends whipped off his outer covering, while he whipped round back through the gate as a painter going the other way. Unfortunately our NCO asked for his civilian's pass, and found he had caught Lieut Delarue!

Towards the end of the month Lieut Lee and Flight-Lieut Tunstall were court-martialled for 'misuse of musical instruments', i.e. unseemly bawling with their trumpets. This meant another trip to the Leipzig court-martial and as the two demanded four witnesses, we scented an attempted mass break. In Leipzig Lieut Lee and Flight-Lieut. Forbes broke away in the crowds but were recaptured. The NCO in charge of the escort marched them all back into the station with their hands up. The accused got three weeks' cells.

A great obstacle to overcome in our searches was the quantity of personal belongings that the prisoners accumulated over the years. Shelves upon shelves of books, amounting to private libraries, had to be gone through to see if there was paper money or passes in the leaves. Even by throwing handfuls of books on the floor, and we often did this, it wasn't possible to open them all up properly. Masses of clothing, for both summer and winter use, lay around collecting dirt. Boxes, cupboards, shelves, home-made stools, photos in frames, musical instruments, papers, boots and shoes by the dozen – all these made concealment the easiest thing and discovery the most difficult.

In due course we decided on a spring-clean. The British quarters were the worst. Far more was sent out to them from home than to the prisoners of any other country, and we determined to clear their rooms out down to the barest minimum of personal effects.

The orders were – 'All superfluous private belongings to be packed today in a downstairs room under the supervision of our Quartermaster. The cases then to be removed to a store-room in the German yard, date 7.9.42."

The room in which all this packing was to be done, packing by over a hundred officers in turn, was a small room about twelve by twelve feet, the 'Evidenz', a small conference room between the canteen and mystery space on one side, and the prisoners' kitchen on the other. It was, of course, much too small and the job was obviously going to take (or be made to take, as we soon realised) several days. A smallish quantity of kit was brought down by the British. It was all heaped up in the courtyard and had to be dragged and struggled with into this tiny room and packed in boxes under our eyes. Then orderlies came and took these out into the yard and loaded them on to a flat handcart. The British orderlies accompanied this almost traditional vehicle to our yard, and shifted all the junk up to one of our storerooms on a third floor.

Of course we had the usual friction before the operation started. We had to submit to a heavy attack on our morale from the Senior British Officer, Colonel W. Tod, as to the justice of the whole affair. After all, these things were private and personal property to which the PWs were entitled under the Geneva Convention. Fortunately for us, the Convention does not say how much personal property a prisoner may retain, and so we won that point.

The next attack was on the impossibility of each officer

coming down with armfuls of kit, queuing up outside the Evidenz Room and then packing what he had with him and then going back for more, up and down the stairs and in and out of the conference room. In the end we submitted to a suggestion from the British that the boxes might be packed in the quarters and brought down into the yard, tied up and labelled with the owners' names, ready for transfer to our store.

The orderlies were now to bring the boxes straight down, and load up the cart right away without any check by us. We merely tallied what arrived in the storeroom. This was upstairs on the south side of our yard, with a window looking out over what had been the moat.

Our Security Officer was not quite sure whether all this was a good thing. It was not quite in the spirit of the orders which he had had – 'effects to be packed under supervision'. However, as none of these containers was actually going to leave the castle, he agreed to the British request, that they should pack their things up in their own quarters without supervision.

To hasten the operation we supplied a large number of Red Cross three-ply cases, about three feet each way in size, which had held food supplies in bulk.

By the evening of that day, our eyes nearly dropping out of our heads from the watching of the dozens of cases and the officers milling around them, the storeroom was finally locked and barred, and the job was done.

Next day, we had a visit from a top-ranking officer, the Officer i/c Prisoners-of-War in Army District No. 4, Dresden, General Wolff. He turned up at about half past ten. Our new Kommandant made some important suggestions for increasing security, which were all agreed. The general inspected the premises, and about half past eleven gave us a 'pep' talk. He too had been a bit of a rebel in his younger years. He knew what sort of attitude people could work up against authority. He advised us to be strict, but fair.

The general left at midday.

Half an hour later a report came of a rope of blue and white bedsheets hanging down the outer wall of the German yard buildings overlooking the moat on the south front. *Du lieber— !* The Security Officer and I rushed to inspect. There *was* a rope hanging from a window – from the very storeroom we had crammed so full of boxes and cases of clothing and so on only last evening. *Gott sei Dank—!* The general had not seen it. It was in full veiw from the main gate and he could easily have done so.

Up in the store we found a Red Cross box broken open and on the lid was written in German, 'I don't like the air in Colditz. *Auf Wiedersehen.* Ex-PW Flying Officer Bruce.'

Bruce was quite the smallest officer in the British ranks. He must have got into the box up in the British quarters where we had allowed them to pack the cases unsupervised. He had been lightly nailed in, the orderlies had struggled down with him and loaded him on to the cart, and had then carried him from the cart up into the store. Even with his small size, it must have been a very tight fit in that box. Bruce wasn't caught until just on a week later, near the harbour basin at Danzig. I imagine he had made use of one of those silk maps from the cover of a book from the Lisbon agent. His story there was that he had jumped from a British plane over Bremen and had arrived in Danzig on a stolen bicycle. His bicycle, unluckily, had a local number on it. He was, however, sent to the RAF camp at Dulag Luft near Oberursel. There, he was recognised by members of the German staff, and for the second time he left there for Colditz. It was perhaps tactless, though polite, of Bruce to write '*Auf Wiedersehen*' on the box when he really had 'Good-bye' in mind. It was indeed tempting fate.

## CHAPTER IX

## Strange Faces – Red Faces

SOMETHING WAS obviously up. Now indiscipline, almost mutiny, could be felt everywhere. The early morning parade was due to be taken by two of us LOs. A lot of people seemed overcome by sickness that morning, and could not bring themselves to get out of bed, and come down on parade. They lay there coughing and groaning on the bunks. Things were so bad that in the end we called off this first parade, and ordered a second one for 9.15. This was playing into the prisoners' hands, as we very soon discovered. On top of all this we still had Bruce's escape of the day before to worry about.

At 9 o'clock a report came through that a woman from Commichau, coming to market in Colditz through the Tiergarten above the park, had found two boxes with Polish uniforms in them. We looked at each other. 'That's why there's all this trouble with that *Sauhaufen* (pigmob) in there this morning.'

At 9.15 we went into the yard with reinforcements. To begin with, ten officers seemed to be missing. We got that number down to six. Then I found two British officers standing in with the Dutch company. We checked the Dutch from their photographs, and found three of them absent. During this operation a bucketful of water crashed down from the British quarters, alongside the table holding the files. Flight-Lieut Tunstall was seen up above and later court-martialled on my report.

We now found that five British officers were missing. But one of them, surely, I had just seen in the yard.

We were in some confusion.

To make this even more confounded, we had something desperately serious to worry about now. We discovered that our basic security check, tallying identities of appearance in the flesh with appearance in photographs, was not infallible.

I pulled out the identity card of Lieut Keillar, and called him forward. I looked from face to photo and back again. 'Who are you?'

'Lieut Malcolm Keillar – Number 310.'

I looked at his identity disc. It tallied. I asked him for the personal details on his card – birthday, father's Christian name, and so on. He couldn't give them.

'Give me your real name. You are required to do that under the Geneva Convention.' He said he had orders not to tell. I pressed him. He asked to speak to his Senior Officer, and finally claimed to be a Corporal Hendeen, whom we had, we thought, transferred two months ago to a soldiers' camp in Silesia with several other British orderlies. It turned out that Keillar had changed places with him, and the corporal had been living in Colditz for eight weeks under an assumed identity!

We collected Lieut Keillar later on, pleased to have got something out of the confusion of that day. But still, the price of this discovery, that our security check, the final one, was not as good as it should have been, was highly disturbing.

By the end of the morning we found that six officers in all were missing. However, Lieuts Donkers and Wardle, RN, were brought back the same morning, and next day Lieuts Lawton and Beets also returned. The two others, Flight-Lieut Fowler and Captain van Doorninck, got to Switzerland.

Security had now to discover how these officers had made their escape from Colditz. We searched, and re-searched, and in the end, after lengthy questioning of the sentries, we found how it was done.

The six, disguised as a German officer and NCO in charge of apparently four Polish orderlies, had come out of a store-room on the north side of the castle, just after the guard had been changed in the early morning. But how had they got into the store? The sentries naturally thought that they had gone in by the outside door (the one they came out of), shortly before they, the sentries, had been changed. We discovered that, in point of fact, they had got in from our Sergeant-Major's office on the inner side of the castle. The exit hole was actually dug under Mussolini's table! His office was entered from a corridor leading from the north-west corner of the prisoners' yard to the hospital. The hole had been made at night after opening two types of locks on the office door, and closing them again afterwards, twice over. The hole had been enlarged night after night, and covered up each morning before it was time for an accomplice to let these night shift workers out! There must have been a great deal of assistance given by way of watching the sentries round the outside of the building, and also by keeping an eye and ear open for sudden irruptions of the Riot Squad. This 'stooging', as this type of PW surveillance was called, was probably carried on either from above Mussolini's office, or from the infirmary across the corridor. Our locks were no damn good, nor our damn sentries either.

To make things worse, we found that a gate had actually been unlocked for the party, as they made their way towards the road, by one of our own NCOs. This ass had asked them – 'Are you going to Zschadrass?' The answer was, 'Yes.' – 'Then I will open the door for you' – which the soldier did. They may have had a false key but it didn't follow that it was going to work, and the arrival of this NCO with the proper key was a godsend. He thought they were taking spare clothing to the loony bin. We told him that's where he ought to be himself!

Security measures. We played hell with the Guard Company. 'Haven't you been told to demand passes from every Tom, Dick and Harry who comes along, if they don't show them first?' and we moved the infirmary from the ground floor to the first floor in another part of the yard.

During the identity check some of the prisoners hurled water from their windows on to us in the yard and it seemed to me I was the primary objective. Flight-Lieut Tunstall was court-martialled for his part in this affair at Leipzig just before Christmas. Counsel for defence was the same local German lawyer who had been a British PW. His defence was, that the accused could not be charged with aiming intentionally at me personally, since he was up on the third floor behind barred windows, having concealed himself before parade. The bars were set so far back from the edge of the sill that they prevented him from seeing who stood directly underneath. There was no question of his leaning out between the bars and looking down. Tunstall, a bomber pilot, admitted that he threw the water but said he just splashed it about in a general way. Defending Counsel also said that in PW camps there should not be bars on prisoners' windows, under the Convention, although they were allowed in punishment cells. The sentence was the fairly mild one of four weeks' arrest. I must say that I always suspected that someone down in the yard gave the tip when I was directly under the window, and so a suitable target for a bucket of water. But I could not prove anything.

A central escape museum had been organised about this time in Vienna. We sent some specimens of our best escape material, or photographs of it, to this exhibition, and they were favourably received, as being quite unique. It was very easy to replace the specimens we sent away, from further items provided by the prisoners. Our own collection of photographs of tunnels, contraband, false passes, keys, disguises, etc., reached over a hundred by the end of the war.

Our Kommandant went to Vienna to have a look at the museum and brought back some really good ideas aimed at increasing the areas under observation by our sentries around the castle buildings.

We put up a 'pagoda' or machine-gun tower in the northwest corner of the terrace, giving a sight down most of the northern and western sides.

We also put up a catwalk running in mid-air well out from the outer wall of the approach yard, covering the fifty yards of the Saalhaus buildings, plus the two buttress-type buildings standing out at each end, namely the archway with its cells, from which two escapes had already been made, and the guardroom. It was down the front of this guardroom, the sheer face of about eighty feet high, that Lieuts Chmiel and Surmanowicz had slid on their rope over eighteen months earlier.

On the park or east side of the castle we put a sentry up on a catwalk over the barbed wire gateway to supplement the sentry whose beat ended at the gate. This also gave a better view of the ground floor windows in the prisoners' quarters, as it was now possible to watch what had been dead ground.

Furthermore, we decided to face the wall surface in a passageway that ran along the back of our quarters (overlooking the prisoners' yard), with an alarm net of wires. This corridor ran above the single-storey kitchen buildings, and so on, and was accessible to the prisoners both from the Senior Officers' quarters on the south-west corner of their yard and from several levels above the canteen on the south-east corner. When I say accessible, it wasn't officially accessible, but there was nothing but an eighteen-inch wall between the quarters at the upper levels.

On receipt of these instructions I went up with a man to measure the area that had to be covered. And there, in the passageway, which we called Hexengang (or Witches' Walk), we came upon two Polish officers who had got through a hole from the Saalhaus!

The very same night we found the iron door at the other end, which was a connecting link through the wall between our yard and the attic over the Conference Room, unlocked and ajar, but we did not catch the persons who had opened it. Plainly, several minds were thinking alike.

We also put up a stronger light in the yard. It suffered destruction more than once from well-aimed catapult shots, as did a picture of the Führer, which dominated the small Evidenz or Conference Room.

In spite of having all the resources we wanted for material security, two whole years were yet to elapse before Colditz became anywhere near escape proof. By then, the autumn of 1944, the prisoners had mainly decided that they would wait for liberation to come to them.

By October 1942, Colditz had become known even to the deadbeats in the OKW, as something to open files on. They finally sent the general in charge of prisoners-of-war, OKW, down on a visit of inspection (for what good that might do!). He inspected the prisoners' quarters and O.K.d everything that we had done to keep them inside the place. I doubt if he could possibly have made any practical suggestions to augment our precautions without having spent at least twelve months in the camp. But we did get it out of him that the order to hand-cuff British officers for certain periods of the day did not apply here. This was a reprisal measure ordered by Hitler that summer, but from the text of it it could be read to apply only to prisoners in British PW camps. We were glad of the general's interpretation of the order. Colditz, he ruled, was not a British Prisoner-of-War camp; it was an international PW camp, and the order, therefore, in his view, could not apply. I must say this order hadn't much success elsewhere, since the prisoners always managed to get their handcuffs off in good time. We thought what splendid raw material this type of metal would have afforded the Colditz workshops had we been compelled to handcuff the British in our camp.

By now the war outside was taking an unpleasant turn for Germany. Partisans in Russia were declared to be beyond the law. Our civilian population began to take its revenge on bomber crews who came down by parachute. These pilots were safe, and by that I mean comparatively safe, only when they got into Wehrmacht hands. With Partei authorities their fate was uncertain.

In the middle of October I went to a conference held in Dresden. We discussed new Wehrmacht orders, which were to reduce personnel in Home Front Commands, and defined ways and means of employing as many prisoners-of-war as possible in the ranks of German industry. What we needed was replacements for the terrible losses we had suffered and were still suffering and were estimated to suffer on the East Front. There in Russia we had come to a standstill. Our high water mark in Africa, at Alamein, had been reached. The tide was beginning to ebb, though it had a long way to go.

I returned from Dresden on October 15th and found all passengers being checked by the police when I changed trains at Döbeln. My heart sank. I knew without asking. 'Yes,' they said. 'Four prisoners missing from that *verdammte* Sonderlager of yours!'

That morning four British officers had been found missing after the usual hullaballoo. These were Major Littledale, Lieut Stephens, RN, Captain Reid, and Flight-Lieut Wardle, Royal Canadian Air Force.

Once again it was a report from a civilian coming through the Tiergarten which had warned us that something was up. She had found some suspicious blue and white material (the usual bed-sheets) under some bushes. The dogs were not successful in following the trail outward, but worked back to the castle wall on our south front and then stopped. The code-word 'Mousetrap' had gone out at once down all available telephone wires to authorities and security personnel within the five-mile radius of Colditz, but by midday we had spread the search net to the twenty-mile limit with the word '*Hasenjagd*'. That means 'Hare Drive', but it was often taken to indicate 'Wild Goose Chase'. By 5 p.m. we realised we should have to rely on railway and criminal police along the railway line to the south-west, the regular home-run to Switzerland.

For days we searched inside the prisoners' yard and quarters looking for an exit. On the 18th we found a hole in the Dutch quarters, in the thickness of the wall, a secret passage of some kind, dating from the Middle Ages. This was the principal Dutch hide-out. We collected three home-made German officers' uniforms, plaster moulds for buttons and emblems of rank, and so on, as well as a quantity of tools. This hole was under their washroom floor, and we got it because their warning system against the Riot Squad again failed, and we were on them before they could close the hide-out down.

As the dogs seemed to have found some kind of clue at the outside foot of our south wall, we searched around in our own quarters on the ground floor and in the different basements of that side of our yard. The Riot Squad produced what they called evidence to support a crazy theory that an escape had been made across the German courtyard and out of the cellar under our south buildings looking over the dry moat. The dogs had indeed sniffed their way back to the outside wall close to an air-shaft that came out there. It was claimed that footprints could be made out in the flower beds close to our Kommandantur wall by the moat. English toffee papers were found in one of the cellars, and a bar was found bent on the outside of the air-shaft. This all seemed very nebulous to us at the time. How could anyone get past the sentry who was parading back and forth in the middle of the German yard? How could any prisoner get out of windows on the prisoners' side of that yard in the full glare of the searchlights without the sentry seeing him? Security did agree to board up the air-shaft, but as for the rest we concluded that probably one of our own people had been given sweets and had eaten them unobserved in the cellar on some occasion, while the footprints on the flower beds might have been made by anyone, or even by one of the dogs.

In spite of our searching, by the 23rd of the month, we had still found no sign of any exit from the camp, and no news had come in from outside of the four British escapers.

One evening in November we nearly caught someone in the passage that led from the top of the guardroom building stairs back over the gate to that hole under the stage which we had blocked off in January, after two successful escape attempts. Whoever it was this time, he got away back through into the theatre dressing-room before the Riot Squad could get up there to cut him off. We then wondered, was this the exit from which the prisoners had escaped the previous week? They might have opened up and used this old and successful escape route, again going out dressed as German military personnel. We had moved our Mess from over the guardroom, so there was one less obstacle to pass on their way down. Where they would have gone after that we could not work out.

Shortly afterwards, we discovered a loose bar at the back of the prisoners' kitchen. One side of the kitchen was entered from their yard; the other side had no door, but just windows, which overlooked our yard. It would have been possible to get out of these windows, and on to a low roof and drop into the German yard, but where would you go after that? There was a sentry in this yard, night and day. We checked with the sentries who had been on duty on the park gate the night the four got away. They all swore that no one had gone past them in the early morning without showing his pass. In the end, so far as we were concerned, escape of the four British officers took place from the theatre, and once again down past the guardroom, and then out by some route never discovered, and away. We thought they might have gone down below the guardroom, into the cellar, and so out to the lower ground terrace on the south front and so perhaps through the wire, but there was a sentry on the terrace which ruled out that theory.*

It was obvious that autumn that the work of the Oil Commission, which had sat earlier that year in Colditz to prepare for the exploitation of the Russian oilfields, was going to be in vain. Germany was not going to get any oil out of the Baku fields. We had admittedly flown our flag from the top of Mount Elbruz, the highest in the Caucasus range, but that was only a gesture. Perhaps from this peak our climbers might have seen the oilfields, but that was about as near as we could be said to have got. We now pinned our hopes on the submarine campaign. Definite consolation was found in our potato and root crop, which that season was a record, and thank heaven, it was a lovely autumn. No night frosts at all in October. The coal ration had been dropped by 30 per cent.

On November 3rd, two British officers arrived from Poland. They were Lieuts Silverwood-Cope and Crawford. As escapers their cards were marked in the register with the usual green tag, but these two were escapers with a difference. They had escaped originally from a camp at Posen, and had been in touch for some time with the Polish underground in Warsaw and Radom. In these cities they had hidden for several months. We never found the agents mainly responsible for their care in Warsaw,† but they were picked up by the Gestapo in a *razzia* (street check), along with Poles and a number of Jews.

They had themselves been beaten up with the others in prison, and had seen the most dreadful things – Jews pushed down under manhole covers into drains full of water, for as long as they could survive. From the top of their cells they had seen dogs set on prisoners by way of training in attack. They had seen the prisoners lacerated by the dogs. They had seen prisoners beaten, and hung up by their wrists.

In Colditz these two wrote out statements describing all this. I read through it, and to me it was the first information that I

*Many years later I read the true story of this escape – out of the kitchen, over our yard, into our cellar, through the air-shaft.

†An Englishwoman, who billeted Cope, Crawford, Sinclair and Davies-Scourfield (Colditz inmates) as well as dozens of other British escapers while they were in Warsaw, now lives in Sussex.—ED.

personally had from first-hand sources, of what to me had till then been only rumours, of what went on in Partei concentration camps, and also of *Vernichtungslager* (destruction camps), in Poland and occupied Russia. These reports were sent to the Swiss Protecting Power through us, via the OKW. This was the normal channel of communication, under the Geneva Convention. Although this line of communication was officially permitted, the OKW replied with a threatened court-martial, on a charge of insulting the German Reich. The two accused said that they welcomed this opportunity to prove their story. The OKW then backed out and said that disciplinary punishment would suffice.

Disciplinary punishment was a matter for the Kommandant. He said it was outside his power to award disciplinary punishment on such a charge. He passed the papers to Army District 4, Dresden. Dresden ordered arrest for a considerable period. The prisoners appealed to the OKW from Dresden as entitled, alleging that they could produce proof of the statements from which the alleged offence arose and that their punishment was illegal, since this justification had not been asked for. They could not be punished without trial. The appeal was rejected. The appeal then went to the Protecting Power, who put it before the British Government. At this stage, however, in German law, the prisoners had to submit to the arrest, and punishment. An appeal as far as the OKW only effected a delay. Both officers did thirty days' cells, the limit of disciplinary punishment without court-martial, and by and by the matter was damped down by the passing of time and the eruption of events.

When we discovered that prisoners were missing on parades, the first thing we had to do was to make sure that we had the true number of absentees. This usually took some time owing to the diversions laid on. The next step was to find out who exactly was missing, by checking the identities with the cards in the records. Unfortunately the photographs on these cards grew more and more out of date as time went on. Many had been taken as long ago as 1940. The Poles had been photographed in 1939, but by now were three years (of prison conditions) older. Many now had, or had had then, moustaches or beards, particularly the Dutch. The photographs, therefore, were not too reliable. We had one example of this when we discovered by means of the photos the switch between Corporal Hendeen and Lieut Keillar, who did vaguely resemble each other. It would, of course, have been possible to settle any queries 100 per cent by carrying out a check of fingerprints, but this was too technical a matter for us.

We had quite an identity problem as the result of the arrival of seventeen British officers on September 1st (although to be correct I should say that sixteen came on the 1st and one, Lieut-Commander Stephens, who disappeared at Döbeln when they changed trains, came on later). This party came from a camp at Lamsdorff, in Silesia. For some time, naturally enough, their letters from home went to Lamsdorff and were forwarded from there on to us. By the end of October our censorship had noted that letters addresssed to a Lieut Michael Harvey, RN, frequently had the name in different handwriting from the rest of the Lamsdorff camp address. It appeared to have been written over another name, which had been rubbed out. The letters were signed 'Alice Steele'. Our Security Officer was advised, and sent for the officer concerned, and asked who was this signatory. 'That is my stepmother,' was the reply. We asked him to repeat the personal details on his card and he gave them to us correctly, date and place of birth, etc. It still seemed odd and so we fell back for the first time on a fingerprint check. Here there was a discrepancy. The Lieut Harvey, RN, in front of us was not the Lieut Harvey, RN, on the identity card. There was a facial resemblance, but the prints could not lie. We reported the facts to Lamsdorff. The Kommandant there followed up the clue provided by the name Alice Steele, and found he had recently sent a corporal of that name to Goldberg. On examination, this corporal's fingerprints were found to be different from those recorded on his card at Lamsdorff. Corporal Steele on the card there was not the Corporal Steele who had gone to Goldberg. Lamsdorff therefore returned the apparent Corporal Steele to Colditz. We put the two together, and the swop was plain. The corporal, known to us for some weeks as

Lieut Harvey, went back to Lamsdorff, and Lieut Harvey, RN, who had taken his place there on a working party, got ten days' arrest when he arrived at Colditz.

On November 26th the guard on the gate from the German yard to the park actually did carry out his orders and asked for passes from two German soldiers going through. They had none, being Lieut Barry and Lieut Aulard, dressed up as Germans. After they were caught we had the usual Sonder-appell. Barry was difficult to recognise at first and impossible to identify with his photo as he had shaved off his very heavy cavalry moustache for the purpose of the escape. But we found two more were missing. These were Lieut Sinclair and the French Captain Klein. I was very surprised to be told by the Senior British Officer that the couple we had just caught would have got away the day before, along with the other couple, but that I had spoilt the attempt by suddenly coming up to the theatre just as they were going down through the bars of the air-shaft and so out through the German kitchen route. It seemed extremely odd to me that I should be told all this. I wondered if this wasn't a bluff. Had this other escape really taken place twenty-four hours earlier, and by this old route, which we never thought would or could be used again? It certainly was a good story, and obviously the evening parade the night before must have been faked. But why tell me all this? I thought the prisoners did not want to risk whatever system they had of faking the parades too often; the escapers had twenty-four hours' start anyway and whatever way their absence was covered at roll-call, the method still held good. Although Lieut Sinclair was caught at Tuttlingen on the 30th, and Lieut Klein shortly after at Plauen, we felt there was something cooking. But we couldn't identify the scent!

## CHAPTER X

## Son et Lumière

FOR SOME time now it was becoming obvious that the prisoners had more information at their disposal than they could get out of the newspapers. We allowed them at least a dozen different German papers daily from all over the country, among them the *Frankfurter Zeitung*, the *Hamburger Fremden-blatt* and the *Pommersche Zeitung*. Neither gossip nor incoming prisoners could account for all they now and again admitted to knowing. And now, on December 15th, we made the second only of two finds in the camp in nearly four and a half years, which we could put down to treachery. The first of these was the tunnel under a bed in the infirmary.

The warning cries of the French always seemed a little quicker off the mark and more intensive as the Riot Squad, or any of us, approached the Kellerhaus (Cellar Block) staircase in their north-west corner of the yard. Their quarters ran up four floors, and on the top floor we had once found a wiring system that was not our own. The whole of the Kellerhaus was down for searching that day, and I had the whole of the top floor to go through. Although we had been tipped off, I worked along slowly from room to room. The French padre Congar came with me as a witness. In the room – No. 305 – which he himself shared with four others, including the French priest, Jean-Jean, a large map of North Africa was drawn on the wall.

'Nice map,' I said. 'Very nice.'

We chiselled round the blob marked Tunis. A piece of thick cardboard came out. Behind it there was a socket and wiring. We broke through the wall behind Tunis looking for a radio and, oddly enough, we didn't come out into room No. 302, on the other side. We then discovered that the ceiling there was lower than the one of No. 305, and we were through under the roof. Up there in the attic we found the wireless set, French make, tuned to London. The connections led to the socket behind the map. We never found the plug or the earphones they must have used. The aerial ran up the rafters and along the purlins for several yards, and must have made the set quite selective.

Just to show that once again we could not expect to have everything our own way, during the great deal of coming and going that went on before and after this discovery, Lieut Falk-Bouman (Royal Netherlands Navy) got out of the yard disguised as one of the German personnel engaged in the operation. Where he went from there to get out of the castle I do not know. He was caught near Immendingen four days later and was back for Christmas.

Security scratched its head and racked its brains. How had this set got into the camp? It must surely have come in in parcels, but how? Supposing it got into the parcel office, how did it get out of there and into the French quarters without being detected? The informer who had given the radio away told us that the parcel office used to be opened with a fake key while the yard sentry's attention was distracted, so we rigged up an alarm system that flashed a light in the guardroom whenever the door from the prisoners' yard into the parcel office was opened. That only flashed once in its whole history when we weren't ourselves responsible for opening the door. On that occasion, the Riot Squad rushed in and found nothing. This alarm never went off at any unexpected moment thereafter. And yet there were radios in the camp two years later.

Our Kommandant, who had been with us since August, now took it upon himself to think up a splendid disciplinary Christmas present for his prisoners. *Lagerbefehl* (Camp Order) No. 38, required proper discipline on all parades. No cat-calling, no hands in pockets, no wandering about, no smoking, and no snowballs.

He also put a bell up in the yard to ring a half-hour and five-minute warning, and the exact moment when the parade to be held should have started. The first time this was used, it was greeted with tremendous cheers. Everyone was smoking, hands were thrust through coat pockets, into trousers; everyone was wandering about, and people were calling loudly to their friends in other companies. The count in the yard was now to be taken by two of us at a time. One was to check the numbers present, and the other was to note down offenders against the new rule, and keep an eye also on any possible faking of the parade. Punishments of between five and ten days' arrest were to be distributed for offences against this new order.

We Duty Officers, however, decided it was going to be better to keep our eyes averted. Discipline, obviously, had gone to the devil. If we noted down every officer offending, then the whole crowd would be in the cells, and there would be an impossible backlog of arrest sentences to make up.

The Kommandant once or twice went up to the Hexengang corridor in the wall over the PW kitchens to observe from there how his new order was faring. Viewed from there, it seemed that at any moment he might have a mutiny on his hands, so he set up a light machine-gun in the window. I cannot say that I, as the German officer taking the roll-call, would myself have felt particularly safe in that yard had anyone let fly with this weapon. The ricochets had been bad enough in the British quarters with single shots at their Union Jack from the park back in the summer of 1941. A machine-gun firing down into that stone quarry of a courtyard would have been sheer murder of the prisoners, and undoubtedly for some of us. The machine-gun was soon removed, but we had some more manoeuvring yet before we got much semblance of discipline.

Christmas was coming once again, my third at Colditz. All I got this time for extras was a plate of honey cakes, some apples and some nuts, and, of all things, a mouth-organ! For the first time we, in the Officers' Mess, got no coffee. Even the snow was in short supply. There was none until after the New Year, 1943, when I had my leave.

Willi was the camp electrician. He worked in the castle off and on the whole of the war, together with Slim the carpenter and Slam the mason (who died in 1944), as they were nicknamed. Willi went into the French quarters one late afternoon to mend a blown fuse. Many of us were on leave – the Christmas spirit had left everyone a bit slack. Willi's tools were checked and he was issued with the usual yellow arm-band with Number 54 and the German Eagle on it.

About half past five a French officer came to the gate to hand in the *épées* that were issued on parole for fencing. The gate-man checked them. Willi came back from his job, pushed past the French officer, and so out and on left under the archway and into the German yard. Although Willi was one of the most familiar figures in the camp, at the park gate the sentry asked for his pass. Unfortunately for 'Willi' it was the wrong one, and he was phoney too! The attempt failed. We took a photograph of the false 'Willi' (Lieut Perodeau) and of the real one together. The resemblance was almost perfect, but the scarf that the false 'Willi' wore, wasn't the same colour as the real one.

By New Year 1943, Germany's main weakness on all battle fronts was plain – lack of men. Italy had become a liability, for now she needed precious divisions from us which we could ill afford. We had also recently taken over the whole of France. More men were needed for the complete occupation of that country. In the east, our Caucasus Army just got back over the Don at Rostov, while later on the Sixth Army was caught at Stalingrad and in the end 300,000 men were lost there.

We officers in Colditz had orders to keep up appearances no matter what the morale of our men, and no matter what the news. The notice – 'We do not capitulate', still up on the factory wall down in the town, began to have a double meaning.

Food was short – and getting less – but now and again we had a windfall in the shape of hares sent down by the son-in-law of our first Kommandant, whose daughter had married a sugar-beet grower from the district of Magdeburg. Large areas of land there were under cultivation for seed, as well as for experimental purposes. Here there were hares in large numbers, and in winter time the Kommandant got some of them and invited the officers of his staff for supper at the Weinstube down in the town.

I have left out the tale of quite a few minor escape attempts, but for the true record for 1942, I give the full list here:

Prisoners attempting escape – 84 in 44 attempts.
Fifteen got home (7 English, 3 Dutch, 5 French).
Prisoners caught getting out of the castle – 39.
Successfully out of the castle – 26, of whom 14 were re-
    caught. Of the 26, 12 got to freedom.
Our own prisoners who escaped from hospitals or in transit
    from the camp numbered 19. Of these 16 were caught,
    three got safely to freedom. It was, I think, the peak year.


The morale that New Year among the prisoners was very high.
Prophets were at work, bets were laid. I was even asked for a
copy of the prophecies of Nostradamus. I remember one of his
sayings that the Polish officers always quoted – 'The (Russian)
Bear will go back to the greatest River in the East (a reference,
they were sure, to the Volga), wash his paws, and then turn
and attack the (German) Eagle.' Another was, 'A town in
North Africa will change hands five times' – Tobruk.

The replacements and reinforcements for our East Front
were now put at 800,000 men, and General Von Unruh was
deputed to scrape up this number somehow, from industry,
agriculture, bureaucracy and business. We wondered if the
blow would fall on any in the Colditz Mess. We were all over
fifty except the Adjutant and the Kommandant.

They put us through a medical examination, first at the
hands of the camp doctor. Our second in command seemed
fit enough but we were all shocked at his report. Our doctor
wrote: 'Am unable to decide if fit for any further service at all.
Case referred to Leipzig', and at Leipzig they found him
'Unfit for all service, even Garrison Duty. Failing abandon-
ment of drink and smoking, death may supervene at any
moment.' So he left the army and went to run a school in
Eastern Germany, and in August 1943 was found dead in his
bed.

In Colditz he was not replaced, so now we had only two
*Lageroffiziere* (Duty Officers) left on the strength.

When I returned from leave in January, I was glad to hear
that the troubles on parade had died down. It seemed that the
prisoners were taking some notice of Camp Order No. 38.
Alternatively, I thought they might just have been behaving as

it suited them, order or no order.

'No order' was indeed my correct interpretation of the welcome that I received on my reappearance in their yard. The English led the storm that greeted me, the French supported them strongly. The Poles and Dutch just looked on and listened. It appeared that I had been selected personally to bear the brunt of this infantile behaviour. I felt honoured!

The following day the British came to me officially with a complaint to the Kommandant that I had been pressing for maximum punishment in the cells for recent escapists, and also that I had not offered Lieut Sinclair any food when bringing him back from Weinsberg in October. This they alleged was 'ungentlemanly' conduct. In point of fact I had given Sinclair a bottle of lemonade at Heilbronn and some soup at Leipzig, to supplement his rations. The complaint was 'noted'. A day or two later snow fell and as the weather remained mild, snowballs began to liven up the parade.

One day, while I was speaking to a British officer after the parade, a snowball smashed against the canteen door behind me. It was thrown with such force that in the mush left on the door I found a piece of glass stuck into the wood.

'You,' I said to the officer, 'are witness of this.' I extracted the glass and made a report of the incident to the Kommandant. He asked what suggestions I had in the matter. I said we should photograph or film the parades and make a sound recording as well, as evidence of the disorder in case something serious should occur.

So for a few days we mounted a camera instead of a machine-gun and took photos of the parades from the Hexengang window. But then on January 14th the French priest Congar saw what was going on and protested. I told the French Senior Officer what we were doing and why, namely to have available evidence of disorderly conduct in case some serious incident should occur.

The Senior Officers among the prisoners must have seen our point and accepted it. From the following day, rioting on parade generally speaking came to an end, to my very great personal relief. A *modus vivendi* was established, and Order No. 38 disappeared crabwise into the sands of time.

My satisfaction at this little victory was heightened by the success of our monthly search.

From under the floor in the Dutch quarters we collected three hundred and sixty German marks, eleven French francs and, more important still, fifteen rubber or linoleum stamps of all kinds, used for the 'authorisation' of false papers. We also got the apparatus that Captain Van Doorninck used for measuring the drops and distances in our Zeiss Ikon locks. At the same time the Poles lost a splendid collection of false passes. And under the chapel floor the Riot Squad found fifteen yards of tunnel.

A second *Prominente* turned up this month. This was Captain Michael Alexander, a nephew of the Field-Marshal.

Our 'detectives' covered him in the same way as 'Emil' and we made the two share the same room to simplify our two-hourly controls of them.

By mid-January the temperature was well below zero. So that meant an end to snowballing, thank heaven!

On the 30th, however, the anniversary of the National Socialists coming to power, the Partei made its usual effort throughout the country to boost morale with parades and speeches. But for the first time, in many towns these celebrations were called off. Not so, however, in Colditz, where several of us were detailed to attend the Partei Show down in the town. I noticed that the Kreisleiter (District Party Leader), a healthy-looking master fitter, barely fifty years of age, together with a local Leader of thirty-five years of age, seemed to have been missed by General von Unruh's *Heldengreif* (hero snatching) Commission – as we sarcastically knew it! Maybe Partei members were outside its scope, but ordinary mortals certainly were not. All men from 16 to 65, all women from 17 to 45 had to register. There were, however, Partei exceptions. By April 1945, I remember these two had still not been called up for military service.

Next came the news of the capture of Stalingrad by the Russians and of Hitler's promotion of General Paulus to Field-Marshal – a sorry gesture which did not conceal from anyone either the military disaster of the capitulation, or the blow to the Führer's prestige, who had given his word that he would relieve the surrounded Sixth Army.

To show how low stocks were running, I remember that winter having the job of getting something out of the Colditz shops to serve as prizes for football competitions the prisoners had organised. It was extremely difficult to collect even twenty items as there was hardly anything at all for sale, only pencil cases, vases, book-ends, and so on. Any goods at all were reserved for the black market.

In February our only Indian prisoner, the doctor, Captain Mazumdar, went on hunger strike. He had repeatedly asked to go to a prisoner-of-war camp for Indians, and practise there, as he was entitled to do under the Geneva Convention. But this was repeatedly refused by the OKW, in whose files he was down with a red tab as '*deutschfeindlich*' (hostile to Germany).

For a week Mazumdar lost a great deal of weight, and after a fortnight the OKW gave in, and he was moved to a camp near Bordeaux.* Mahatma Ghandi was also on hunger strike at that time in India. His fast lasted for twenty-one days. The Viceroy, however, remained unmoved.

During February our Kommandant was posted to a PW camp in South Russia. He was replaced by a forty-three-year-old Lieut-Colonel who had been studying form in the camp since Christmas.

With this change of teacher, the 'bad boys' in the 'classroom' began to take the measure of the new arrival. The French opened up the barrage. We found broken razor blades in the kitchen waste. These had been upsetting the pigs in the Zschadrass asylum for some time, and we traced the source back to the French quarters. In reprisal we withdrew all privileges for them (walks, theatres, football).

On March 18th the French blew their electric light fuses one evening and for once we did not send Willi in immediately to mend them. As the French had apparently no spare wire, or at least did not care to use their stolen stocks, they had to sit around in the dark. This went on for several evenings, and made them extremely cross! On the evening parades they would set up a howl of '*Lumière!*' and throw burning news-

*Dr Mazumdar escaped successfully to Switzerland from this camp the following year.

papers or toilet paper about to light up their staircase when they came down and went back up after roll-call.

The British smoked demonstratively on parade by way of illuminating sympathy.

We took no notice for quite a while.

When their lights were eventually restored the French cry changed to '*Promenade*'.

We said they could go down to the park again on March 20th if there had been no more sabotage '*schweinerei*' by that date.

Next we stole a march, as we thought, on the prisoners, by moving out all their metal bedsteads without warning, and replacing them with wooden ones. Most of the beds were double-deckers of wood, but there were quite a few metal ones still about, single size, especially in the infirmary. Naturally we could not whip out a hundred beds in one fell swoop, and by the time the last one was out the angle braces had gone from the last dozen or so to come out. Metal was the most precious raw material for escaping purposes, especially for tunnelling and making screwdrivers, keys and crow-bars. We riposted with an immediate general search and got most of this valuable stuff back into our hands. The tug of war continued – pull devil, pull baker – a day or so later, when we sent a lorry into the yard with mirrors and fittings for the barber's shop, to be set up in a spare room off the yard. Two sentries went in with the lorry to keep an eye on it while the unloading was going on. The prisoners had their eye on the lorry as well and when they too had finished their 'unloading', a set of maps, a tool kit and a jack had disappeared.

While in the Conference Room complaining to our Security Officer, who had been summoned by the agitated sentries, the owner of the lorry incautiously removed his hat and let it go out of his hand, placing it on a ledge by the window. In due course it went, not only out of his hand but completely out of his sight, for evermore. The prisoners just reached in with a wire and hooked a splendid catch.

'For heaven's sake,' the lorry owner shouted to his men, 'get going – before they steal the wheels off the axles. This is a madhouse.'

Flight-Lieut Dickinson's second escape from the town goal took place on March 7th, 1943. Once again the few prisoners down there filed in from the yard after their exercise. One stopped to light another's cigarette in the doorway, and the file spread out. Neither the front nor the rear sentry noticed this. Dickinson, who was ahead of the two smokers, slipped under a table on the half-lit ground floor, close to the door. The file carried on past him and up the stairs, the second sentry bringing up the rear. When the second sentry had gone up the stairs, Dickinson slipped back quietly through the yard door and again over the wall, and again had the luck to find an unlocked bicycle to get away on. However, 'Mousetrap' caught him yet again, as the previous August, heading for Chemnitz. This time he had money on him, fifty marks in all. I was particularly annoyed to find this money because he had been very thoroughly body-searched before he went into the cells.

On April 5th, no less than 150 officers turned out for the afternoon walk in the park. Most suspicious! They moved off in due course, but as the party reached the German yard, a Dutch officer at a window called out suddenly, 'All Dutch officers come back. There is a lecture on.' The Dutch turned back although they had no right to do so – the others carried on. There was confusion in the ranks and among the guards.

Suddenly two German officers appeared at the gate leading out towards the park. The sentry there asked for their passes. These carried the signature of our Adjutant and Kommandant over the office stamp, authorising the bearers, officers from the OKW, Berlin, to visit the castle and grounds.

Fair enough – the sentry clicked his heels. But by chance the Post Sergeant 'Nicht Wahr' (to the English), or Beau Max, arrived on the scene. He took a look at these two 'German officers', and thought he recognised one by his gold teeth. 'Who the devil are you?' he asked.

They cursed him fluently in the appropriate German.

'Who *are* you two? I'll bash you if you don't say.'

These officers cursed him more than perhaps German officers normally should.

The walk having by now sorted itself out, came on through

the gateway and the NCO in charge arrested the two suspects. They turned out to be Captain Dufour of the Dutch company and Flight-Lieut Van Rood, an RAF pilot of Dutch descent.

We were suspicious of all this to and fro – had other 'German officers' gone through this gateway to the park about this time? The sentry said no. We had a special roll-call. We were right – two more officers were missing. These were Lieut Michael Harvey, RN, and Flight-Lieut Jack Best, RAF. Obviously they too must have got away during the confusion at the gate disguised in our uniform as well. We reported them missing to the OKW on April 5th.

With the reopening of the escaping season in April our new Kommandant ordered four counts a day at 7, 11 and 4 p.m., and the last parade at any time between 8 and 10 p.m., at half an hour's notice on the yard bell.

One day the Kommandant attended the 11 o'clock parade. His reception was particularly noisy, and in view of this indiscipline he threatened to order six, seven or even eight parades a day. The prisoners didn't really worry at this prospect. They had nowhere to go, they said, and nothing to do – they might just as well stand around in the yard day and night being counted. It was not they, they hinted, who would tire of this.

A week later we took up all the linoleum off the floors – splendid raw material for rubber stamps and German belts. Searching around doing this operation we found a hole under the chair in the surgery where the French dentist worked. We also found a trolley in the French quarters fitted up with rubber wheels and several yards of tow rope. It looked as if a tunnel was in contemplation.

The same month a fire broke out in a heap of straw in the yard as we were refilling palliasses. We sent men in to put it out with a hose. The French tried to put them out with buckets of water flung from their windows. Again we withdrew all the French privileges.

At the beginning of May, Flight-Lieut Tunstall, who held the record for time in arrest and courts-martial, came again before the Leipzig court on a charge of striking one of our medical orderlies. Unfortunately the plaintiff collapsed during cross-examination. Tunstall sprang to his assistance with a glass of water, and the case was dismissed.

After Mairesse-Lebrun's escape over the fence and wall in the park, those under arrest in the castle cells took their daily exercise along a terrace on the west front of the castle instead. On the morning of May 11th, three prisoners were let out of their cells for exercise on this terrace. One of them was Flight-Lieut Don Thom (Royal Canadian Air Force). Thom was an athlete. He was the only officer I ever saw using the parallel bar we set up in the park. He could stand on this, ten feet up, and do back somersaults to the ground successfully.

As Thom came through the door at the back of the guard-room that morning, he dropped his jacket and dived straight over the balustrade at a window just below it in the wall of the guardroom building that projected out at right angles from the terrace. For a second he hung on to the cross bars of the grille, then dropped to a lower window, catching the bars of that again as he fell. He was on the ground before any of the sentries reacted. As they opened fire from both terrace levels, in danger as much of hitting each other as getting Thom, he raced to the dead ground under the pagoda, and then up over the barbed wire curtain untouched and down into the park beyond. Here Thom made away down among the trees, but ran into coils of wire which brought him to a halt. Here the park sentry got hold of him. It was the maddest attempt of all and but for those final trip wires I think Thom would have got out of Colditz, though perhaps not very far thereafter.

Shortly after this episode two representatives of the Swiss Protecting Power visited the camp. The Kommandant announced that he personally would conduct them round the prisoners' quarters. I accompanied the party into the yard, and the order 'attention' was given. None of the prisoners in the yard took any notice at all. So I cleared the yard and showed the Swiss into the Conference Room.

While we were talking, shots were heard outside in the yard. I explained to the Swiss that the prisoners were probably cat-calling from the windows and that an order must have been given to them to withdraw from the windows under the threat of shooting. I pointed out some must have ignored the threat and a few warning shots would have been let off to impress them. The Swiss, I regretted to note, were not themselves impressed in the way I could wish.

However, the Kommandant then suggested a visit to the quarters. We spent ten or fifteen minutes in the British rooms, on several floors of the east block, and then found ourselves and the Swiss locked in at the bottom of the staircase! The British had simply turned the key in the lock and taken the door-knob off after we had gone up the stairs.

After a lot of shouting an NCO came over from the guard-room and levered open the door with the end of a French bayonet.

The Swiss report on this visit must have made very impressive reading, for within a fortnight we had a visit from the General in Command of Prisoners-of-War in Berlin. He informed the prisoners' Senior Officers that under the Geneva Convention they were subject to all the laws, instructions and orders of the holding Power. He further added that he approved each and every measure taken by our Kommandant in support of his own orders, with the use of arms or not. Discipline must be enforced.

Among our visitors was the French general Scapini. He represented that public opinion which in 1940 was against a continuation of the war by France, even from the colonies. Although the picture of Marshal Pétain was to be seen in some of the French rooms in Colditz, by 1943 the sentiment behind these pictures was wearing a little thin. At the best, the feeling was 'wait and see'. Scapini, who represented the government of Pétain and Laval, and was in charge of prisoner-of-war matters, was allowed to speak to the French on his own. I don't think he had very much success in his arguments for collaboration.

Shortly after Easter 1943, my decoration with the War Service Cross (second class) was received with howls of delight by the members of the 'Grande Nation'. Not 'Pour le Mérite' but 'Pour la prison' was their cry. Plainly the French had it in for me personally.

## CHAPTER XI

# End of the International

IN THE parcel office our X-ray machine kept finding contraband in any and every kind of solid object, such as hairbrushes, cotton reels, gramophone records. Pencils showed lead each end, but in the middle we often found rolls of fine paper with messages written on them. It seemed that the British authorities were really letting themselves go on behalf of their men in captivity. We made our own efforts in that line – both to stop them and to improve on them for our own purposes.

In Colditz, as in all PW camps, the Abwehr (Security) Section had as its first task the prevention of escapes. A PW returning to his homeland might take with him information of value not only as to camp conditions, but also as to conditions among civilians, or concerning transport, or indeed as to practically anything he might have noticed as he travelled through Germany. He might also bring with him code arrangements for communication back to the camp he had left, by which a steady supply of information could be assured through the medium of prisoners' letters out and home. In this way the prisoners could receive information and advice as to escaping.

It was a security officer's job first of all to keep his prisoners in. To achieve this he advised the Kommandants in the camps, in the first instance, as to direct prevention methods. These would be the siting of barbed wire fences and searchlights, the disposition of guards, the methods of searching individuals and quarters, the arrangements for in-going and out-going checks, the roll-calls, and so on. Security also had to decide what should be done if and when an escape should actually take place. The arrangements taken under the above heads I have already described as they were in force and as they were not effective in Colditz. A further matter coming under the control of Security was sabotage and the bribery of German personnel.

Since written communications were allowed between prisoners and their home country, and vice versa, the necessity for censorship arose, to cope with this obvious though official leak in any country's security ring. We could not very well control incoming mail as to quantity, but we rationed the prisoners to three letters and four postcards a month outwards, written on special forms provided by ourselves.

Unlimited food parcels through the International Red Cross were also allowed.

Private clothing parcels were rationed to four a year per head, and the IRC was responsible for their transport only. Food parcels from occupied countries such as France, Poland and Holland were sent privately and only on the production of the appropriate forms, obtainable in the countries themselves. It was in private parcels that we found quantities of forbidden material, as described. Independent charitable organisations such as the YMCA also sent gifts to individuals or for general camp use.

Letters were checked visually and chemically for codes or secret writing, while parcels were X-rayed for forbidden goods. At Colditz we allowed German newspapers in, provided we found nothing in them which might be of use to the prisoners by way, for example, of train timetables or similar announcements. Some books and authors were on a blacklist. Technical books were, as a rule, allowed, but, of course, there were exceptions.

All this is mainly passive defence. However, active defence on security matters consists, among other things, in the acquisition and posting of agents in the ranks of the enemy. 'Security without agents is like a housewife without a broom,' a Russian once said to me.

In Colditz we had no broom, no listening post at all. There were only two traitors the whole time I was there, and they came forward by chance, and on their own initiative and not as a result of any plan of ours, and betrayed their people only once in each case. One other was spotted in time by the other side and rendered ineffective.

We collected and confiscated a mass of escape material from parcels, and our museum was well worth a visit, including not only these articles, but finished objects in the shape of uniforms, passes and civilian clothes of all kinds manufactured by the prisoners either with the help of contraband or by themselves alone. But in many respects I am bound to admit failure, failure in some cases only suspected and never proved until after the war. There must have been something wrong with our practical arrangements, as shown by the many occasions when prisoners got out. I felt there must also be gaps somewhere, through which information and material assistance were getting in.*

We never discovered any British codes or secret writing, and only one or two instances of such among the other nationalities, mostly fairly harmless, dealing with personal or political matters.

What we did find above all was money, German military passes, civilian identity cards, escape maps, even with details of frontier guard posts, tools (especially hacksaw blades), miniature wireless parts, compasses, dyes, blankets for civilian suits with patterns marked out on them, pills for producing symptoms of various illnesses, and so on. Certainly, we could not complain of nothing to do in that camp at Colditz, or indeed of nothing to learn. In due course, even the OKW in Berlin began to take notice, and began also to use its head. By the summer of 1943 it had formed an idea, and then a plan. Why not copy the methods of the British War Office, and communicate with our own prisoners in Allied hands in the same way as they were attempting (only attempting?) to do with their prisoners in Germany?

Since the Security Office at Colditz had more experience than that of any other camp in this matter, due to its continuous instruction, as one might call it, at the hands of the British Secret Service, the OKW picked on us to fix up this link with our prisoners, who were mainly in the United States.

*Not until I read the prisoners' books after the war did I learn o the success of Lieut. Guigues in his by-passing of our parcel office alarm circuit, which completely neutralised the Colditz security system at one of its vital points.

Local Partei leaders in Germany were required to give us lists of reliable Partei members in captivity. Letters to them were passed through our hands for 'treatment'. Articles were sent down to us from Berlin for inclusion in parcels once contact had been established with these addressees, and we spent a lot of time making up consignments to these men, 'dynamited' according to the approved British or French methods.

To begin with we had to establish communication back to ourselves. For this purpose we sent out a plastic substance in small wrappers with the instructions printed on them. This stuff was called 'Philip' – if a fingernail or a matchstick were pressed into it and then written with, invisible writing remained on the paper. Questions were written on the finest Japan paper and compressed into soup cubes, or dried peas, for example. These methods were in fact successful. We never established a communication by code in what one might call plain letter-writing. Monthly we sent out from Colditz over one hundred 'dynamite' parcels to different addressees. None of the parcels resembled each other in any way, as to packing, labels, senders' names, or so on. The whole operation was code-named 'Ekkehard'.

The great difference between us and the British and French was that we did not set up a traffic in escape material in any shape or form. No money or passes or tools were dispatched. I mentioned that 'articles' were sent to us by the OKW for onward transmission to certain of our prisoners. That is exactly what I meant – newspaper articles, propaganda articles, and extracts from Hitler's speeches. Or from Himmler's. But how often did we not have to cut out portions of these, when events had contradicted the prophecies or assurance those two had made!

We did not find any propaganda articles in the prisoners' mail – the British War Office never even thought to boost its men's morale with political speeches in print. The chief question that we put to our prisoners was, are the Partei members still loyal? Are attempts being made upon their loyalty? But no Colditz prisoner, as far as we discovered, was ever asked by the War Office, for example, if his own loyalty was still 100 per cent. In fact, had such a question come at all, I imagine the prisoner might well have replied that, having regard to the nature of the question (and therefore the sanity of the questioner) he required notice before giving an answer.

We had reports on camp conditions and requests back from our prisoners, in secret writing, for radio sets. Thereupon the OKW told us that if the British could send these things to their prisoners why didn't we go ahead and do the same? Hell, yes – but none of the parts that they sent over ever got past our X-ray machine. The OKW replied by asking, well, then, how did the French officers in Colditz get their radio past it? Our answer to this was that they had stolen it out of the parcel office with a false key after distracting the sentry, as a traitor had told us. 'Yes,' continued the OKW, 'and since then you've had an electrical foolproof warning system on the door. Are you sure there are no more radios in the camp?'

'There are no more radios in the camp.'

'Well, perhaps our prisoners-of-war will also make false keys and knock parcels off out of the Allied parcels stores before they put up alarm systems. Give them something worth trying for.'

In vain we replied that German radio sets at the time were far too big for the concealment of their components in cakes, in soap or in tobacco parcels, by the British method. The OKW then ordered all prisoner-of-war camps in Germany to send to us whatever miniature radio parts they had or might collect from prisoners' parcels or from their quarters. We in Colditz were then snowed under with sets of every kind, size and shape, both new and old – but no miniatures at all! These seemed to be reserved for Colditz only, or else had already got into other camps and been successfully concealed.

Before we got down to even trying to send out concealed radios, the war, and 'Ekkehard' too, came to an end. We had indeed tried to copy the Secret Service but with other ends in view.

There was only one successful escape home of a German prisoner – that of Lieut Von Werra, who got from Canada to the then neutral United States, through to Mexico and home by U-boat. Generally speaking, escaping was not in the forefront of our prisoners' minds. To most of them, getting home from the USA was an enterprise almost beyond the bounds of possibility.

However, the British had by far the best of this smuggling service, although I treasured for a while a letter to a British prisoner which had slipped back into the mail, from which the English censor had removed it. His remarks to the loving writer of it were a model of sarcastic reproof!

Although we seemed to have closed all gaps in our lines a tip from 'Security News' indicated another one we hadn't spotted. We read that the laundering arrangements had been exploited in other camps, and that officers had been establishing contacts as a result of permission to send their clothes out for washing and ironing. They had found another channel for the bribery and corruption of our civilians.

So one day we decided to give the Colditz dirty linen a public airing and opened up all the cardboard laundry boxes before sending them on. Among the bundles of clothing we found evidence of quite a traffic of coffee and chocolate one way, and liqueurs another way, together with love letters from impassioned washer-women to French and Polish officers.

Parties on both sides of the wire were appropriately punished with solitary confinement.

Meanwhile, the loss of Tunis, and so of the whole African front was greeted appropriately on subsequent parades by the prisoners. Holland was put under martial law. We had air-raid alarms several times a week now. The enemy's shipping losses were dropping. We wondered what had happened to our submarines.

Another example of the result of excessive contact came when the dentist's attractive assistant fell victim to the tall, dark and handsome personality of Flight-Lieut Chaloupka, a Czech RAF officer. We had to make use of the town dentist in his own surgery, because he refused to come up to the castle again to give treatment after once losing his coat there to his patients. Repeated dental appointments indicated that Chaloupka's teeth must be in a bad way! and finally we had to have the girl moved in her own interests. I do not know what contraband passed between them but it was suspected that the girl's soft heart must have provided something more than love letters for her amorous airman.

One could philosophise here quite a bit on sex as a driving force, the ultimate one, perhaps, that will throw overboard everything that religion, custom, social instinct and practice command. Of course, there was a sex problem in Colditz. I cannot say whether married prisoners were better off than un-married in this respect, but I don't think that after two or three years there was much to choose between their different states of mind.

Occasionally we had glimpses into the prisoner's condition – from their letters.

Once an officer posted home a drawing of himself, idealised perhaps, but a good likeness, in perfectly fitting uniform, smiling, well and fit. The paper seemed unusually thick and heavy, so we slit the picture, looking for concealed messages behind it. There was indeed a second sheet. It contained a message – a very passionate one – and again a sketch of the writer, not this time in uniform, but in all his (perhaps imagined) olympic nakedness, the true representation no doubt that he would wish his sweetheart to see and keep in mind.

Once at the beginning of morning roll-call I found in an open doorway in the north-east corner of the yard a birdcage in which was suspended a figure of the Führer, a very cheap form of insult I felt, but what could we do about it by way of discipline?

In June 1943 we saw the beginning of the end of Colditz as an international camp, except for a few weeks right at the end of the war. The first change was the arrival of two batches of sixty-seven British officers in all, who had made a mass break from a tunnel at Oflag 7B, Eichstätt, in Bavaria. One of this group was Captain the Earl of Hopetoun, son of Lord Lin-lithgow, one-time Viceroy of India. He was shortly promoted by the OKW to the rank of *Prominente*, thus bringing the number in this category at Colditz up to three.

The concentration of *Prominente* in Colditz gave rise to rumours of an increase in British military interest in the camp that held them. Swiss papers even reported that a plan was on foot to liberate them by some parachute attack, and get them away by plane. The OKW went so far as to organise a kind of Riot Squad on our own Colditz model, on permanent standby for action at the training camp at Leisnig. The unit consisted of tanks and lorried infantry to be rushed to Colditz should any air landing be reported in the vicinity. More spectacular rescues did, of course, take place during the war, in particular that of Mussolini from the Gran Sasso by Otto Skorzeny.*

Next came the transfer of the Dutch company to Stanislau in Polish Galicia. We sweated at the thought of their impending departure, our hearts bled for the Kommandant at Stanislau.

We lost only one of the Dutch company on the way to Poland, one of the van Lynden cousins, but the sixty of them made a veritable hornet's nest out of Stanislau, and many more of them got away from there than would have done from Colditz. Indeed this was again an example of another of the OKW's big mistakes in that it mixed hardened escapists with comparatively harmless prisoners. The old lags got away from an easier clink – the innocents became infected with the same idea.

In July came the order for the French and Belgian companies to go to Oflag 10C at Lübeck. They went in two groups of about a hundred each. The first left on the 7th and arrived at full strength without incident. The fun began with the second group six days later, by when I suppose the prisoners remaining in Colditz had worked out the routine of departure.

The amount of luggage to be taken each time was enormous. It always was. There were boxes, sacks, cartons, bundles of blankets, cardboard suitcases and so on. Our one cart was heavily overworked, between the Schloss and the station.

We dug two would-be escapers out of the stacks of personal belongings: one was Lieut Klin, a De Gaullist officer, the other was Giles Romilly! We only caught the latter because we had virtuously set a guard on the railway baggage between cartloads to prevent pilfering, and the sentry caught Romilly

*And, of course, the body-snatching of German top scientists and rocket men by both sides at the very end of hostilities.

breaking out of his box. Our Kommandant ran his finger reflectively round his collar when he heard that Romilly had been recaptured. It was he who would have had to answer, and with his head, should 'Emil' have got away.

In due course the second group of French officers arrived at Lübeck, also without loss. Too good, I wondered, to be true? Sure enough, after a while we spotted three strangers in the British company, which was by then the only nationality represented in what they called 'Allied Occupied Territory in Germany'.

We discovered there had been a switch. Three French officers had stayed in Colditz, and three changelings had gone up to Lübeck in their place. We sent the three French off, and Lübeck returned their namesakes, so they thought.

But, actually, of the three who came 'home', only two were the right British officers, the third was still a Frenchman. He spoke good English just as Lieut Barratt, being a Canadian prisoner from the Dieppe raid, spoke good French. This was bluff upon bluff and Lübeck fell for the double bluff. Back went the Frenchman and in due course back in exchange came Peter Barratt, whose place the Frenchman had taken.

The confusion in these large camps of several thousand officers was so bad that, in the end, security just went by numbers, as complete identification became practically impossible. Fingerprint checks were all right as proof positive, but what if a couple of dozen prisoners were shown to be fake? I think in some camps they found it better to let sleeping dogs lie.

With the departure of those who gave Colditz its international character, I could not help reflecting about these various national groups who had been there.

We on the staff at Colditz knew, and accepted, that the prisoners would consider it their duty to continue a sort of cold war against us even in captivity. We should have been surprised had it been otherwise. We knew that collaboration during hostilities ranked as treason and of course disgrace. We on our side were brought up to the same standards of military duty and honour. After all, the tradition of the different European Officer Corps have the same source, hammered out in centuries of continual war between the nations.

While we were in Colditz my rule was, 'Do as you would be done by', and I say that I stuck to it throughout.

It is perhaps rash to identify the particular with the general and vice versa but the Dutch company were, in my view, unique. I think one could fairly say that they were indeed all for one and one for all. We never had any 'nonsense' from the Dutch. Their escape average was the highest of all nations in Colditz. Their behaviour as a military unit was impeccable, not only in their discipline but in their unrelenting and active hostility to ourselves.

Admittedly these were the *élite* of the Dutch Colonial Army, some of them of mixed blood, but in spirit they were all from the same mould. I would rather have had them as allies than enemies.

French ingenuity and energy was something to be wondered at, but why so often did they, if I may say so, let themselves down, with stupid and empty personal attacks, on myself and on others of the German staff? Could not the French company have been satisfied with their great contribution to the common stock of prisoner successes, without indulging in childish and, as it turned out, utterly ineffective, reactions, which served, surely, only to reaffirm the legendary hate-complex between our two countries? What I have never been able to swallow is the assistance given by the French religious and medical personnel to escapers. These people were privileged under the Geneva Convention. Their actions were, in my view, an abuse of the privileges granted and in consequence of the Convention itself.

The last of the Polish company left Colditz for Spitzberg in Silesia in August 1943. The Poles had two fanaticisms that impressed themselves on my mind. One was love of their country, the land so seldom their own, so long desired, so briefly known – a mere twenty years – from 1920–1939. The other was hatred of Germany. The Poles seethed with hatred of us, but in Colditz their behaviour was exemplary.

CHAPTER XII

*Franz Joseph*

WITH THE departure of the Polish officers, Colditz was no longer an international camp. Two-thirds of its occupants had been moved, leaving about two hundred British officers, including De Gaullists, and one or two Americans. We on the Kommandantur staff began to wonder whether, taking all in all, life would not quieten down in the camp in its new shape and form. There were several reasons for this wishful thinking.

In the first place German reverses on the main war fronts might make the prisoners believe that the end was so near that to escape was taking a needless risk. In the second, escape was now becoming increasingly difficult. We had microphones all round the outside walls, which recorded even the pacings to and fro of our sentries. The wall surface at the seam between their yard and ours was networked with alarm wires under the plaster on our side. We tightened up again on the order to sentries to demand passes from everyone who came past them, and punished those who failed to do so. But the weakest point in all our security was again not the mechanical but the human element.

On one occasion we found in a hide-out a comparatively perfect pass – bearing so good a copy of the Adjutant's signature that it must have been drawn from an original. It purported to be an internal Colditz camp pass establishing the identity of the holder as a member of the guard company. All that was lacking was the holder's name. Plainly to obtain this copy some guard had been bribed for the loan of his own pass, perhaps for a short while on more than one occasion.

In reply to this we called all passes in and reissued them. The new passes were printed, however, to our special Security instructions. The printer was told to use, as identification number of the blank pass, not just the one figure for all passes of this same type. He was told to print a sequence of numbers covering the total of the blank passes printed, and to print these figures in very small type. We kept this fact secret. There was, of course, the normal serial number in large print which was usually the only number to which persons paid any attention. As we issued the passes, we noted down the minute special number of each pass and set against it the name of the person to whom it was given. In due course, among the booty after one of our hauls of contraband, we found another perfect pass. In this case once again the prisoners had naturally copied down what they had assumed was the printer's normal identification letters and figure, as well as the serial number printed plainly on top of the pass for all to see. This find gave us the identity of the guard who had lent his pass to copy.

We had the man up and, of course, he talked himself out of it. He said he had once taken his coat off for half an hour while watching two civilians at work in the prisoners' quarters – perhaps in this interval the prisoners had 'borrowed' his pass. There was nothing we could do about it except to warn him to be more careful in future, and also to make certain that he was never again put on the job of keeping an eye on civilians who went to work in the prison yard.

It was now September 1943, the start of the fifth year of the war. Number 3 Platoon of the Guard Company was on duty the night of the 2nd. The NCO in charge was an old Sergeant-Major, over sixty years of age. He wore several decorations from the First World War, including the Iron Cross (First Class). He was a man of middle height, of military bearing, and on the best of terms with all his men. Not only was he well known as a character but he was physically recognisable in the simplest possible way by his outstanding personal feature, his huge Hindenburg moustache – ginger-coloured, grey-tipped, and clipped always in the prescribed regulation manner. Because of this moustache the Sergeant-Major was known to the prisoners as Franz Joseph.

Round about midnight Franz Joseph appeared on his usual rounds outside the castle walls, accompanied, however, by two sentries with slung rifles. He came to the last two of the guard posts on the east side of the castle. Here was the gate with the catwalk above it, that six officers had escaped through almost exactly a year previously. Above the gate we had put a small catwalk after this escape and an extra sentry was now posted on it. The height of the catwalk above the ground enabled him to look over the edge of the canteen terrace and survey what had till then been dead ground all along the foot of the buildings. The last two sentries, over the gate, and on the beat up to it, had been on duty for about twenty minutes.

Franz Joseph dismissed the sentry below the catwalk with the remark, 'Your relief is early tonight. We have had an air-raid distant warning.' The guard was replaced by one of the men who had come with Franz Joseph but did not himself move off towards the guardroom, waiting apparently for his mate on the bridge above the gate to be relieved too and come back with him. The Sergeant-Major then went up to the bridge and relieved the last sentry, replacing him with the second man he had with him. The catwalk sentry, having been relieved, descended the steps from the gate and was just about to march off when, for no reason that he could later define, he decided to ask Franz Joseph for his Sergeant-Major's pass. For once someone obeyed the rules we had been trying to drill into our sentries for years, and obeyed it in spite of himself.

'Are you daft?' asked Franz Joseph. 'Don't you know your own Sergeant?'

The pass seemed in order, but, nevertheless, the guard had a vague suspicion and pressed his warning bell. He also covered Franz Joseph with his rifle and ordered him to put up his hands. Joseph cursed – not very fluently – but did indeed put his hands up. In due course a corporal and one man appeared from the guardroom in answer to the buzzer. Franz Joseph did not know the password when asked. The corporal drew his revolver and demanded Franz Joseph's. There was a struggle. The corporal swore later that Franz Joseph tried to draw his pistol. He himself fired.

'Good God,' said one of our three sentries present. 'You've shot our Sergeant-Major.'

But it was Lieut Michael Sinclair, in almost perfect disguise, who collapsed to the ground. The true Franz Josef appeared next on the scene, having heard the shots, and the two phoney sentries were marched off, Lieut Hyde-Thomson and Captain Lance Pope, leaving Sinclair on the ground. It was as simple as that. Three prisoners disguised as a German sergeant-major and two sentries had tried to cancel out the last two of our sentry posts at this vital corner of the building. They relied on blind obedience to orders on our part, and on the hope that at that time of night our men would not trouble to ask their own Hauptfeldwebel for his pass. It worked with one man, but not with the second.

Above the canteen there had been watchers, ready and waiting to go. Two sets of window bars we found sawn through. Had our sentries gone back to the guardroom, how many prisoners might not have got away in the five to ten minutes that they would have had available before the real Franz Josef came out to investigate? Months of rehearsals, months of run-throughs – all failed because, for once, one of our sentries did what he had been told to. Thinking back on it afterwards he did finally agree that what made him first suspicious of Franz Joseph was the fact that when the Sergeant-Major, as he appeared to be, came up on to the bridge, he did not, as he usually did, look on both sides of the catwalk as he advanced along it towards the sentry.

We held, of course, a special parade right away that night, but all were present. Tempers were extremely high after the tension had broken. There had been, as I said, months of preparation for this, and I do not know how many had hoped by then to be well on their way to freedom. One officer accused us of murder, for which he was later sentenced to two months in Grandenz military prison.

The British witnesses claimed that Sinclair had his hands up when he was shot. Our corporal swore that Sinclair had grabbed for his (dummy) revolver. To settle this point, our Kommandant sent in a report. A military court refused to prosecute, and the corporal was later sent to the East Front. Although shot from three-foot range, Sinclair was comparatively unhurt. The bullet struck a rib and passed out under his shoulder-blade. His disguise was as near perfect as it could be. Only the moustache made from the hairs out of a shaving brush, dyed, was the weak spot. It did not quite curl properly, but was, as we have seen, good enough for the dull light below the searchlights and for the dim intelligence of the first of the sentries to be relieved.

We put Sinclair's uniform in our museum but burned it before the capitulation. He himself was back in the camp after a few days in hospital at Bad Lausick.

The Kommandant was almost beside himself at this escape attempt. The brazen impertinence of not only attempting to impersonate some of his men, but in point of fact the successful impersonation in at least one instance!

Shortly afterwards, an orderly refused to obey an order. The Ferret reported the fact.

'Why didn't you use your gun on the man?' said the Kommandant.

Relations were getting very, very strained.

The Kommandant's deputy, known to all as 'Turkeycock' from his colour, and from the cloak in which he used to strut around, was also a man of violence. Those of us constantly in contact with the prisoners preferred to avoid even the threat of weapons, keeping them only in reserve should it be necessary for self defence.

On October 7th we caught Lieut Orr-Ewing in German uniform, in a paper dump just outside the castle. The British orderlies had taken him there it seemed in a basket of waste.

Shortly afterwards, our Security Officer left. He had his enemies on our staff, and the near escape of Mr Romilly, when the French left, had shaken his morale. He went to Muehlberg. His replacement was a lawyer, who had been severely wounded in Russia. He went about on sticks, but in spite of this disability was determined to go back to the front and win a decoration, and was posted for active service after about six months.*

The Swiss Government, acting as representatives and intermediaries between the British prisoners on the one hand and the German High Command and the British Government

---

*This officer, Major Hans Horn, won the Ritterkreuz in February 1945, after breaking out with his troops from encirclement by the Americans at Echternach in the Ardennes area. He died in Soviet hands at Sachsenhausen.

on the other, visited the different major PW camps three or four times a year. A typical visit took place in October 1943. Two representatives arrived with an officer from the OKW to escort them. The main points for discussion between them and ourselves and the prisoners were (1) the Franz Josef affair – that is, the alleged shooting down in cold blood of Lieut Sinclair; (2) the lighting in the castle; (3) collective punishments. These points were first of all discussed between us and the Swiss, and the results of the conversation were brought up in talks between the Swiss and the British Senior Officer in our absence. Finally the Swiss came back to us again with such of the British views as they thought practical.

As regards the first point – our Kommandant had sent in a report on the matter and we were awaiting the result of the investigation by the Military Court.

On the second point, we agreed that the lighting in the castle was bad, but we confessed the impossibility of providing a new cable two miles long to the power station to take the increased current necessary. We had neither the labour to rig the cable and pylons, nor had we wire in sufficient quantity to rewire the whole castle.

Point three was an old one. We took the view that the theatre was a privilege to be withdrawn at will whenever we required, for disciplinary purposes or even without reason. We won this last point.

On the night of October 19th, there was a very heavy air raid on Halle. Hundreds were killed and thousands injured. The electric current was off in Colditz for twenty-four hours. It was the closest evidence of bombing that we in the castle had ever had. The parade on the following morning was postponed from 7 o'clock to 8 o'clock, and then it was just like old times – shouts, whistles, demonstrations, indiscipline. However, the numbers were correct.

At 11 a.m. the Kommandant called me over. 'Look at this,' he said.

I read a telegram: 'To Kommandant – Oflag 4C Colditz–Saxony. Kindly collect Lieut Davies-Scourfield – picked up on 7th instant near Hildesheim. Signed Kommandant – Lamsdorf–Silesia.'

154

I was dumbfounded. 'Have we a Davies-Scourfield?' asked the Kommandant.

'We had, it seems,' I replied.

'Well, see where he is.'

I went into the camp and asked the British Senior Officer, Colonel Broomhall, where this officer, Davies-Scourfield, was. He replied, 'I'm sorry to say he's not in the camp.'

I answered, 'I'm sorry to say he's back in our hands,' and reported back to the Kommandant.

'Well now – since October 7th, nearly a fortnight ago, there have been about fifty parades. Are you telling me that you LOs have been fooled over the number of prisoners in this camp four times a day for a fortnight?'

I asked for twenty-four hours to think the matter over. In the end I concluded the only possible weak spot, where we might have been misled, was in the count of those who were temporarily sick and who were counted, sometimes rather crowded together, at one end of the hospital ward. But I wasn't really satisfied that I had been fooled this way four times a day for over fourteen days. How had Scourfield been covered up so long? As to how he got out, we reckoned he must have taken the same route as Lieut Orr-Ewing at the beginning of the month – in a box of waste paper. The date, I will quote again, was then October 20th, 1943. When he got back, Lieut Davies-Scourfield said he had left camp on September 30th, nearly three weeks before he was caught. When he was picked up his story was that he was a Sapper by the name of Brown. That was why he was sent to the other ranks camp at Lamsdorf, where he eventually admitted his rank.

It was not until the following March that the mystery was solved as the result of another escape attempt. By that time I had become Security Officer myself, and had never been really satisfied with my explanation of how Lieut Davies-Scourfield got away. One evening towards the end of the month the guard on the catwalk facing the Senior Officers' block or Saalhaus, noticed a rope flick back into one of the windows. Upon his reporting this, the Riot Squad rushed up to the room concerned and found, of course, nothing whatsoever except that the bars had been cut through. Someone seemed to have got out, and when, and where was he by now?

Below this window the small approach yard stretched, from the Archway (which was guarded), between the Saalhaus on the right and the high outer wall on the left – to the guardroom. Sentries were day and night on the catwalk, some way out from the outer wall in mid-air, above the thirty-foot drop from the top of this wall to yet another terrace below.

No one had been seen moving around in the approach yard, about fifty yards by ten, by any of our people in the guardroom, or by the archway sentry. Had anyone got out at all? or was this just a trick?

I ordered a '*Sonderappell*' to establish if anyone was indeed missing. While they were forming up I walked up and down the approach yard thinking. Suddenly someone beat on the inner side of an air-raid shelter door leading into a basement under the Saalhaus. A voice called out from inside the shelter. 'Here we are – let us out, will you – no need for *Sonderappell*.' I opened up and there was Flight-Lieut 'Bush' Parker from Queensland, Australia, and another officer, both in German army dungarees.

'What are you two up to in there?' I asked. 'You've no chance at all – that's an air-raid shelter.'

'I know,' replied Parker. 'We thought there would be a second exit. That's the rule in Germany, must be two ways, one in, one out of all air-raid shelters. This place is all wrong. There's only one door. I'll report you. It's against the rules.'

I laughed and searched both of them, finding nothing. In the shelter I found a screwdriver and a small heap of ashes, probably paper money and passes that they must have burnt when they found there was no way out except through the way they came in. They must have profited by some distraction of the man on the gate and trusted to luck as to where the persons from the guardroom window might have been looking, before dropping out of the window down the rope, and opening the door and getting into the cellar. A slight angle in the Saalhaus building did give them a little cover from guardroom surveillance, but they were wide open to view from the archway. Someone must have distracted the sentry there.

In due course, I let just Parker back into the camp. I had

my suspicions as to the identity of his companion. He said he was Lieut Bartlett. I wondered about this, and having learnt in so many cases that a hunch was as good as a cert in prison life, I sent over to my office for his identity card. I asked the man for details on it and he had them all correct. However, his face did not seem quite to fit the photo. I put him in one of the archway cells.

As I was still suspicious, I sent the Riot Squad in to fetch out Lieut Bartlett. They came out with an officer they said they knew as Bartlett. But he said his name was Camp. This second officer, Camp, looked far more like the Bartlett in the photo than the so-called Bartlett I had in front of me, and I looked from one to the other and back again to the photograph of Bartlett, that I had in my hand.

Again I sent the Riot Squad back into the camp, this time with orders to fetch out the officer whom they knew as Camp. They came out with 'Camp' and I asked him at once, 'Who are you?' and he replied, 'Camp'.

Immediately the first 'Camp' (who had been brought out as Bartlett) called out to the second 'Camp', 'Haven't you been warned?'

It was getting difficult to keep track of all these identities and officers, but it was now plain to me that the third man really was Camp and the second man was really Bartlett. The question now was – who was the first prisoner, the one I had caught with 'Bush' Parker? Bartlett had been in arrest recently. The sergeant in charge of the cells was brought along and he swore that the man claiming to be Bartlett was not the Bartlett he had known in arrest. I told him to go back through the list of names in the arrest book and see if he could put faces to all of them. He went right the way back until he came to Lieut Michael Harvey, twelve months previously. There he stopped. 'The man in front of you,' he said, 'who gives his name as Bartlett, is not Bartlett, but Harvey.'

All details of Lieut Michael Harvey, RN, and Flight-Lieut Jack Best, RAF, had gone to the OKW in Berlin in April 1943, for their 'escaped successfully' file.* We had been informed by the British some time in May of the previous year that these

*See page 136.

two had in point of fact got away to Switzerland. We thought they had got out of the park gate disguised as Germans, when our NCO Beau Max caught two others trying the same trick.

However, I had a spare copy of their photographs, and fetched out Michael Harvey's. As I walked back to the archway I thought, could it be that Harvey had been in the camp concealed somewhere in the course of the last twelve months? I was quite staggered by this thought. The sooner I settled the identity question the better.

'Good morning, Mr Harvey,' I said. He replied, 'My name's Bartlett.'

'Listen,' I told him. 'In three days Lieut Michael Harvey's papers will be back from the OKW. If your fingerprints tally with those on Harvey's papers there is no doubt as to your identity.'

And so he gave up and agreed that he was in fact Lieut Mike Harvey, an officer who had apparently escaped from Colditz just under twelve months before!

Now then – where was Best, who 'escaped' at the same time? Again I sent the Riot Squad into the yard after showing them Best's photograph. 'Get this officer,' I said. 'Go in at about 5 o'clock when it's quiet and they're all having their tea. That's when you'll find him.' Two of them went in, and there was Best leaning up against the wall. 'Come with us, Herr Lieutnant Best,' they said, 'the game is up.'

These two officers had actually been in the camp for one week under twelve months, living at first in total concealment, somewhere we never discovered, and later living in the quarters more or less as they liked, as we let them slip further out of our minds as 'gone away'. When necessary they had stood in to fill up gaps in the ranks on parade, on behalf of officers who had escaped unknown to us, as in the case of Lieut Davies-Scourfield three months previously, as I now realised. For the rest of this time they had lived a normal life in the camp except that they did not turn up on parades.

The Dutch had filled in with Max and Moritz, the dummies. The British had made do with Harvey and Best – the 'ghosts'. Best had actually escaped with Sinclair over the terrace on the west front in January, and on recapture gave himself to be Lieut Barnes. In fact he did twenty-one days' cells under that name, and still he was not recognised. All the real Barnes did was absent himself as a temporary ghost in Best's place, along with Harvey.

It was a hell of a story – I let myself go (in some admiration, I confess) in my report, again direct to Berlin, copy only to Dresden. But the real hell of it was that the OKW just would not believe me! They worked it out that these two had left the camp on April 5th, 1943, and must subsequently have returned at their own convenience! They even sent a detective officer down to investigate.

Our Kommandant thought this a very poor job. 'Is this place a damned hotel?' he asked, 'where people come and go as they wish? I don't believe any prisoner-of-war would ever want to return here once he got out, and I will say that it's nearly as difficult to get in here as it is to get out.'

The detective heartily and amusedly agreed with what were truly the facts, and the first letters home from these two officers confirmed our own reasoning. These were the first letters they had written for over a year and they said in them that the ban on communication home was the worst ordeal of the whole adventure.

On October 31st the Partei again held a demonstration down the town. As the parade crossed the river bridge on this occasion, all windows on the west front of the castle were fully occupied by the prisoners. At a given signal, cheers roared out over the valley, and all the orchestral brass blew in triumphant and welcoming discord. The noise carried even to the Kreisleiter's house. This time his wife rang up and complained. We turned out the guard on to the terrace below the row and ordered the windows to be cleared – 'or else ...'. The prisoners withdrew, only a few pumpkins fell among us.

Later that winter we had visits from all kinds of higher authorities. At one time it seemed possible that the castle would be abandoned entirely as being quite unsuitable for this kind of special camp and special prisoner. But in the end we all stayed put. The Kommandant received confirmation of his right to enforce discipline by any and every means and later he received the personal recommendation of General von

Keitel in this connection.

Not only were relations between us and the prisoners becoming badly frayed by the winter of 1943-44, but among the staff too there was quite a lot of friction. To begin with food was inadequate. Some had lost house and home and all their possessions. And some had lost members of their families as well, either at the fronts or in bombing raids.

All this worked on the nerves of the Colditz staff. Worst of all, however, was the now complete lack of confidence in our military and political leaders. Goebbels' line was, 'We must win, therefore we shall.' It wasn't a very sound line of argument.

Some of our staff left the camp at their own request and were posted elsewhere. Others grumbled because of the 'kid glove methods' of the camp officers, as they held them to be.

'What this lot wants,' said one officer, 'is Napoleon's whiff of grapeshot. That would show them who's boss here.'

In November the Kommandant's deputy appeared at a parade – loud cheers of welcome. He ordered a second parade an hour later – and when it took place the cheers were even louder. So he ordered a third and threatened a fourth, fifth and sixth. . . . Even louder cheers. On the third occasion the Turkeycock pleaded another engagement.

That same month two of the British orderlies escaped from a working party – Corporal Green and Private Fleet. They walked all night to Leipzig and took a train to Kottbus. They had no papers and were caught on the train. We collected them from Finsterwalde.

The fifth Christmas of the war found in most people's minds the conviction that the end was only a matter of time. There was no doubt as to the result, and among the prisoners very few reckoned on yet another Christmas in the bag.

Symptomatic was the British suggestion for a truce – the first time they had ever put this forward, between Christmas Eve and January 2nd, 1944. We naturally agreed, with considerable relief. We had other things to do than relax, however, especially after the air raid on Leipzig on Christmas Eve. But how was all this going to end ? A catastrophe for Germany was inevitable, and to my mind that meant a catastrophe for Europe.

## CHAPTER XIII

## No Co-operation

JUST OVER a fortnight after the end of the Christmas truce, Lieut Sinclair escaped again. This escape was, like so many others, a quite fantastic affair.

The idea arose from the delay which the prisoners had noticed and timed, in our switching on the searchlights round their half of the castle in the evenings. The shortage of current was something we always had to bear in mind and very often it was quite dark before the lights were actually switched on. This meant that the sentry on the lower or garden terrace on the west side of the castle, and the sentry in the pagoda at the north-west corner there, could hardly see that face of the castle in detail. The sentry on the pagoda always left his tower just before the searchlights came on, and patrolled the garden terrace together with the regular sentry down there until relieved. Neither could see on to the upper terrace twenty feet above, from their own level. The prisoners worked it out that they often had several minutes of near darkness before we grudgingly switched the current on each evening. During this time it was, in theory, possible to get out of their windows, if the bars were cut, and down by rope on to the upper terrace and then by this same very lengthy rope over the balustrade and down on to the garden terrace which was about forty yards wide and twenty feet below again. The darkness would be nearly complete, the searchlights not having been switched on, and if it were a dull or rainy evening then their safety was even more assured. Along the outer edge of the lower terrace the sentry paced back and forth. And from the barbed wire fence behind him the ground fell again steeply to the backyards of the town.

The sentry's beat on the lower terrace was right back up against this fence, and this reduced the amount of dead ground concealed from his view by the upper terrace, which jutted out from the ground floor of this part of the castle.

It was January 19th, 1944 – a dull, dark evening with a little rain – time, about 5 p.m. Suddenly the bell on the west terrace rang in the guardroom. One of the NCOs went out through the back door of the guardroom, presuming some officer was going the rounds and wanted to be let in from the upper terrace. The bell-push was not on the back door of the guard-room itself, but twenty yards along, on the balustrade. The searchlights were not switched on. It wasn't time yet. The NCO found no one on the terrace near the bell or anywhere else. He walked a little way further along and suddenly saw a rope whip up over his head and into one of the prisoners' windows. He rushed back into the guardroom and rang up the Security Officer. We all turned out and dashed into the prisoners' quarters on the first floor of the cellar house, where we found the grille of one window sawn through. There was no sign, of course, of any rope. This had undoubtedly been hidden away in the interval between its being pulled in to the room and our arrival some minutes later. We switched on the searchlights and searched both terraces. We found foot-prints on the flower-beds on the lower terrace, and a strand of wire cut in the outer fence. From here a home-made rope hung over the edge. The guards there swore they had heard nothing.

A woman below in the town, however, whose house backed on to the foot of the rock on which the castle stood, said that she had seen two or perhaps three figures climb down from the lower terrace and over a shed in her back garden and away.

We warned the usual circles of authority with the code word 'Mousetrap', and then held a *Sonnderappell* to discover exactly how many were missing and who.

Soon after this famous *Appell* started they put out the main lamp high up on the eastern building with a shot from a catapult. In the weak light of the remaining lamps it was im-possible to count the prisoners. So I ordered the lot up to the then unoccupied first floor across the yard, on the east side. They took so long to get up even this short distance that I literally drove the tail of this funeral up the stairs with gentle pressure from the rifle barrels of my Riot Squad, held cross-ways.

We herded the crowd into two unoccupied rooms up there. I had the identity files brought into a third room which I kept empty. As I knew pretty well all the officers by sight and name, I called the nearest to come in to this room and started to check. After I had got through about thirty, however, someone fused the lights. I shouted to my NCOs to sit on the files, lest they disappear. I called for lanterns, and after an hour and a half's work I eventually decided there were three officers missing. One of them was Lieut Sinclair.

Next morning I checked again and found that only two officers were missing. Apart from Sinclair the other missing officer was Lieut Barnes (or so we thought).

A week later these two were caught at Rheine on the Dutch frontier, were returned to us, and did the usual three weeks of solitary confinement.

The next to go was Lieut Millar, a Canadian officer. We never discovered with certainty how he got away, nor was he ever seen again by us, nor did we ever have any news of him from anyone else. A jacket that could have been his was found on the road some miles away and was brought back into the castle.

A few French orderlies still remained in the camp after the departure of the main body of French prisoners to Lübeck the previous summer. Mixed parties of British and French orderlies used to go out for exercise outside the castle, under guard. Mussolini had been posted to the east front that winter to fight against the partisans. There he was killed. His successor in Colditz was not so familiar with the faces of the other ranks in his care, and on one occasion this month Lieut Orr-Ewing took the place of one of the Frenchmen. He got away from the walk and away into the woods. The only sentry with the party chased him as far as the river Freiberger Mulde, having left his rifle behind so that he could run faster. Orr-Ewing felt that he could not stop simply because of the river, waded into the water and swam across. The guard funked the swim, but yelled to a railway worker on the other side who caught the escaper when he reached the far bank.

In February 1944, the Security Officer left and was due for replacement by a nominee of Dresden (Ast. 4). Our Kommandant thought this a poor idea, and rang up to say that to put a newcomer in charge of Security in Colditz was a complete waste of time, and would play straight into the prisoners' hands. In point of fact he told Ast. 4 that if they insisted on their own appointment, he would make them completely responsible for security in the camp, as he could not possibly accept that responsibility himself with a man who in the circumstances would be in no way equal to the task. He suggested that I was the only person who could do the job properly, since I had been in Colditz over three years, knew practically all the inhabitants by sight, and was familiar with all the tricks and all the attempts and the details of nearly every escape that had ever taken place. The Kommandant had some influence with the OKW in Berlin to whom he referred the matter in the end, and finally Dresden gave way and it was I who was appointed to be Security Officer as from that month. I held the post till April 1945 – over a year later.

It was for me a fateful step, but I did not think so at the time.

At that period of the winter it was extremely cold. There was deep snow everywhere, though the weather was lovely. It was, in fact, just right for the bombers. Heavy raids went on all the time, on Leipzig, on Halle and all around Colditz.

It was some time before the prisoners realised that I was now Security Officer. I had been one of the Duty Officers for so long that I was a familiar figure in the camp. As I alone on our staff spoke English, I was more often than most inside the camp during searches and checks, and for the purpose of negotiations and so on. If things had continued on their old plan. I should, as Security Officer, have done less duty inside the prisoners' yard than as an ordinary Duty Officer. But as the number of Lager Officers had been reduced from four to two I had now to do ordinary Lager Officer's work as well as what should have been the rather more backroom job of Security.

So life in Colditz for me continued much along the old routine. My promotion did not in any way change my relations with the prisoners. It merely increased the amount of work and of responsibility which fell on my shoulders. It was in some ways quite a relief to be so busy on this small battle-front. It momentarily enabled me to ignore the mounting catastrophe outside.

I thought that as a new broom I would strike an original note and sweep round for the first time in some corners which hitherto had been quite overlooked. I therefore arranged a search of the rooms occupied by our three *Prominente*. Two of these, Lieut Alexander and Giles Romilly, shared one room, while Captain Earl Hopetoun lived in a second. This was my first effort as a Security Officer, and I cannot regard it as a success. During the search of Hopetoun's room a hammer disappeared from our tool kit. Alexander told the sentry I had given him permission to get some water from the kitchen and the sentry let him out, against my orders. Alexander had picked up the hammer during the search and whilst out in the kitchen presumably passed it on to some one else before he came back.

I did not report this loss. In point of fact I felt too stupid. But Captain Hopetoun found out about it, and pointed out to me that this hammer was the one he always borrowed on parole for stage work. He was one of the theatrical producers in the camp. Hammers were fairly easy to make, but we always collected any unauthorised ones. Hopetoun got this one back for me, and so I was able to hand it out to him later on parole, whenever it was wanted. I thought this was a nice gesture, as my face was completely saved in my own Mess where this loss was never known.

In March of that year, 1944, the camp staff was again reduced. Fouine the Ferret went to Italy and never returned. His successor discovered a tunnel in the showers when he went in there one morning rather earlier than the Fouine was in the habit of doing. The cover over the hole in the floor was hardly noticeable and was also quite watertight. That afternoon the General came on a visit from Dresden. To show him the sort of job we had, the difficulties we were up against, and the calibre of the experts on the other side, we stood him on the cover to this tunnel and said, 'There is a tunnel here in the floor, Herr General – now see if you can spot it.' Not being trained as a PW detective, he failed – but this gave him some idea of my job, and I hope he realised why our Kommandant had made such a fuss about his Dresden Security Office appointing or trying to appoint a complete novice to the position of Security Officer in Colditz. At the time we could not think why this tunnel was being made just at this spot, until we remembered a previous hole near by. It seemed they were still aiming at the yard drain.

In March, too, I began to turn my attention to the foot of the clock tower where the great French tunnel of two years previous had been discovered.

There were several odd haphazard pieces of building in this north-west corner of the yard, the tower, the cellar, the chapel, air-shafts and so on. They had all been built at different times and had all been joined on to each other wherever it seemed handy. There had been no master plan for the construction of that part of the castle. On the ground floor of the west side, or cellar house, we still kept the parcel office and store, but the upper floors were now occupied by the British. It was noticeable, just as it had been with the French two years ago, how smartly they raised the warning cry of 'Goons up', when the Riot Squad, or indeed any of us, wandered in their direction.

Through a hole in the cellar wall between the tower and the chapel we were able to reach into a shaft that led back upwards to ground level and here we found odd material which varied from time to time – sacks, a piece of copper piping, odd pieces of rope. Something obviously was going on around here but our microphones gave no sounds from the outside of the buildings of any work in progress. I decided it was better to keep just a casual eye on this corner and the circular staircase that led up from it, and let the prisoners carry on with whatever work they were doing. At least it would keep them occupied and so comparatively happy. Until the microphones gave notice of work within their range, the prisoners could not be considered occupied in any particularly dangerous way. Should the microphones eventually begin to record sounds of tunnelling, then it would be high time to investigate, if we had not done that already.

However, I went into this corner of the yard and began to carry out a search of the ground floor, then of the first floor, then of the second floor.

I had the mason and the carpenter with me and one sentry just to keep an eye on things. The inner wall of the building, the courtyard wall shall we call it, was about four and a half feet thick at the base here, rising at that thickness for two floors. It was quite wide enough for a tunnel, or even just a hide in the width of it.

We found nothing on the ground floor or the first floor but when we came to the second floor, there in the bottom of a built-in cupboard, we did find a hide.

We were really looking for an entrance to some tunnel which we were sure was being dug in the cellars three floors below. Our experience with the French chapel tunnel had told us that the entrance might be absolutely anywhere however deep a tunnel might start horizontally. In that case, the entrance to the tunnel started four floors up the building, at the top of the tower. So we had therefore to search everywhere. In the bottom of this built-in cupboard we found a hide which was in effect an absolute gold mine in both senses of the word.

The British had boasted once, nearly three years previously, that they had over two thousand German marks in their treasury. This boast had rankled in my mind for years and I had always hoped that one day I would find that money. And now under the floor of the cupboard we found their main hoard: 2,250 marks, 4,500 French francs, plus passes, tools and some clothing – two sacks full. To crown it all we found a miniature radio. This was the real thing. We had, in fact, come upon the very first miniature radio ever discovered in any PW camp. We reported this directly to Berlin, as well as to Ast. 4, Dresden. We had found some spare miniature valves earlier in a parcel of tobacco and now we had the set they were meant for.

Pleased though we were with this very worthwhile discovery we still had not found the tunnel entrance. Indeed, we had given ourselves another worry. How had this radio got into the camp? We assumed that it had been smuggled in by guards or had come in in some parcel which had not been properly X-rayed.

Next day, acting on a hunch, I broke into a bricked-up space at the bottom of the circular staircase to the British quarters, and there was the tunnel we were seeking. It was about twenty feet long. The entrance to this was in a window seat on the first floor up above. The seat was in the thickness of the wall, and under it the tunnel entrance dropped down to the ground floor. It was a very narrow way down in to the main working tunnel and I think only those of very slender build could have been employed on that job. So far as I recall, this working was referred to later as 'Crown Deep' because only officers of the rank of major were working on it. Apparently they had some sort of monopoly in the affair.

The British thought they had reason to suspect a stool-pigeon over either 'Crown Deep' or the hide in which I discovered their treasure the day before. Indeed, Wing Commander Bader shouted down that second morning, 'Pay the fellow who gave the hole away, with your own food parcels, and not with ours!' He was, however, quite wrong and attempts on our part to get information from prisoners were hardly ever successful.

I have already mentioned cases of collaboration that we discovered between our own guards or civilians and the prisoners. We became aware of the extent of this more and more, as we continued to discover hides containing tools, passes, maps and money. Much of this must have come in concealed in parcels, but much must also have come in through guards and civilian workers in the camp. Bribery and corruption was going on the whole time and the dice were fully loaded on the side of the prisoners.

They had more food than they wanted and with this they used to bribe our men. Occasionally they would make a straight swop of food for food, chocolate or coffee for eggs or fruit, and so on, and even for alcohol, although this they made for themselves quite successfully in the last two years of the war. Their best medium of exchange, however, was in the form of the thousands of cigarettes which they could lay their hands on. Coffee also they had at their disposal (Nescafé usually), a commodity which had entirely disappeared in Germany by the end of 1942. It was easy to understand the success that the prisoners had on the bribery front.

The question arose, had we anything comparably desirable to offer any prisoner should he offer himself to us for the purposes of acting as a 'stooge' or informant? We could, of course, offer a man his freedom but that would only bring suspicion down on his head. As Propaganda Officer and later as Security Officer, I often pondered over this problem and I must say that at no time did I get beyond the first step – making an offer. I got nothing back in either case. In the three cases reported in this book, information was offered voluntarily.

One of the British orderlies wrote repeatedly in his letters home that he was sick of acting as servant to officers and wished that he could go and work again in the mines, which was his job at home. The censor told me of these comments and I had the man over.

'I could send you away, you know,' I told him, 'but I should want some information in exchange – as to what is going on inside the camp.'

'Captain Eggers,' he replied, 'I may not like it here but I am still British.'

I could not but admire his reply and in due course I did have him transferred. But he never gave me the slightest information.

However, again in March 1944, I had a chance, this time a real chance, of an agent of my own. A British Merchant Navy officer was sent to us by the OKW. He said that he had been broadcasting propaganda on our behalf from the 'Concordia' Studios in Berlin, where he'd had a row and been sacked. I mention no real names as the matter is now over, and the man has been punished in England as far as I know. I will call him by a name which was never known in Colditz – I will call him Grey. When Grey arrived, he at once offered me his services as informant. He said he had lived eight months in Berlin on his own, and drew a salary from our authorities of 800 marks a month (about £50). He broadcast for us and wrote scripts as well. He had a girl there. He had been a member of the British Fascist Party before the war.

Now he offered to pass back to me such information on escape and security matters as he could collect in the camp. All this seemed too easy, so I put a few questions to him first.

'Who's going to win this war.'

He replied, 'England, of course.'

'What's going to happen to you then?'

'Oh – I'll go back home and spread National Socialism in England.'

It occurred to me the fellow was a bit weak in the head.

'Well – be very careful inside the camp. You will be suspect until you are cleared. I think a Canadian officer, a lawyer, is in charge of the PW security. Have your story ready.'

'I'll say I escaped from Oflag 3D, and hid in Berlin for several months until I was caught in a *razzia* [round-up] in the streets after an air raid.'

'Where were you captured in point of fact?'

'At Narvik.'

It turned out he knew some prisoners in Colditz who had been on his old ship.

'That's fine,' I said. 'They will speak for you if there is any argument.'

Lieut Grey went into the camp. I brought him out two days later, ostensibly for photographing. He had not much to say, but what he had was interesting.

'I asked someone if I could get a letter out to a German adressee without going through the censorship. I was told to hand my letter to an officer I was shown. Don't know his name yet. I did so, and later in the day I was told the letter had already been posted.'

Here to me appeared proof of bribery among the guard company. Someone was acting as a carrier pigeon. I never caught this go-between. At that moment I thought my stool-pigeon would do the job for me in time.

That was all Grey had to tell me. Two days later the British Senior Officer handed in a note as follows:

'We do not recognise the man Grey as a British officer. I have given him an escort by day. I will not guarantee his safety by night.' After a brief discussion with the Kommandant we decided to remove Grey for his own safety.

He told us how he had been discovered. On the third day he had come up a second time for questioning in front of the Canadian, Colonel Merritt, V.C., and had been asked again for the full story of his whereabouts since capture in 1940. When he had finished his tale, the remark came, 'And you have just been eight months in Berlin, broadcasting from the

Concordia Studios.' He knew at once the game was up.

How did the Colditz prisoners know this? They got their answer as they got so much of their information, from the stream of experts we kept sending into this special camp, bringing in both hard news, rumours and gossip.

A Captain Julius Green, a dentist, had been sent to us from the other ranks camp at Lamsdorff. His patients there came from among those in the camp itself, numbering many thousands, and from those who worked outside on the surrounding farms, and in the mines all round that area.

Now and again a party would go off to Genshagen, at our invitation. This was a camp near Berlin, a propaganda camp. Both British officers and NCOs were there at different times.

We ran a camp, too, for disaffected Irish in the early days, but we found the Irish worse than the Poles when it came to making decisions. We tried to find possible collaborators in the base camps and then sent them off to Genshagen for a rest and for submission to the delights of freedom. After that we asked for active collaboration.

Grey had been one who had gone the whole way. He had broadcast for us. There were also others. But most of these who went to Genshagen decided in the end they had had enough of it, they were not going to play with us and they returned to the different camps after a nice rest, bearing with them interesting information. Some of them, of course, went back to Lamsdorff. Some talked to the dentist, Captain Green. Captain Green remembered. He remembered names. He came to Colditz. Grey came to Colditz. Captain Green remembered Grey's name.

We removed Grey from the prisoners' yard and installed him in one of the archway cells, until Berlin should decide on his disposal.

While here, Grey was fed on normal German rations, which he found not very satisfactory. He asked for Red Cross food and cigarettes. The British Senior Officer refused them. We had nothing extra to give the man, but in the end the Kommandant decided he was still legally a prisoner-of-war and therefore entitled to food from his own country. So on our own initiative, we took one parcel a week for Grey out of common British Red Cross stocks.

It was some months before I got him transferred.

In the end Grey joined the British Free Corps, a volunteer unit which we recruited, largely for propaganda purposes, though ostensibly to fight with us on the East Front. It was not a particularly successful venture and never went into action. Other volunteer units against Bolshevism were made up from White Russians and from races such as the Ukranians, and so on. These did actually get to the front, so did the 'Viking' unit of Scandinavian volunteers.

In June 1944, just after D-day, we had two visitors to Colditz, in the uniforms of the British Free Corps, whose initials were on the arm-bands they wore. These two said they wanted a chance to talk to the prisoners, with a view to getting some of them to join up in the BFC. This did not seem much of an idea to me, even in my capacity as Propaganda Officer. It was hardly the moment, June 1944, for the British to start active collaboration with the enemy. Anyone who knew Colditz could be certain that, first of all, there would be 100 per cent non-co-operation, plus, if possible, violent reaction against these two men. Second thoughts, I imagined, might produce a crop of pseudo-volunteers, whose sole purpose would undoubtedly be to escape at the first opportunity, from any line of march to Berlin and the East Front beyond.

We could not see that these two had the slightest hope of attaining their object, but I felt it my duty to help them as best I could. So while we would not take the risk of any trouble that might arise from escorting these two 'recruiting officers' around the castle, we did do them at least the favour, and I don't think it was any more than that, of distributing their leaflets among the PW mail. In these leaflets it was stated that no action was intended hostile to the British Crown. The war was condemned as the work of Jews and international finance, and it was declared to be a betrayal of the British Empire. The pamphlet ended with an appeal for an Anglo-German alliance.

The prisoners at first burnt all the pamphlets, and then, on second thoughts, demanded more as souvenirs. The visitors by then had gone – we had no more of their leaflets left.

## CHAPTER XIV

## Waiting for the Bell

TWO MORE attempts were made in April 1944 to break through the 'seam' where the buildings of the prisoners' and the German yards backed on to each other.

When the snow tunnel was discovered two years previously, we had found a small three-cornered empty space in the south-east angle of the yard between the then canteen and the Evidenz or Conference Room. And now, one morning about 7 o'clock, the cleaners were busy on our side of the 'seam', when they heard a banging on the iron door at our end of the short passage through the wall from the attic above this room. They at once fetched the guards who were surprised to hear a cry of, 'We want the Kommandant, we want to visit the Kommandant——' 'Fetch us some coffee,' and so on, in English!

I opened the door in the wall and found three officers there in the six-foot passage through the thickness of the wall. They had apparently spent most of the night sawing away the hinges of the door on their side, but were rather tired when they came to the second door on our side. There was no lock to force, but only bolts and hangers to be cut through. They had got the first door off its hinges, but had no time to do the same with the second one. They had been very careful not to touch off our alarm wires which did not cover the doors but only the walls up to them on our inner side. We had originally intended to use this way in the other direction – should we ever want to get quickly from our quarters into the prisoners' yard. For this reason we had left these two doors free of warning wires and this the prisoners had somehow discovered. They were profiting by this gap in the alarm circuits to turn our entrance into their exit.

About the same time two officers broke into the Hexengang

corridor again in our wall over the prisoners' kitchen, with the window in it overlooking their yard. Unfortunately for them during this incursion they cut the alarm wires, the warning light flashed on, and they were caught by the Rollkommando when it dashed off to discover why the red warning light was flashing on that stretch of the circuit.

Towards the end of the month we had instructions to draw up a list of serious medical or wounded cases for presentation to the International Medical Commission, with a view to their repatriation upon the Commission's advice. This 'Repat' Commission was entrusted with the task of examining prisoners who claimed repatriation on grounds of chronic illness, or high degree disability from war wounds.

The Commission consisted of two Swiss and three German doctors. Its recommendations were final.

Our own camp doctor and English doctor were thereafter busy for some months dealing with the many applications made to appear before this Commission upon various grounds, genuine, specious and spurious. In the end they agreed on a list of twenty-nine names to be forwarded as prospective candidates for repatriation. Security approval was required for the applicants and the OKW right away ruled out the two De Gaullists on our list.

They also objected to Captain Green, the dentist from Lamsdorff, possibly because he had been responsible for spoiling my plan to plant Lieut Grey in the camp as a 'stooge'. They also objected to the presence on the list of Flight-Lieut Halifax, an officer who had been very badly burnt when shot down during a raid over Berlin. He had expressed himself in the very strongest terms, as dissatisfied with the medical treatment that he eventually got for his wounds. Later in the year he was allowed to go on parole to the University Hospital at Halle. He stayed there for many weeks and was treated by first-class eye specialists. I took him there and back and learned that he was very satisfied and had good relations with the staff.

When the Commission turned up at Colditz the Senior British Officer announced that if the whole twenty-nine on the original list could not appear then not one of the remaining twenty-five would do so. However, we replied that we had our orders from the OKW and that these must be obeyed. We could therefore present only twenty-five of the candidates to the Commission. As no one at all appeared at the gate to see the Commission at the appointed time, we ordered a special parade. When I went in to pick out the twenty-five sick and wounded the parade broke up in disorder. I thereupon called out the entire guard and posted them round the milling, yelling mob in the centre of the yard, forced my way into the thick of this and hand-picked the twenty-five myself, knowing them all by sight. I marched each and every one of them away at the point of the rifle and eventually got them all over to the Kommandantur and up in front of the Commission. The four 'exceptions' I left behind.

As the Commission had been waiting a good hour while all this was going on, the President demanded the reason for the delay. He could not believe that prisoners who had a hope of repatriation would be late for so important an appointment. The reason was explained. It was stated that our higher Security authorities had banned the presentation to the Commission of four members from a list agreed by both sides in the camp itself. The Swiss President then refused flatly to examine patients who had been brought up before him at gun-point. A call to Berlin by the German members of the Commission was necessary to break this deadlock. After some wrangling the OKW agreed that the four officers the trouble was about should be presented to the Commission after all.

I made a sorry 'Cannossagang' back into the yard to fetch them. The welcome that greeted this 100 per cent capitulation beat all records. However, neither Green, nor Halifax were repatriated, but nine of the others, including the two De Gaullists, were passed by the Commission.

This extraordinary reversal of its decision by the OKW brought us in Colditz up against a situation we had kept trying to avoid. The inevitable sequence was order, counter-order, disorder. This was a small matter admittedly, in a small place, but at this time Hitler had shot seven of his officers for expressing doubts as to the ultimate victory – and we older officers began to wonder at the value of any instructions which were likely, as we had just seen, to be cancelled just because some prisoners-of-war objected to them. Security at Dresden had all along taken the view that the medical condition of PWs and their suitability for treatment or repatriation was no concern of theirs. The OKW burnt its fingers badly in this matter and put our own noses in Colditz very badly out of joint.

The early summer month of May was fine and warm that year of 1944. With only 200-odd prisoners to guard on the one hand, yet with all this worry from bombing on our minds, on the other, and at the same time waiting anxiously for the next inevitable step in the war – the invasion – surely we might be excused from thinking that as all the old exits from Colditz were by now securely buttoned up, then only by means of spectacular and therefore, one might conclude (given the psychology of the prisoner who sees the end in sight), inadvisably risky new schemes, could any further escapes take place, if at all.

It was May 2nd. The walk in the park came trailing back up the steep path, apparently overcome by springtime heat and fever. They passed the basement of the house that stood out from the upper roadway. No chance of escape there any more. Just by was an old rubbish dump overflowing with tins, cardboard, branches, paper, old sacks, wood wool, rags, and so on. It didn't actually stink, but it looked so untidy and horrible that no one on our side ever cast a glance at it. The prisoners, though, were less delicate. They had second thoughts in the matter.

When the walk got back to the prisoners' gate there was a bit of long-drawn-out trouble over the count. Everyone looked so dumb and stupid that our people never thought to speed it up.

When they had checked and recounted two or three times they woke up to the fact that the walk was one short. At once '*Kartoffelsupp*' for a special turn-out, and at the same time the telephones all round began to ring – 'Mousetrap', an officer missing, again from Colditz, details to follow (we hoped). Out went the Riot Squad on foot and on bicycles to their different posts – at railway stations, crossroads, bridges, etc.

One cyclist had to check the footpath from Colditz to Gross Sermuth. This ran for some way along the east bank of the River Mulde in open land through the meadows. Our cyclist met there, about two miles off, a slight, fair-haired young man, trotting along with a rolled-up blanket under his arm.

'Who are you, where are you going, and why? And what's in that blanket?'

'Well – actually – as a matter of fact . . .' and the blanket was unfolded to show, sewn all over it, tins, cardboard, branches, paper, old sacks, wood wool, and so on. It was Lieut John Beaumont, the oboe player in the camp orchestra. He had dropped down under the rubbish dump under this camouflage on the way back from the walk, while the sentries allowed themselves to be distracted for just a few seconds by the other prisoners. Beaumont was lucky to get away unseen, but he was asking too much of fortune in hoping to get right away over the fields in broad daylight. He would have done better to hide up somewhere until nightfall.

On Whit Monday when some of the staff were on leave, we had an unexpected piece of good luck. I took a walk that afternoon in the Tiergarten up the little valley from the enclosed part of the park. Idly I wondered whether the prisoners would be up to anything on that sunny peaceful day. Everything was quiet, with the trees in full leaf. The people were in holiday mood, although that meant, those days in Germany, only that it gave them time to think about things they would rather forget. Were the prisoners up to anything? Of course they were! And by a fluke we caught them at it.

One of our handymen, an old chap who'd lost a leg in China, suddenly bethought himself of a small repair job he had to do for his wife. He took his bunch of keys and went across our yard to the workshop on the south side of the castle. In the carpenter's shop there, he was startled to flush two figures in khaki shorts and shirts who rushed out of the door and disappeared up the stairs. He gave a yell to the sentry outside, and had a quick look into the next room. There was another figure, similarly dressed! The old man stood with his back to the door and waved the largest of his keys – it was pretty old-fashioned and heavy – and said, 'If you try and come past me I'll strike you down.'

The Riot Squad came in and collected Lieut Hamilton-Baillie, who was engaged in sorting out what might have been a magnificent collection of booty. He had opened several drawers and had on the floor in front of him a heap of wires, switches, fuses and electrician's tools of all kinds.

The rest of the Riot Squad meanwhile had roared on up the stairs on the trail of the two who had got away. They went right to the top of our quarters, searching all floors, and finally came to the attic. They followed in the attics round the south and east side of our buildings, and at last came to a hole in the end gable.

Outside this was the roof of the buildings in the prisoners' yard. This roof was two feet lower than ours. They got out on to it and from there into the attic through a window. The floor of the attic was the roof of the circular staircase which ran up from ground level to the top floor in the canteen corner. By the time we trundled through all these obstacles – the trail was cold.

The prisoners had now tried to get into our quarters, at this point of junction, at every single floor level – the canteen, the lavatory tunnel from their Long Room – from the Dutch quarters on the second floor, through a hole in the back wall of the third-floor Mess – and now through the attics! By the greatest good fortune we had found this new way into our own quarters in good time to prevent an escape, and also just in time to save ourselves from a serious loss of electrical equipment.

Three days later the Riot Squad caught Major Anderson and two others changing shifts in the tunnel under the operating chair in the dentist's room. Plainly there was going to be no letting up in escaping however the war might be going elsewhere.

Now and again during searches in 1944 we came upon home-made telescopes, or even found people standing at windows scanning the near or distant horizon with these useful instruments.

These were constructed basically of rolls of cardboard. Two

or even three cylinders were fitted into each other loosely, so as to slide in and out – with lenses at either end of the whole construction. The lenses came from broken-down spectacles, and were of two kinds, each to its proper position. The outer lenses magnified the image, the ones at the inner end reduced it. These telescopes gave a multiplication of up to X 3. Earlier prototype models were up to six feet in length, and very shaky, requiring a crew of two besides the 'viewer', to keep them straight and steady, but the superior types which developed from these, with multi-lens end-pieces and three inter-sliding tubes, did not come to more than eighteen inches in length when closed and so were easy to conceal. With these primitive but effective instruments the prisoners were able to scan the landscape and pick up such details they required from the houses and streets of the town below and the fields beyond. They were also able to mix pleasure with business and cast their eyes upon sunbathers (sunbathing is a widespread habit in Germany) by day, or on less intentional exposures indoors at night, or at dawn. Harmless though these reported activities may well have appeared, the existence of these astronomical instruments could prove dangerous to us, and so we collected as many as we could.

With the whole of the town under surveillance the norms of traffic could be established. Anything untoward on the railway, on the roads or over the river bridge could be instantly noted and reported by the prisoners to their own Security Officer.

We had often thought that surprise was not always achieved when springing our monthly searches. For one reason, we gave the guard company a general warning of 'Search in the next twenty-four hours'. This made it all the easier for anyone on our side passing information to the prisoners to cover up. He might be off duty when the search actually took place. Apart from that, the Reich Security Office insisted that a dozen or more CID officials from Dresden now and again should take part in these searches. These people were more trouble than they were really worth to us, but it had to be.

The Dresden party began by coming as civilians, but by 1943 they resembled a small army as they marched over the bridge from the station in full uniform. The word must have flashed round the prisoners' quarters, 'Goons up for search'. The Dresden people had no cars to spare for this jaunt, and necessarily came by train. There were not all that many trains and whichever PW was on 'Station Control' would know exactly when to make a special report. He would certainly have had a detailed time-table to hand, made from observations over a period of the times of railway traffic, both goods and passenger. The rough date of the departures in 1943 could have been guessed from the prior arrival of goods trucks to take the baggage of the French, Dutch or Poles, a day or so previously. Once the counter-alarm was given among the prisoners, deep hides would be securely battened down, temporary hides evacuated, and expressions of bland innocence rehearsed to greet us when we arrived *en masse* to break up this or that room or floor in the early hours of the dawn.

Indeed, we found far more contraband with snap searches or irregular patrolling by the *Rollkommando* or myself, with just a couple of men, working to a small scale plan, than we ever did in major search operations. For some time we kept two NCOs on permanent patrol 'snooping' in the quarters wherever they might choose to go, day and night.

Mass attacks were extremely destructive, necessitating repairs to the walls we had broken open, and hence to risky contacts between workers, extra sentries and PWs. They often lost us valuable material ('borrowed' by the prisoners), and were quite nerve-racking as to the precautions and preliminaries. In addition, they usually left a trail of protests and complaints and appeals to Dresden, the OKW, and the Swiss Protecting Power in their wake. All these had to be dealt with by Security and the Kommandant, requiring lengthy reports to higher authorities, copies all round.

All this paper work might take weeks to thrash out. Very often it took seven to eight weeks to clear up the aftermath of one search and by that time another was long overdue. In fact, I think the prisoners made it their business to spin out the consequences of any search as long as possible in the hope that we would not care to run another one (which according to our orders we should do every month), before the last one was cleared up. In this way they could gain extra weeks of comparative quiet on their own escape front.

Not content with extending their observations by means of telescopes beyond the walls of the castle into the immediate vicinity, the prisoners, we had reason to believe, were trying to establish some sort of contact with the outside world by signalling. There were two ways of doing this. One was by ordinary flashlight and the other was by radio transmission. Whether they actually did try either of these two methods I cannot be sure, but we certainly thought we had sufficient indication to that effect to make counter-measures advisable. The morse code is international in its application and after we had received certain reports we posted a couple of signallers in the back room of an inn down in the town, thought to be the receiving end of a lot of dots and dashes flashed by some kind of amateur heliograph in the castle by day. Our men could not make anything out of the presumed signals that they did receive, so maybe it was just a diversion for our benefit.

Some time after this a signal unit of ours carried out an exercise in the Colditz forest and reported that an unauthorised transmitter was working somewhere in the direction of the castle.

The Kommandant was quite certain that there was a radio somewhere in the prisoners' part of the camp. We had found a lot of components as well as a complete set before now, and if there were a receiver, then there might well be a transmitter as well.

We kept a listening post in the woods for several weeks with a direction-finder, but in the end they could not report any concrete results.

As from May 1944 we noticed on our visits that the prisoners were giving the usual warning signals to each other in a visual form rather than acoustically.

This seemed rather odd until we worked it out. What we noticed was that, whenever we went into the yard, squares of cardboard, coloured diagonally or across, would be shown from one particular window in the east block. This was the wing directly opposite the entrance gate. We reckoned that these signals indicated who had come into the yard on any particular occasion. Maybe it was a stray 'Goon', maybe it was the Riot Squad, or maybe it was just myself. However, the cards could also indicate in which direction we were moving. We might be going half right past the Saalhaus door on towards the kitchen; we might be going more dangerously perhaps, half left past the cells to the north-western corner staircase by the tower. It seemed to us that whoever was being warned was working in some clandestine way from such a position that the entrance gate, in the west side of the yard, where there was a break in the buildings, could not be directly observed. It took a week or two for us to solve this riddle.

I expected at any time, such was the ingenuity of the prisoners, to find a complete telephone system linking all the floors and all their rooms, and if I had found a public telephone with a coin box installed in the yard one morning, I should not have been very much surprised.

Once again about this time our human material let us down badly in a case where the mechanical system had done its job 100 per cent.

At 1 o'clock in the morning a red light showed on the alarm switchboard, somewhere in area 9. This was the kitchen, through which several attempts had been made down the air-shaft from the prisoners' quarters above in the Saalhaus. We sent a man in to investigate but he found the kitchen door locked. This was a case where our own security measures worked against ourselves. The key for the kitchen door was not on its hook at our main gate because the paymaster responsible for the kitchen had taken it with him and was not to be found. We rang up the gate, and found that he was marked down in the book as having left earlier in the evening. He had not come back by that time and indeed did not return until the morning, the key in his pocket.

Meanwhile, the red light had gone out. Perhaps, we thought, it was just a local disturbance due to damp or maybe some dust or some plaster had fallen on the wires. And so the guardroom let the matter drop.

Next morning when our kitchen was opened up we found that an inner door had been broken open. An exit hole to the Saalhaus was also discovered from our storeroom to the ground floor changing-rooms in the prisoners' quarters.

It was this last piece of work which must have set off the warning light in the guardroom. Our alarm wires must have been cut when the hole was made. We assumed that the reason why the red light went out again, giving the all-clear, was that subsequently a bridge across the circuit had been effected by means of a spare piece of wire.

However, from this day, the signalling with cardboard squares, which we had noticed when we came into the yard, came to an end.

We did not think this kitchen incident worth making a special report about, so we put it only in our monthly bulletin to Ast. 4 at Dresden, and not to Berlin.

Oddly enough, Ast. 4 raised quite a stink about the matter. It was, they said, the first time that anyone had succeeded in by-passing an electrical warning system. Did this mean that these wall-surface warning grids were no good at all? It appeared that someone had something to worry about – namely the firm who installed these systems. We discovered later that their director was an officer at Dresden and had an interest in the matter. However, we beat off this attack from our own Security HQ and in due course they left us alone.

CHAPTER XV

## *Breaking Point*

D-DAY. Here was what we had all been awaiting for months.

Our immediate reactions were – what has happened to the Atlantic wall? Where are our U-boats? What has become of our Luftwaffe? What was the V.1 doing – that wonder weapon which had only just been put into use against London?

Before we had time even to find our own explanation or form our own estimates, in spite of our own Press – the Russians had started a general offensive in the east on the anniversary of our attack on them three years before, June 21st. Our front was by then back on the old Polish eastern frontier.

In the south Rome was abandoned.

The optimists among the prisoners, thinking of the First World War, said the second would be over in the autumn. But before November 11th had been March 1918.

The realists said November 1918 came because of a political defeat which had been accepted by our government, whereas this time only a military capitulation would be acceptable, and to the Allies. The war would go on until the Russians met the Allies in or near Berlin.

In all our doubts at the time I feel that our course was nevertheless rigidly determined by the other side. 'Unconditional surrender' was what they demanded. That left us no alternative but to go on to the bitter end. If the Allies had suggested an alternative – had they treated with the opposition in 1943 or 1944 . . . then more among us would have risked disgrace, torture and death. But the feelers put out by our opposition in 1943 were turned down flat by the British Government. Only force should decide.

The prisoners were, of course, much satisfied at the turn of events on the wider wheel of fortune. But they still played their luck merrily on the little roulette wheel at Colditz. Round and round the circle they flipped the ball – we waited wide-eyed to see into which of the many compartments it would drop. There it was running again on June 16th, but it came to rest on zero for the prisoners.

That afternoon the guard under the archway heard a noise beneath his feet. At this spot there was a manhole cover. There was another one further up the approach yard towards the guardroom and a third just outside the courtyard gate. All were in a stretch of about fifty yards of cobbles. The guard gave a shout and out came the Riot Squad and in due course the Security Officer. 'Up with all three drain covers' was the order. Altogether we found six tunnellers in the drain. Four of them were half-way back to the gate, two of them were under the archway drain cover. The diameter of the drain was about two feet six inches, and it ran out under the gate from the prisoners' courtyard. At the point where it passed out of the yard there was a grille across the whole width of the pipe but this had been sawn through.

We found the miners trying to dig a tunnel at the archway end, where the drain narrowed to a pipe about eighteen inches across. The two officers here were knee-deep in the foulest black mud. They had been levering away at the stones around the narrower pipe with iron bars wrapped in sacking. It was this noise that the sentry had heard.

Our Paymaster came by at this moment. He was very hostile to all prisoners and, as I have already mentioned, he had lost his two sons at the front. He could not restrain himself and spat at the two in the drain, calling them 'stinking swine'.

A protest was made officially by the Senior British Officer and in the end our officer had to declare that his remarks and behaviour were not directed personally at the two tunnellers, but were a generalisation.

In the spring of 1944 some seventy-six British officers escaped from the Air Force camp at Sagan. In June a British doctor, Captain Henderson, came from that camp to Colditz.

Shortly afterwards the SBO asked our Kommandant if it were true that fifty of these escapers from Sagan had been shot on recapture. Had the Wehrmacht changed its attitude to escaping? Was it a matter for other than the disciplinary punishment of arrest? The SBO also asked if he might send a list of names to Sagan so that the prisoners in Colditz might know if any friends of theirs had been among those shot.

All we could say in reply was that we did know of this mass escape and we did also know there had been some shootings among those who had been recaptured afterwards. We did not know how many in all had been 'shot while escaping'. The OKW, as far as we knew, had not given any new instructions as to the treatment of escapers on recapture. We did know that about thirty of the Sagan group had been brought back and, as far as we knew, were still alive.

Escaped prisoners picked up by other than Wehrmacht formations, such as police, Gestapo, Sicherheitsdienst (Himmler's security organisation), and so on, were not the responsibility of the regular armed forces until returned into their hands. Escapes of PWs had increased to such a degree that Himmler had ordered that any recaptured PWs were not to be sent back to their camps but were to be handed over to the SD. It was as a result of this order that over half the members of the mass break from Sagan were executed.

We sent a list of British names to Sagan, and when it came back a number of them were marked with a cross to show they had been shot.

As things got worse Himmler began taking it out of the most helpless of all, the prisoners and the KZ (concentration camp) inmates. He announced that he did not propose to over-exert himself in protecting bomber crews who were shot down during raids. Those descending by parachute were in many cases left to the fury of the population. What a change since 1939! Then, British pilots shot down in battle were given a proper military funeral. Sometimes these ceremonies were broadcast on our radio networks. Even Flight-Lieut Tunstall admitted that during the first six months of the war, if he could not find his military objectives he would take his bombs back home. Who was the first among us to take the gloves off in the aerial war? Each side, of course, accused the other.

Later in that summer Security Officers from different areas

were ordered to visit Sagan to study the security methods of that camp.

I went there myself and was amazed at the simplicity of their arrangements. Admittedly the siting of the place made things easy. The camp was in a clearing in the woods and built on sandy ground. The Kommandant and staff numbered barely thirty. The guard company totalled 250 in all. There were at the time no less than seven thousand British and American Air Force personnel in the place. At Colditz we had at times as many guards as prisoners! I noticed sourly that discipline on parade was perfect.

The total number of escape attempts from Sagan was much less than from Colditz. Yet we had less than one-twentieth of the number of prisoners to control.

The only chance the prisoners at Sagan had of getting out was by tunnelling. The only place where they could safely build tunnels was under the barrack stoves. The barrack floors themselves were raised off the ground and it was easy to see anything that might be going on underneath. But the stoves were built on concrete slabs in the ground, which slabs were held up by a four-square brick wall. By lifting the stoves and prising up the slab, a perfect entrance hole was provided, completely screened from all observation. The barracks were raised from the ground but no one could see into these brick shafts. In fact, here again was an example of the vertical approach, provided by ourselves once more, to a horizontal tunnel.

That was how the famous Sagan tunnel came to be built. The main trouble with tunnelling in Sagan was the provision of fresh air. In the camp museum they had several specimens of air-feed mechanisms. Football bladders were far too small to be effective. Watertight bags of linen, fitted with two-way valves, were mostly used to aerate the working faces of their tunnels. The sand made the work fairly easy and in the large compounds it was not difficult to dispose of the spoil. But these tunnels in sand had to be shored up all along with bed-boards and other pieces of timber.

After the big escape of seventy-six officer prisoners, the staff at Sagan was largely replaced and the camp was wired for sound all round the perimeter with microphones to give warning of underground workings. 'Shot while escaping' – only once did we make a report in these terms from Oflag 4C at Colditz.

We were playing Skat in Zschadrass on the evening of July 20th. Suddenly the radio programme broke off to give the news of the bomb attack on Hitler. We thought this must be an Allied propaganda broadcast, but no, the set was correctly tuned and the programme continued as usual. At 1 o'clock in the morning Hitler himself came to the microphone and confirmed the news.

On the 21st, the first names of the plotters began to filter through. People at all levels started to cover up. Hypocrisy was by now so deep-rooted in everyone's behaviour in Germany that the true reactions of the people were not to be perceived.

Among the Colditz staff no one would catch another's eye. It was best to keep a straight face over this affair. How would the Armed Forces as a whole come out of this plot formed within their ranks?

The Officer Korps had its answer very shortly. From now on the Forces were identified openly with the Party, not merely as their own preference had been, with the people. Up to now the Hitler salute had been given by German officers only when entering or leaving their Mess, or as a form of unofficial salute when not wearing their caps. From now on it was to be used officially between ourselves and also as between officers and prisoners. The Wehrmacht salute was replaced by the raised arm salute of the Partei.

We had to put up with a great deal of ridicule in the yard for the next day or two after this order was propagated but in the end things quietened down and the Nazi salute came to be taken as something in no way out of the ordinary.

On July 24th a parade was held in the town to 'Express thanks for the safety of our Leader at the hand of Providence.' All those in the castle who were not on duty had orders to attend. The function went off as expected, perhaps with rather more enthusiasm than was normal being shown, because people were afraid and did not wish to seem lukewarm in their loyalty at that moment.

Himmler was by now not only head of the State Security Service, and head of the SS. He was also head of the Home Army.

Now he began to roll the heads. Those in the plot and their families were liquidated. More distant relations lost their jobs. Duesterberg of the Stahlhelm went to Dachau concentration camp. Jüttner had changed his coat long since and became Hitler's Deputy. In Ast. 4 at Dresden, a chilly wind blew several out of the door, including one of our own Security Officers who had been posted there.

A million marks were offered for Gördeler's arrest. A Luftwaffe telephonist got 800,000 marks for recognising him, and two others got 100,000 each after his capture.

Having settled the active reactionaries, Himmler again went for the old Socialists and Communists, and ordered more of them off to concentration camps. They must have felt that with the bomb attack on Hitler by Army officers their own time would come soon. The movement would spread downward.

We found a pamphlet near the castle, no doubt from an Allied plane, saying that revolution would come but it must come from the factories and not from above. There, among the workers, lay the key to revolution. Maybe the Allies would have been very glad to see Hitler shot, but perhaps they had different views as to whose finger was on the trigger?

But what was the answer for each and every one of us to the question, the more immediate one. 'What shall I do when ... they arrive? And who will "they" be – Americans or Russians?'

When we felt safe, with the Partei men outside the door, some of us did discuss the point – what to do if and when, and as, the end came. Although with all of us the unspoken hope was, 'may the Americans get here before the Russians,' there were differing reactions even to this possibility.

One said, 'I'll shoot myself and family. But before that I'll go into the yard and finish off a few of the prisoners first.'

Another said, 'You can do what you like with your family, they're your affair, but the prisoners are the responsibility of

189

all of us, and what one may do may be avenged upon the whole lot of us here.'

A third said, 'I'd shoot myself if I hadn't got a family.'

A fourth – 'I'll go as a prisoner. If Colditz is a sample of PW life – it can't be as bad as all that.'

Yet Doktor Goebbels assured us we must win, therefore we should win. 'Never were we so near to victory as now. Let us give up space to win time.' We lived in two worlds – of fact, and of illusion.

On September 1st the Kommandant received the War Service Cross (First Class), yet on the very next day he was holding a conference over measures to be taken when the enemy arrived at his gates.

The British Senior Officer asked if he might take part in these discussions, and the Kommandant replied that he had no instructions to sit at a round table with the prisoners in his charge in this particular matter. Months later it came about that the Kommandant pressingly requested the Senior British Officer's participation in discussions on this identical point.

Himmler's next move was to approve a scheme for the retirement of all active officers over fifty-eight and all Reserve officers over fifty-two. They were to be transferred to industry or they were to be re-enrolled to work with the Army in civilian capacity. Half the Colditz staff would have had to go, but nothing came of this order in the end.

The new head of the prisoner-of-war section at Dresden, after the clean-up, was a high SS police officer widely known in central Germany as 'Bubi'. The Partei was digging itself into the Wehrmacht – older officers were pushed out, younger Party men came in.

More demonstrations took place in the town on October 4th. Once again the order in our Mess was, 'All not on duty will attend.'

On the 19th, General 'Bubi', head of Ast. 4 at Dresden as well, came round the castle and showed himself very friendly. The Kommandant seemed pleased to have gained his favour. 'Bubi' was a very useful friend at court, if indeed he were not the court itself! On October 21st, there it was again, a mass demonstration down in the town – 'All not on duty will attend.'

On the same day came the first secret order for the evacuation and break-up of the camp on the eventual day.

On November 12th the Partei March took place in Munich. This time there was no speech at all from the Führer. It was whispered abroad that the 'home' of the Hitler revolution was becoming the 'home' of the counter-revolution. On the same day members from more age groups were scraped up in Colditz town for the Home Guard. Being a question of military service, most obeyed their orders and turned up, but for the first time there was a strike among the spectactors at the call-up ceremony. Practically none of the public attended. Of the fifty seats reserved for the relations of those killed at the front only ten were occupied. How could one take an oath (or even show approval of it by attending this ceremony) to a government that had told such lies ? And yet – some wondered – the V.2s had just started on London. Could they do the trick ? Was it perhaps better to wait before passing judgement on our Leader ? Give him and the secret weapons a final chance ?

What of the attitude of the prisoners by this stage ? They were now all agreed that our unconditional surrender could be the only end to the war. Typically British, they began to feel sympathy for the under-dog. I quote from a prisoner's letter in August 1944: 'It is no longer fair to organise demonstrations against the Germans as things are going now.' But the escaping spirit was dying hard, in some cases it would not fade at all. And in Colditz the greatest escaper of them all found his own end in his undying example.

## CHAPTER XVI

## The Great Escaper

IF THERE is indeed a Valhalla, for the heroes of whatever
nation, if the men who go there are men of courage and daring,
if their determination springs from one true motive alone and if
that motive is love of their country – then in our own German
tradition, Valhalla is the resting-place of Lieut Michael
Sinclair. Whatever his secondary motives, it was plain to all
that, for him, the highest was that of service, to regain which
in full right and duty Lieut Sinclair felt he must at all costs
get back to England by his own efforts. The number of his
escapes, the distances covered, the variety and ingenuity
resorted to and displayed, the thoroughness of preparation
and the exactness of execution, all added up to unparalleled
accomplishment and example.

Lieut Sinclair's first escape was from a camp in north-east
Germany. It led him through Poland, Slovakia, Hungary and
Yugoslavia, until he was caught on the Bulgarian frontier. He
was then transferred to Colditz, escaping for a short time
while on the way. His third attempt, from Leipzig hospital,
ended in Cologne. By then he was known to our guard company as the Red Fox.

Sinclair's fourth attempt ended in south Germany and both
at Weinsberg and on the way back, he tried again to get away.

His seventh attempt, disguised as Franz Josef in October
1943 nearly came off, and with him would have gone a mass
break-out in grand style. This was the time he was shot at
point-blank range and by sheerest luck escaped alive.

An eight attempt, over the west terrace at Colditz in January
1944 one evening, got him as far as the Dutch frontier.

By the summer of 1944 the war could only go one way,
but perhaps Sinclair felt that captivity was a disgrace, even
though by that time it had practically lost its meaning.

On September 25th the walk was down in the park – moving around and chatting in groups, in the afternoon sun. The leaves were just turning on the trees, preparing once again the finest view in Colditz, when seen from the eastern windows overlooking the valley, with hornbeams, beeches and sycamores flaming away up through the Tiergarten out of sight to the south-east.

Suddenly, without warning or any foreknowledge among those present, Lieut Sinclair broke away from a small group walking round inside the wire. He sprang across the trip-wire and reached the main fence. Up over it he went, his thick gloves helping him to grip in spite of the barbed wire. Down he came on the other side.

An NCO close by shouted to him to stop. His revolver misfired. Sinclair ran forward down the ravine to where 150 yards away the stream ran through a grid under the foot of the ten-foot park wall. He could not climb this wall. He could not get through the grid. What could he have hoped to do?

Several sentries opened fire. Even then, the shot that killed Michael Sinclair was not aimed true. Fate seemed to hold just one more chance in store. But just as one year previously a bullet from three-foot range had glanced off Sinclair's ribs and out of his body, this time the bullet glanced off his elbow and inwards to his heart. He died instantaneously – 'Shot whilst escaping.'

He was doing his duty as he saw it – our men were doing theirs. There was no dispute this time over the shooting. Sinclair was buried in the military cemetery at Colditz with full honours.

A week or so after Lieut Sinclair's death, the Senior British Officer, Lieut-Colonel Tod, announced on parade, 'It is no longer an adventure to get out of this camp. Anyone escaping will get home too late to take part in the war anyway. Furthermore I disapprove of kicking a man when he's down. There will be no further demonstrations on parade.'

One line of attack upon us by the prisoners in Colditz, of which I strongly disapproved, as already mentioned, was the misuse of the medical services which we provided for them.

Some escapes out of hospitals have been told in their due place, but I will group several together now regardless of chronology; it may serve to emphasise what I felt to be a grave abuse of humanitarian concessions on our part.

The prisoners made it their business to show how incompetent our doctors were – and how insufficient were our medical supplies. Medical staff among the prisoners were privileged personnel under the Geneva Convention and were normally entitled, and in most were allowed, to practise among their fellow-countrymen. On repeated occasions they requested permission for medical supplies to be sent from home where these were not supplied by ourselves or by the International Red Cross. I think they would have accused us of being inhuman had we refused these medical necessities. What were some results of our agreeing to these humanitarian requests ?

In the summer of 1941 we found the following message concealed in a parcel of medical supplies addressed to the French captain, Arditti:

'I hope you won't need the enclosed [false] papers, but will soon be able to get home in a legal way. If necessary I will send you 1000 francs and 100 Reichsmarks, together with a worker's permit valid for France. The papers herewith are quite in order so do not worry if you have to travel on your own and not with German authority. Don't talk too much while you are travelling. Remember that you have worked in Coswig, near Dresden, and that you live at Dijon, 12 Rue de la Gare. If you are travelling home on these papers, don't stop in Paris. There are always sudden searches in the streets and it is the most dangerous place in the whole of occupied France. Keep to the line Riesa–Leipzig–Erfurt–Kassel–Cologne–Liege. I take it you have all the civvies you need.'

Soon after this another parcel came from France to this officer, and inside a hairbrush we found three ampoules, and a note signed apparently by a French doctor stating that Arditti had suffered since his sixteenth year from gall bladder trouble. In consequence a trip to hospital for Arditti was cancelled.

Subsequent supplies of medicine from France were then sent for testing to Leipzig University, and if found to be genuine were kept in our hands for ultimate distribution among the prisoners.

In spite of this, prisoners were able on various occasions to obtain transfer from Colditz for treatment, by simulating the appropriate symptoms without help from their friends abroad.

Gall bladder trouble seemed to be the easiest of all diseases to fake. The Polish Lieut Kroner was having terrible pains that summer, it seemed. The *Tierarzt* was suspicious but finally conceded that the symptoms were genuine. His fury at the escape of two previous 'patients', Lieuts Just and Bednarski, in April, had died down somewhat. Kroner also went to Königswartha, where his condition gradually improved. So did his escape preparations, and in due course he changed his blue and white hospital garb for civilian clothes, and disappeared under the comparatively unguarded wire all round the place. We never heard of him again after August 20th, 1941.

A little over a week later, a suffering Frenchman escaped from the hospital at Schneckwitz. At Mainz the Gestapo took Lieut Mascret out of the Paris train and returned him to Colditz to continue his hospital treatment at the hands of his private doctor, the *Tierarzt*.

The French Lieut Boucheron had an inflamed appendix. There didn't seem to be any doubt about it at all. The *Tierarzt* sent him to hospital at Zeitz. On September 25th, 1941, Boucheron broke into the hospital store and exchanged his hospital clothes for civilian and left. His appendix went with him, and it seemed he did not worry that it might burst. In any case it was still all right on the night of October 7th when he was caught near Bonn and deposited in a Stalag at Arnoldsweiler. They asked us at Colditz to collect him, but by the time we got there Boucheron had again been moved. He had persuaded the Stalag doctor that his appendicitis was extremely serious and he had been transferred to the hospital at Munster-Eifel. From there he had again got away, appendix and all, and eventually arrived safely home in France.

'That appendix would have made interesting medical history,' observed the *Tierarzt* sarcastically when our party came back from the Rhineland empty-handed.

Four French officers were sent by the *Tierarzt* to the hospital attached to Oflag 4D, Elsterhorst. As this was part of a PW camp for French officers, the surveillance was fairly strict and none of the four had a chance of escaping. In due course, on October 15th, 1941 they set out to return to Colditz. The first part of this journey was on foot for a mile or so through the woods. They were, of course, under guard, but being hospital cases the guards presumably thought there would be no question of their being fit enough to escape.

At a given signal, while still in the woods, all four ran in different directions, and all four succeeded in getting clear away. Of the four Charvet got to Kassel where he took a ticket to Aachen, but unfortunately changed there on to the wrong train and came back to Düsseldorf. Here by merest chance he met up with another one of the four, Levy, and the two travelled together back to Aachen and spent the night there in a wood. On the morning of the 18th they took a tram into the town, but unfortunately were caught. They said they were French other ranks and so were sent to the Stalag at Arnoldsweiler where they stayed for three weeks. During this time they told differing stories as to their identities, but in the end they let it be known as certain that they came from Oschatz in East Germany. On their way back there, Charvet jumped out of the train, but was seen and retaken at Helmstett. He then admitted that he was an officer prisoner and came from Colditz, and we collected him from a camp at Fallingbostel. He returned to Colditz without any further trouble, and when he got back there he found that Levy had already been caught and brought back as well.

Lieuts. Navelet and Odry, the other two who had broken away from the guards on leaving Elsterhorst, eventually arrived safely home in France.

In October 1941 the French were playing stoolball – a kind of Rugby handball invented by the British – in the yard. The ground was cobblestones and very dangerous for this kind of play. Lieut Diedler broke a bone in his leg and was sent again to Elsterhorst for treatment. On the 22nd of the month, however, when his leg was nearly healed, he got into the hospital garage, and climbed into the boot of a car there. He was just taking a chance. He spent the whole night in the back of the car. Next morning someone took it out on to the road, and after a short time the car stopped. Diedler crept quietly out of the boot, but unfortunately he was seen and driven back smartly to Elsterhorst and so eventually back to Colditz.

April 1942. Three French officers went for medical attention to Leipzig. On Colditz station Lieut Manheimer tried to jump across the line and put an approaching train between himself and his guards. He fell on the line itself and was dragged clear just in time. We wondered perhaps if he had had a brainstorm and was attempting suicide.

June 20th, 1942. It was the anniversary of our attack on Russia the year previously. The weather was fine. The evening was one of the longest of the year.

The prisoners started throwing water at each other from their windows for some reason unknown. Soon a great water battle started. Water bombs fell from the windows, buckets of water were slung around in the yard. Gradually a kind of hysteria built up. We were the ones to provide the climax. The Duty Officer received reports that the prisoners were getting rather disorderly. He went into the yard and ordered the prisoners back into their quarters. They ignored him. He turned out the guard. The prisoners moved off up the corner staircases shouting and catcalling. When they got up to their quarters, water bombs began to fall in our ranks. Someone in the French quarters began yelling abuse out of the window. The Duty Officer lost his temper and fired a shot from his revolver. The bullet struck a French officer – Lieut Fahy – in a room on the first floor where he had been quietly reading a book all this while. That evening we sent him to Bad Lausick hospital, but his arm never healed properly, for a nerve was cut.

But one of the great lessons that all the prisoners learnt in Colditz was, that there was no situation, however unpleasant it might look at first sight, from which some profit could not be obtained, and Fahy's case was a good example of this.

Nearly twelve months later, in the spring of 1943, he contracted scarlet fever and went to Hohenstein-Ernstthal. For a long time he had been hoping for repatriation because of the shooting and the partial loss of the use of his arm. This repatriation did not seem to be going to materialise and when

Fahy recovered from his scarlet fever, he found himself ordered back to Colditz. So he left the hospital that afternoon in broad daylight on foot and headed for home. He was picked up in the evening at Kaufungen and taken to Hartmannsdorf, from where we collected him. Fahy had a first-class faked pass on him when taken, which we only just prevented him chewing up and swallowing.

Another hospital escape in June 1942 was successful. The incident really started back in April, when Lieut Bouillez was sent to Lörrach in Baden, for a court-martial. He knew the district well and he knew the Swiss frontier was fairly close.

He jumped out of the train on the way to the toilet. The train was immediately stopped, and Bouillez was picked up with head and arm injuries. At the court-martial he was acquitted and returned to Colditz. Later he was sent to hospital from which he successfully escaped to France.

One last successful escape under false colours was that of Lieut Darthenay, again from the military hospital at Hohenstein-Ernstthal.

I would only comment in all this that no British or Dutch officers appear on my list of escapers from hospital, though Lieut Michael Sinclair had attempted to get away when he was sent to Leipzig for sinus treatment.

## CHAPTER XVII

## The Fading Light

CONDITIONS AT the end of 1944 were getting steadily worse. In Oflag 4C, Colditz, we reached the lowest level ever in food supplies for the prisoners. A bare 1,300 calories a day was the best we could scrape up after the New Year. Fuel was nearly gone. We were reduced to allowing officers out in the woods on parole and under guard to collect branches for their own fires. No more parcels came from the International Red Cross because the railway to Switzerland was cut. The prisoners ate up most of their last food stocks at Christmas, and their own internal market prices rose to fantastic heights – cigarettes were £10 per 100, while chocolate and raisins were proportionately high. A pound of flour obtained on the black (German!) market was priced at £10 sterling.

The meal programmes for the week showed little more than bread, potatoes and cabbage or swede soup. There was no jam to be had – but we did manage to get hold of some sugar-beet syrup in barrels. We made some of this, too, for ourselves, steaming the roots in the big kitchen boilers.

Morale among our people was reduced to mere stoicism. Thousands were buried every day under the bombed ruins of their houses. The survivors lived as they might through that dreadful winter. Worst of all was the misery of the endless trek of hundreds of thousands of refugees from East Prussia, Silesia, Pomerania and Transylvania, fleeing before the Soviets.

The Party machine ground out just the one theme – 'Time, we must gain time. Hold on and we shall win.' But how? That was the question. V.1 and V.2, our only possible hopes, were having no real effect. We were promised V.3, V.4, and so on.

Someone that winter brought a rumour in to Colditz, which we, anxious though we were to snatch at any straw, discredited as too fantastic for belief. It was the hint of the atomic bomb.

This was too much for any of us to believe. Not even the Party men in the Mess would credit the mere thought of putting into effect atomic destruction as a weapon of war. The propaganda men must be raving! It was just a story to save their skins for a little while longer.

Every day we read in the papers or heard on the radio that men and women had been shot for lowering the national morale with defeatist talk. The new propaganda line reported Germans found dead in the already occupied areas, with notes on them – 'Killed by the avengers of the German honour.' We could hardly blame the French in Colditz, then, for not having collaborated with us earlier. Would they not have reason to fear similar treatment on their own return home, at the hands of the 'avengers of the honour of France'?

Other propaganda lines at this time ran as follows, 'What does not break us makes us stronger.' 'The worse things seem to be, the greater our confidence in the ultimate victory.' Hitler's New Year speech was simply a call to fight on in whatever circumstances might arise.

In Colditz, by the end of 1944, the guard companies were formed almost exclusively from old men between the ages of fifty and sixty-five. These had all gone through one world war already, and had known two political revolutions. They had served the Kaiser, the Weimar Republic, and Hitler's Third Reich. Small wonder if in due course they were to accept without too much question the Hammer and Sickle as their emblem. What could they do?

Our Christmas celebrations for that last winter feast of the war were, strangely enough, a little more worthwhile than the year previously. For one thing this Christmas could only be the last. It was the sixth Christmas of the war. Now that we were up against the abyss perhaps our ignorance of the future gave us all just that much more momentary happiness. It must all soon be over, and things could not get worse than they were.

I remember we even had goose for our Christmas dinner. The camp poultry stock under my care had flourished well and we decided to eat our way through what there was. We had bred rabbits, hens, ducks and geese, and we finished the ducks off at New Year. After that, at midnight, we went out on to the

200

bridge and sang the New Year in with our German hymn, 'Wir treten zum Beten, vor Gott dem Gerechten', and 'Now thank we all our God'. I think with most of us tension was relaxed. We were beyond all further anxiety. At 7 o'clock that evening the sirens had given us the distant warning of a raid on Berlin.

In the camp there was again a kind of armistice from December 24th to January 2nd. The prisoners were also eating up their stocks. I remember only one incident of note – Lieut Chaloupka running around the yard three times stark naked on Christmas Eve, having lost his bet that the war would be over by then. The usual tumult in the yard was missing, even on New Year's Eve, perhaps for one or other or both of two reasons, (a) food was going to be short, (b) the prisoners were asking themselves – are we all going to be treated as hostages like the Prominente?

On January 4th, 1945, Flight-Lieut Tunstall came up once again for a court-martial in Leipzig – was it his fourth, or fifth? I had lost count. He was charged with referring to 'b—— Germans'. His defence lawyer pointed out that the offending word was a botanical or zoological expression for a cross as between species. But the Court accepted the applied meaning in popular speech, and Tunstall got three months in gaol, less his six weeks in cells while awaiting trial. The war ended before the balance of his sentence could be carried out.

On January 9th, the American Captain Schaefer was court-martialled at Gnesen. He had been in Colditz since December 28th and was charged with obstructing a German NCO in another camp and disobeying his orders. The sentence was death. We put Schaefer in solitary confinement when he came back. Hitler himself had been advised of the affair, as head of the Holding State, but in the confusion of the last two months of the war appeals to the different Swiss and German authorities never got disposed of, and Schaefer survived.

In the middle of January we were advised of the arrival of five French generals from Oflag 4A, Königstein – Generals Flavigny, Buisson, Boisse, Daine and Mesny. They travelled to Colditz in separate vehicles, and the first four arrived safely. We waited a long time for the last car, but in the end a telegram came instead from Dresden, 'General Mesny has been shot on the autobahn while attempting to escape.' As he had said nothing whatever to any of the others about any intention of escaping General Flavigny spoke most harshly of his murder.*

The anniversary of the Party take-over came round again on January 30th. It hardly seemed the moment for celebration.

At the beginning of February we were warned of the transfer to us from Warsaw of General Bór Komorowski and his staff of about a dozen. These were the men who had planned and fought the Warsaw rising. They arrived in Colditz on February 5th – an impressive band of men with heroism and tragedy behind them. The rising had not been supported in any way by the Soviets who were the Allies closest to hand. These had simply waited inactive on the east bank of the Vistula while our SS slowly broke up the Polish resistance and destroyed whole quarters of the city. Bór admitted to me his hatred of all things German, but his greater hatred of all things Soviet. 'Even if you occupy our country for twenty years, both of you,' he said, 'my people will remain Polish, the race that they are born of.' That was the spirit which had helped General Bór to raise, equip and organise his Home Army of two hundred and fifty thousand men under the noses of our own occupation forces and police. And when this rising was broken and he surrendered, he obtained for his men the protection of the Geneva Convention. We agreed to treat them as prisoners-of-war, and not as partisans. It seemed a long way back to the Berlin Olympic Games of 1936, when General Bór, on behalf of the Polish riding team, received a prize for horsemanship out of the hands of Hitler himself.

On February 9th, the SBO, Lieut-Colonel Tod, asked for a meeting with the Kommandant to discuss the procedure and steps to be taken on the approach of the Americans. The Kommandant again replied that he had no instructions on the point.

*Over fourteen years later Polizeigeneral Panzinger was charged with the shooting of General Mesny, 'in reprisal'. When the police went to arrest him in Munich, he poisoned himself. An SS officer was also charged in Essen a few months before, with being an accomplice in the affair.

On the 15th of the month three Royal Air Force officers came in. Their camp at Sagan had been evacuated in the face of the advancing Russians, and these three had got away. They were recaptured and dumped on us. We passed them on to Nuremberg. A few days later the Swiss turned up again, for the last time. They held a small tea party in a café in the woods for some of the *Prominente* and others, but not including General Bór or his group. Their Herr Denzler appeared to be on a round of leave-taking. His OKW escort told us that these farewell parties were becoming quite the rule.

Between February 14th and 16th there were three very heavy air raids, two British raids in one night and an American raid by day, on Dresden – a city which up to this time had been untouched by bombing. The wife of the Kommandant, who was a refugee from Silesia, was at the time staying in the city with her baby in the house of our Paymaster. The Paymaster went off to help as best he could and was caught in the second raid and barely got to his home through the fire and destruction. He came back to Colditz and next morning a young paymaster of his staff went to Dresden with a lorry, got through, found the women and the baby safe and brought them back to the castle.

My clerk asked for leave likewise to go to Dresden to help his family. When he got home he found the house burnt out and his family all dead, along with other unidentifiable bodies in the cellar. He told me that in the old market square in Dresden corpses had been piled up high and burnt with flame-throwers. The inner part of the city was completely destroyed, and to prevent the spread of disease it was barred off even to those who had property and relations there. Some of the approach streets were actually walled up. Many officers of the Army District Command No. 4 in Dresden were killed along with their families in these raids. People in the city were quite demoralised by these massive attacks, even to the point of openly mocking at officers in the street that they should still wear Hitler's uniform.

At the time of the raid Dresden was full of refugee treks from the east, convoys of horse-drawn wagons making their way to some hoped-for safety in Central Germany and away from the Russians. For them there was no shelter. All the parks and avenues were full. There was nowhere for them to go. The fire bombs set the asphalt of the roads afire and they burnt to death where they stood. The estimate of deaths in this air raid is between 100,000 and 300,000 – at least double that at Hiroshima.

On February 24th Hitler again spoke to the nation. 'Let there be no doubt about it,' he said, 'National Socialist Germany will fight this war until the scale of history is turned, as it will be, in this very year. No power on earth shall weaken us. This Jewish-Bolshevik world destruction, together with its West European and American supporters, can be met with only one reply, the utmost of fanaticism, the most resolute of determination and the very last of our strength – all this we must throw into the scale in one final effort such as God in His mercy will grant to any human being who draws upon his final resources to save his life in the darkest hour.' And he reminded his hearers with the following, 'Party comrades – twenty-five years ago I pronounced the victory of the Movement. Today I prophesy, inspired by my belief in our people, that in the end Germany will win through.'

On February 26th, Oflag 4D, Elsterhorst, about sixty miles north-east of Colditz, was evacuated of its 5,000 French officer prisoners. They descended upon Colditz town and camp in a kind of barbarian horde. How they lived during the several days' march I did not find out. I had enough difficulty trying to fit 1,500 of them, as ordered, into Colditz Castle before even attempting to get something for them to eat.

They came like any other refugees, carrying their precious belongings on their back, pushing them in wheelbarrows, in perambulators, in home-made carts called 'chariots' – dragging small trolleys along behind them, through the frozen mud, laden, you might think, with the barest necessities ? Far from it! We collected two radio sets, and a nice collection of tools during our very cursory search at the Colditz gate, and I must say I admired the devotion to entomology of the officer whose collection of mounted moths and butterflies I allowed through. We quartered these unexpected and rather unwelcome guests wherever we had floor space in the castle – on heaps of loose straw all over the chapel floor and up in its galleries as well. The now overcrowded 'local inhabitants' we compressed into the smallest possible space in the Cellar House on the west side of their yard, and somehow we got the whole of the 1,500 extra prisoners under some roof and shelter.

To the general delight (ours included), a huge lorry-load of food arrived one evening – food parcels sent by the International Red Cross by road as the railway service had broken down. The Danish doctor in charge said he had come from Hamburg with his load and had orders to deliver it to the prisoners of Oflag 4C. We asked if the recently arrived prisoners from 4D were to share in this manna from Heaven? The Dane pondered a while and then fell back on the letter of his orders – the food was for the prisoners in 4C Colditz. The question of sharing this windfall with their French comrades was apparently hotly debated in the British quarters. In the end it was left to individual Messes to 'distribute' by invitation to the French such of their share of the food parcels as they wished.

After a couple of dreadful weeks with 2,000 near-starving men on our hands, 500 of the French were moved on further to Zeithain. Most of their kit went by lorry, this transport fleet being just a collection of wrecks which we scraped up and strung together for the occasion. They were driven by wood gas, and we had the greatest difficulty in even starting them up. We had to push them downhill and perhaps back up hill again if they missed their gears and didn't start the first time – and then downhill again once more to get them going. The prisoners suggested that they would get there just as fast if they towed these vehicles!

Food and fuel supplies decreased steadily during February. Offices and barracks were often no longer heated at all. In Colditz this was the case after March 1st. The baker supplied bread to the camp only when we provided the fuel for his ovens. Army rations went down again. Members of our own guard company frequently complained that they were always hungry. The prisoners made themselves, where possible, extra soup from potato peelings and swede trimmings scraped up sometimes from the floor of the kitchen.

Our Press took up the challenge of Yalta – 'worse than Wilson – worse than Versailles' – 'unconditional surrender means mass deportations, hunger and slavery'. They might be right – but so what?

Our deputy Kommandant took over command of an anti-tank unit 'on the East Front' for the protection of Dresden. He came to Colditz now and again to visit his family in the castle. 'Defeat?' he said, 'there is no question whatsoever of it.' Blindly confident he was to the end. Yet this front where he was now posted, which for so long had been hundreds and even thousands of kilometres away to the east, was now almost on our own doorstep.

At the beginning of March we had an evening of Skat with friends down in the town. There were seven evacuees from Silesia besides the nine people already living in the house. The sirens were on and off all evening – flares hung over Leipzig – we heard the planes, the crash of the bombs. 'How can we possibly win this war?' some of us asked openly. A woman among the refugees asked, 'Is that the best that you Army people can say at this moment?' We replied, 'Why should we dope ourselves any more with illusions?'

In the middle of the month another public 'day of rejoicing' came around again – Armed Forces Day. This time we did not allow the public to visit our 'escape museum' as they had done in previous years, nor did we serve up in the usual way to visitors 'pea soup and bacon' out of our field kitchen. Such luxuries were no longer to be had, and furthermore I doubt if we could have scraped up enough fuel other than by burning the chairs and tables, to light up the 'goulash Kanone' (kitchen artillery), even if the food had been available!

On this occasion was held the last ceremony, as we all knew it must be, for the garrison of the castle as a military unit. We had the usual speeches. The Kommandant gave one last *Sieg heil* for the Führer. We sang for the last time together '*Deutschland über alles*' and the Horst Wessel song. I think for everyone present on that occasion something had broken, were it a kind of religious belief for some, or just a hope for others. For some of us it was as though a shabby adversary had collapsed, his bubble of pride pricked for good and all, and we found no triumph in his fall. Some of us saw this adversary as a leader who had failed. Some perhaps saw this adversary in themselves. The fall of a leader could not fail to bring misery and suffering upon everyone, from his fanatical adherents, through his tolerant collaborators, to the neutral sceptics, and so on right on down to include even non-political soldiers and civilians. The extent of this ruin could not possibly be measured by anyone present at that last celebration in honour of the Wehrmacht, but we all were aware that the future was black and held nothing but disaster for each and every one of us.

Down in the town the Party again mustered a few faithfuls from its ranks and from loyal members of the boys' and girls' organisations.

Chaos on roads and railways affected everyone – but Party infiltration at all levels and denunciations by *spitzels* (stooges) kept the people quiet. To the very end the illusion of unity remained, as between Government and governed, though daily every individual could see and hear and feel the contrast between the facts around him and the assertions of our propaganda.

Our Foreign Office at this time opened its eyes a little wider than usual and began to peer into the future. It held, at last, that the moment might well have come to profit by possible contacts among the prisoners. Officials were sent down to sound the senior French and British officers in Colditz. Private conversations were held between them. I don't know if anything ever came of these meetings – it seemed a little late in the day to resort to rapprochement measures, however insignificant. The French general, Flavigny, indeed, with General Mesny's death still in his mind, refused even a formal meeting with the official to whom he was invited to speak. He was therefore sent back to Oflag 4A, Königstein, a few days afterwards – but (and I say it thankfully) arrived safely, contrary to the general expectation that he, too, would be announced by telegram as having been 'shot' on the way, 'while attempting to escape'.

One small incident to illustrate the chaos that was boiling up around us. One evening the Bürgermeister from a neighbouring village sent us a small party of all sorts – Russians, French, Yugoslavs, and two Negroes – who had belonged to working parties in what had become a forward area to the east. They had simply set off together towards the west like so many hundreds and thousands of others. Tired of wangling food, they had taken to stealing. The Bürgermeister had rounded them up at the point of a gun and passed them on to us as the nearest still-functioning military organisation.

I put these forty odd refugees, call them what you like, into a spare building we had at the back of the castle and got them such food as I could scrape together in our mess and kitchen. They literally fell on the stuff (a fair description) when my men brought it in, with the result that half of them got nothing at all. So I collected some bread and jam, one slice each, then showed them in at the point of my revolver, and doled out the food to them one by one. I could do that with forty men, but if the 2,000 others in the castle ever got to that stage I wondered if I would even try.

Government instructions on food rationing, poultry-keeping, rabbit-keeping, allotments and so on poured out daily. All were utterly impossible to follow and as was to be expected all ended with threats of heavy prison sentences or death.

I went home for Easter and had a lucky escape in an air raid. The bomb fell about twenty yards from my house while we were in the air-raid shelter. It was the afternoon of March 31st, Easter Saturday. I spent the rest of my leave resetting panes of glass or tacking up windows with cardboard in my own and my neighbours' houses. On April 4th I returned to Colditz.

## CHAPTER XVIII

## The Highlights Go

THE SMALL group of prisoners known as *Prominente* in Colditz grew that last winter of the war from three to twenty in number. We never discovered exactly who it was among Hitler's entourage who was looking for a likely swap in his own personal interests, should things ever fine down to the end of an unsuccessful war to the point of horse-trading in hostages. However, since it was in 1941 that the first *Prominente* was so graded, someone must have been looking a very long way ahead indeed.

In November 1944, the three *Prominente* Romilly, Alexander and Hopetoun, were joined by three more – Captain Earl Haig, Lieut Viscount Lascelles and Captain the Master of Elphinstone. It will be recalled that the majority of the 1940 prisoners were provided by the old 51st Highland Division from whose ranks most of our *Prominente* came. Shortly afterwards a Lieut de Hamel, who like Romilly was also related to Sir Winston Churchill, made things a little more uncomfortable in the now cramped *Prominente* quarters.

A last-minute shuffle through Debrett having failed to turn up any more really big social guns in our hands, Berlin played a long shot with the son of the American Ambassador in London, and Lieut John Winant got to Colditz a few days before his countrymen arrived to relieve the castle. He spent all his short time with us working out an arrest sentence in the cells. He was, of course, not present when the Americans arrived, having been removed with the other *Prominente* forty-eight hours earlier. We concluded that it was less the persons concerned than their important connections that made up their exchange value. What we should have really liked to discover was who was going to be offered for whom in the final Bunker in Berlin or the Southern Redoubt. Who, or how many, would be suggested in exchange for the Führer – for Himmler – and so on ? As things turned out no such bargain ever got into the Peace Treaty. For one thing there was no Peace Treaty, or indeed any terms of surrender. For another, the *Prominente* had left Colditz before the castle was relieved, and such was the confusion in South Germany that they eventually reached the American lines without hurt.

General Bór Komorowski and his staff were classed as *Prominente* for more obvious reasons, but having regard to the fate of that other group of Polish Staff officers who went to Moscow about this time and were held there by the Soviet in spite of Allied objections, I do not think the exchange value of our own Polish group would have been very high.

On April 11th a secret order came from Glauchau, now the seat of the Army Command Area, that on receipt of the code word '*Heidenroslein*', the *Prominente* were to be removed to Oflag 4A, Königstein, about fifty miles from Colditz. Two coaches were sent to us and made ready for the transport of the group. They were parked in the German yard, for all the prisoners to see and speculate upon.

The following day between 5 and 6 p.m., although telephonic communication was often broken, the code word came through, with details that the move was to be made within two hours of its receipt.

The Kommandant discussed this point with myself. He and I were the persons to suffer most if anything went wrong with this move. I suppose we could have ignored the instructions altogether. The Americans were in Halle, only fifty miles away to the west. We realised that if we went straight in and told the *Prominente* to pack up and be away in half an hour's time they would simply disappear into some hole, or disguise themselves as any others of the 2,000 British or French officers. In those circumstances we should never catch them at all, even inside the castle, without possible bloodshed. Two thousand men can be very obstructive, while tension by then was very high indeed.

It did not occur to anyone on our side to point out that if this were the sequence of events nobody could blame us in that case for failing to carry out this transfer. If we stuck to the 'two-hour' ruling, the operation could not but fail. And then what – a visit perhaps from an SS detachment? Shooting? The *Prominente* were too hot for us to hold. At all costs we must take this chance of getting them off our hands.

We therefore said nothing until after the last roll-call that evening. By 10 o'clock the yard was clear and all the prisoners were locked in their quarters or in the chapel. The *Prominente* had been locked in since 7.30 as usual, all but Captain the Earl of Hopetoun who was ill in the hospital ward.

Not until late in the evening, therefore, did we inform the *Prominente* and the SBO of the intended move. Lieut-Colonel Tod and Brigadier Davies requested to see the Kommandant immediately.

At this subsequent interview they demanded that the Kommandant ignore the order to move the *Prominente* since with the movement of the front there was no longer sure contact with Glauchau, where our next superiors were. He could claim the right to act independently in view of the altered, and hourly altering, situation.

It would be madness, they said, to send out two bus-loads of prisoners through an ever-narrowing corridor between American and Russian forces, exposing them to certain risk of death or injury at the hands of low-flying aircraft strafing the roads. The Kommandant replied that he would stick to his orders. In any case the journey was to be made at night.

'That's even more dangerous,' said the British. 'People will just snipe at suspected unauthorised transport before you have time to establish yourselves.'

But the Kommandant stuck to his orders and insisted that the move should and would take place by night, and that night. Then arose a further point. We had been forbidden to indicate the destination of the party, and the British in reply told us that the Kommandant and I (as Security Officer) would answer to the Allies with our heads should any of the *Prominente* be shot as hostages by any subsequent unit, even though they had by then passed out of our hands. The Kommandant replied they were being moved on orders to another prisoner-of-war camp further to the south of the approaching lines of the east-west advance. He added that Colditz was responsible for the move to this other camp, and the party would be accompanied by his deputy and by his Security Officer (myself). He further agreed that I should return to Colditz with a letter signed by the *Prominente* announcing their safe arrival at wherever it might be. The discussion ended.

As was to be expected, the amount of luggage the *Prominente* took with them was colossal. The Polish group had brought its own orderlies from Warsaw, and the British now demanded some of their own men. Eight officers, they said, were, under German military law, entitled to at least two orderlies. I agreed with this, and their Orderly Officer was instructed to find two other ranks. He climbed to the top floor of the British quarters in the Cellar House, where the orderlies, too, had been packed in on the arrival *en masse* of the French from Elsterhorst.

In due course he came down again to his side of the locked staircase door and I let out to my surprise two New Zealand troops, Maoris, who had volunteered to take this trip with their officers into the unknown.

About midnight the buses, laden to the roof with kit and containers, of all kinds, passed over the castle bridge and checked out of the Schloss *en route* for Dresden.

The leading driver knew the district and we made good time until we had a flat tyre. Thank God there was a spare. My head was a target from both sides in this affair, from my own and the Allies. If the *Prominente* escaped Hitler would get me and my family too. If the *Prominente* were killed, even accidentally, no one would believe me, nothing could probably ever be proved, and the Allies would finish me off as responsible for their deaths.

I prayed that Dresden might be spared further raids at least for that one night.

As we drove through in the early dawn the city looked a ghastly sight. Not many of the *Prominente*, except of course the Polish party, had seen a major city bombed and burnt out. I was past commenting. We all had one thought in our mind – to get to Königstein and out of the battle area. Most of the villages we passed were fortified to some extent with primitive tank traps. We argued our way through them, fortunately well supplied with genuine papers. On we went through Pirna and so, at 8 a.m., up we came to the plateau at Königstein which I had not seen since nearly three years previously, when I visited the camp after General Giraud's escape. The Kommandant at Königstein greeted us with the news of the death of the American President – Roosevelt. My mind flashed back to the death of Elizabeth of Russia, which saved Frederick the Great at the last minute during his almost disastrous struggles to establish Prussia against the Russians, Austrians and French in the eighteenth century. Was history going to repeat itself in our favour?

I handed over the party and all the papers and got a notice of safe arrival to be delivered back to the Senior British Officer in Colditz. The buses unfortunately could take us back only as far as Pirna before they went off on some other assignment. From there we got a train to Meissen, and there we stopped.

After several hours the local Commanding Officer ordered all military personnel at the station to fall in for the defence of the town. We were allowed through, however, on to the platform and into a departing train since our papers showed that our journey was taken on secret instructions of the OKW. The train took us as far as Tanndorf, and at about 1 a.m. after an hour's marching we got back to Colditz and reported the successful completion of the operation. We also handed over the 'safe arrival' chit to the Senior British Officer.

The next day the British put up a plan to get the *Prominente* back into Colditz from Königstein. We said this was quite impossible. We could hear artillery and tank fire to the west, and no village, we were quite certain, would now let anything through its tank traps. The plan was dropped, and the curtain, too, was soon to fall.

During Saturday, April 14th, the gunfire from the west slowly moved towards Colditz. We had had a visit a day or two before from the Commanding Officer of what was left of an infantry regiment in our immediate neighbourhood. If he had orders to make a stand at our river bridge he would need all the men and munitions that we could muster, and demanded to know what we had.

The Kommandant gave him the figures. We had 200 men between the ages of fifty and sixty-five, armed partly with German and partly with French rifles, with fifteen rounds of ammunition per head. We also had ten machine-guns of four different makes and calibres, with 3 000 rounds each. In addition we had a few hand-grenades. If our guard company went into action, it was a fair guess that the 2,000-odd officers and men, prisoners in the castle, would also join in somehow.

Would it not be best for us to neutralise this last threat, with our 200-strong guard company? The Hauptmann agreed. He insisted, however, that no white flags were to be raised on the castle, otherwise he would shoot the place up. Still in search of reinforcements he turned to the Partei Kreisleiter, who mustered his Volksturm Battalion. These had enough rifles for barely one in ten, plus a few bazookas. The Kreisleiter set up some sort of a barricade for the defence (?) of the town out of a few carts and rolls of barbed wire at the far end of the Mulde bridge, an idea no doubt from Napoleonic days, the last occasion when war had come to Colditz.

I saw no sign of any troop concentrations, artillery, HQ posts or supply units at all on our side of the river. The situation was obviously hopeless.

During the morning Generalkommando, Glauchau, late Generalkommando, Dresden, phoned through the code letters 'ZR'. This meant '*Zerstorung – Raümung*' (destroy – evacuate). All papers were to be burnt, all stores to be distributed or destroyed, our warning systems to be broken up, and so on. Furthermore, we were to evacuate the camp of all prisoners and move off 'to the east' using such transport as we still had at our own disposal, namely, one antique motor vehicle, barely working, and two horse-drawn carts.

The Kommandant passed these orders on to us and informed the SBO. Colonel Tod refused flatly to allow his officers to leave the Schloss. The Kommandant phoned this refusal back to Glauchau, at the same time saying that he did not intend to carry out the evacuation order by force. Glauchau insisted, but refused pointblank to accept the consequences of any such attempt to enforce its orders. The Kommandant declined responsibility. Glauchau eventually allowed the castle to be surrendered at discretion to the Americans when they should come. At the same time they insisted that the British Senior Officer accept responsibility for any injuries suffered in possible American shelling or bombing of the castle, since he had refused to take his men away when the opportunity was offered. Colonel Tod accepted these conditions, and Glauchau hung up on us for the last time.

We breathed quietly with relief. First of all we should never have got the prisoners out of the castle, and secondly no one relished the prospect, even if we had got them out, of trying to keep them together on a trek 'towards the east' in the path of the advancing Russians, then just the other side of Dresden.

My next job as Security Officer was to burn all papers. I took five men and stoked up the fires in the boiler-house and began to work. All offices in the camp then produced mountains upon mountains of paper – nearly five years' stock of what you call 'bumf', and the work began. Around about tea-time I went to see how things were going. Nothing was going. The men in fact had gone! and the furnace was out, too, stuffed solid with files. The boiler-room itself was piled half-way to the roof with masses of paper and cardboard. Have you ever tried burning files in quantity – or even just a few magazines ? I found some more men and started again. We got through the job by midnight.

Administration had the most colossal amount of paper – like all their kind the world over. But that was not all. They turned out secret hoards of things that we, clever enough at discovering prisoner's hides, had never even suspected in our own quarters – heaps of real leather soles, real coffee, real soap, sugar, and so on – things that we hadn't even seen for goodness knows how long. But there was no alcohol of any kind, I remember. We shared out the food. We gave a couple of carts to their drivers, but bicycles, blankets and other stores were left where they lay, instead of being distributed to the towns-people as might have been done.

My contribution to the funeral pyre in the boiler-house was also considerable. Secret, most secret, top secret – out came the files in dozens. 'Not to be passed on without an officer's receipt.' That was the note on top of the heaps of Japan paper with Hitler's speeches in miniature print from the Government stationery office. This was the stuff that we had to send out to our prisoners in other parts of the world, in operation 'Ekkehard'. I remember reading through one sheet before I consigned it to the flames, 'The Soviets will not take one square foot of East Prussian territory' – and here they were, twenty miles east of us in Saxony at that very moment.

On the afternoon of April 14th I handed over to the British all the 1,400 personal items of prisoners' property which we had in store, among them a golden cigarette case that had turned a bullet in the pocket of Brigadier Davies, before he came to us from the Balkans. Other items were fountain pens, and English bank notes. I was offered a general receipt but I refused it. I had had enough of paper and ink!

Each of us on the German staff had, as a prospective PW, his luggage ready. Luggage in this case meant just what one could carry in a small suitcase as entitled – innocents that we were!

All that now remained was to hand over the castle officially to the British. We kept the sentries posted for form's sake, as agreed, and stored all the arms and ammunition under lock and key.

Colonel Tod, General Davies, and Lieut-Colonel Duke (of the US Army) appeared in the Kommandantur for the surrender of the camp. The French played no part in this, which made things all the simpler, as we had to translate then only once, this time from the language of the other side into our own. The surrender document was signed, together with a safe-conduct for the staff. The British drew a line through the past, a line broken by two exceptions to be taken up later, or not, as the case might be: (a) the shooting into the British quarters in the spring of 1943 on the occasion of the Swiss visit, (b) the *Prominente*, if they should have been injured or killed since leaving us a few nights before.

Down in the Schützenhaus, the 500 French officers had taken over simultaneously with the departure of their guards.

There was another prison camp, of a kind, in Colditz, a concentration camp for Hungarian Jews, in the china works. They were in the charge of an SS unit, with whom we in the castle had had practically no contact at all, beyond a visit from the officer in charge when he first arrived.

The next day was a Sunday, bright enough with the breath of spring. In all Europe at that time, there was hope in the air – the war must end soon. For a Sunday it was quiet. I wondered what was wrong – of course, no church bells. Yet today, of all Sundays, there was surely more reason than ever to invoke the protection of the Almighty. Nature carried on, but men and women took cover, wondering who would die and whose house would be destroyed before nightfall.

The front windows of the Schloss were crowded with spectators from early dawn, both in the Allied and the German buildings. From there was a splendid view high across the town and clear to the woods two miles away at the top of the rising ground from the river below us. It was all open and slightly rolling country. The village of Hohnbach lay between Colditz and the forest. A few hollow tracks led out from both town and village and across the landscape in all directions, some of them lined with bushes or small trees. Generally speaking, there was very little cover apart from these tracks for the whole distance between the town and the horizon woods, except for folds in the ground.

Upstream from the town, the river ran between cliffs about sixty feet high. That way, on the other bank, was the china clay works, where a few machine-gun posts were established. The local Kreisleiter with his Home Guard was in the Hain-bach valley this side of the river with three 3-inch guns.

A little after 9 a.m. five American tanks came out of the woods to the west and advanced on Hohnbach. They set fire to a couple of houses without reply. One tank moved forward and then out of sight to the south. Suddenly a shell hit our guardroom close to the main gate. The castle made a good target, standing high on the skyline and dominating all the surrounding buildings and countryside. The American gunner lifted his sights and moved along the building. Crash! – he hit Wing Commander Bader's window, on the third floor of the Saalhaus, where it overlooked the German yard. No one killed yet. The room was empty.

The next shot skimmed the north-west corner of the castle, crashing over the pagoda and through the tree branches. Then a couple of high ones – one short and one over. He had us now!

As the lower walls of the Schloss were proof against 2-inch shells, the next thing was that a 6-inch howitzer came into action. All of us, prisoners (were they still prisoners?) and Germans descended from the upper floors. Broken fire from the howitzer continued throughout the morning, and one of our sergeants was killed near the bridge outside the castle. Two shots hit the Kommandantur building, but that was all the damage we suffered.

In the afternoon, finding little resistance from the town itself, the Americans shifted their attack north to the kaolin works and after some resistance got over the river by the railway bridge. An attempt was made by our own troops to destroy the town bridge over the river below the castle, but although over a dozen shots were fired at thirty yards' range with a bazooka, less than half the central support was destroyed. They tried to blow it later, but the charge was too small.

The Allied officers and men in the castle spent most of the time on the ground floor or in the cellars, where it was safer. If the Americans had set fire to the place, they were all going to move out down into the park below the eastern front, where they would find some shelter.*

During the night the Americans came round into the town from the north, working downstream against stiffer resistance, but by the morning of the 16th there was no further firing from our side. A mortar battery fired spasmodically in the direction of the town and over it, perhaps so that we should keep our heads down while the infantry filtered forward. White flags appeared from various windows in the town, and in due course one or two civilians went over the bridge and told the Americans that there were no more German troops about.

*Lieut. H. E. R. Wood, in *Détour*, writes that the US gunners were on the point of firing the Schloss when someone put a French flag up on the roof, which stopped them.—ED.

## CHAPTER XIX

# *Rôles Reversed*

A SERGEANT and three men crossed the bridge and soon established contact with the castle.

The German staff and men still present were then all formally down-graded to the status of prisoner-of-war.

Being the only English speaker among the German officers, I was marched back over the river to the American Command post where I reported from 'Officer PW Special Camp 4C – 1,500 Allied officers and men, all unhurt. Nominal roll herewith.'

They took me back again to the castle and we were all told to wait. I went aside a moment into one of the cellars to collect my 'luggage' and when I got back again, all our officers had disappeared, leaving their PW kits behind them on the grass. It appeared they had all been called for from over the river.

I set off to follow them on my own and then was stopped. I had not realised I was a prisoner and might not move about unless under guard. However, I then left the castle for the last time, with a British officer – and also without my small suitcase! N.B. – Memo. PW Rule 1. Never let your kit out of your hand or sight!

In the market-place there was quite a crowd of US troops. I was in the charge of a British officer, but in spite of that, the American troops all yelled to me, 'Stick 'em up' – and I thought it advisable to overlook the formalities of seniority and command and obey.

'That's right,' was the approving reply.

I remember seeing a hand microphone in action on a portable transmitter, something that we had never seen in the German Army at all.

Back for the second time at the Command post, I found all our officers standing in line in a lane at three paces interval, facing the hedge. I began to wonder if this was the well-known 'sticky end'.

They searched me and I lost a razor and two candles. I took my place at the end of the line.

After about half an hour standing and waiting, which as I now realised was to be the most marked feature, or the most unmarked feature, of prison life, we were marched off and placed under guard in a house nearby.

All the camp staff were here, prisoners of the Americans, except for Hauptmann Püpcke, Duty Officer, and our Officer Quartermaster busy scraping up food for his former charges but under their unsympathetic direction. These two had some astounding news when they joined us later at the US PW camp at Wellda. There had been radios in the camp after all! No less than two were in full blast in the yard during the few days before the ex-prisoners were moved. Over ten years later, I learnt from the book by Captain Reid (*The Colditz Story*) that in the upper attic over the chapel a glider had been built, in sections, for eventual launching if the castle had been attacked and surrounded. This, too, was on show during those last days, apparently.*

Several hours later we learnt that bodies had been found in the concentration camp down in the town where the Hungarians had been working, and they were trying to pin the shootings on us. This was an SS matter. They had had orders to leave, as we had, and had moved out with their prisoners 'to the east'. But some had refused to go and had been shot. Others hid, and so were released by the Americans. It was they who proved that we in the castle had no responsibility at all for this SS work, so for the time being we were reprieved. There was, however, still another matter the uncertainty of which was to dog us for a week or two yet.

*Although photographs were taken of this glider, it has not so far been possible to trace them, in spite of a lengthy and almost world-wide correspondence. Dr Eggers did not hear of this undertaking until his release from Torgau prison in East Germany in 1955. He has, however, since learned from an official of the town museum at Colditz that the townspeople had seen the glider. Its significance was not appreciated and eventually it was destroyed.—ED.

That evening, late on April 16th, 1945, the order came, 'Commandant and Security Officer outside.' We two were still being held responsible for the fate of the *Prominente*, whom I had escorted to the PW camp at Königstein. About a fortnight later, though, word did eventually come that all these officers were safe in American hands, but it was not until then that we lost our own 'special' status.

The curtain fell for me on Colditz. When it rose again the tables had been turned. It was I who was now a prisoner, but the play continued. Was it to be comedy? – was it to be tragedy?

# HIMMLER
## by Roger Manvell
## and Heinrich Fraenkel

Heinrich Himmler became the most hated and feared of
the Nazi leaders – for it was in his activities as head of
the S.S. that Nazism found its most complete expression.
Yet his character was strangely at variance with his
political role: he was unassuming, pedantic and dull.
How, then, could he have been responsible for the mass
murder of European Jews and the terrible cruelties which
accompanied it?

This is the essential contradiction that the authors
reconcile in their masterly biography. Drawing on
hitherto unpublished documents, interviews with his
family, friends, members of staff and the S.S. they show
how Himmler's intensely superstitious nature led him
to adopt many eccentric beliefs, culminating in the most
dangerous of all – the superiority of the Aryan peoples.

'Anyone who wishes to study the great German aberration
can have a field-day with Heinrich Himmler, the latest
book by two talented authors.'

**The Times**

**NEW ENGLISH LIBRARY**

# NEL BESTSELLERS

**Crime**

| | | | |
|---|---|---|---|
| T013 332 | CLOUDS OF WITNESS | *Dorothy L. Sayers* | 40p |
| T016 307 | THE UNPLEASANTNESS AT THE BELLONA CLUB | | |
| | | *Dorothy L. Sayers* | 40p |
| W003 011 | GAUDY NIGHT | *Dorothy L. Sayers* | 40p |
| T010 457 | THE NINE TAILORS | *Dorothy L. Sayers* | 35p |
| T012 484 | FIVE RED HERRINGS | *Dorothy L. Sayers* | 40p |
| T015 556 | MURDER MUST ADVERTISE | *Dorothy L. Sayers* | 40p |
| T014 398 | STRIDING FOLLY | *Dorothy L. Sayers* | 30p |

**Fiction**

| | | | |
|---|---|---|---|
| T013 944 | CRUSADER'S TOMB | *A. J. Cronin* | 60p |
| T013 936 | THE JUDAS TREE | *A. J. Cronin* | 50p |
| T015 386 | THE NORTHERN LIGHT | *A. J. Cronin* | 50p |
| T016 544 | THE CITADEL | *A. J. Cronin* | 75p |
| T016 919 | THE SPANISH GARDENER | *A. J. Cronin* | 40p |
| T014 088 | BISHOP IN CHECK | *Adam Hall* | 30p |
| T015 467 | PAWN IN JEOPARDY | *Adam Hall* | 30p |
| T015 130 | THE MONEY MAKER | *John J. McNamara Jr.* | 50p |
| T014 932 | YOU NICE BASTARD | *G. F. Newman* | 50p |
| T009 769 | THE HARRAD EXPERIMENT | *Robert H. Rimmer* | 40p |
| T012 522 | THURSDAY MY LOVE | *Robert H. Rimmer* | 40p |
| T013 820 | THE DREAM MERCHANTS | *Harold Robbins* | 75p |
| T018 105 | THE CARPETBAGGERS | *Harold Robbins* | 95p |
| T016 560 | WHERE LOVE HAS GONE | *Harold Robbins* | 75p |
| T013 707 | THE ADVENTURERS | *Harold Robbins* | 80p |
| T006 743 | THE INHERITORS | *Harold Robbins* | 60p |
| T009 467 | STILETTO | *Harold Robbins* | 30p |
| T015 289 | NEVER LEAVE ME | *Harold Robbins* | 40p |
| T016 579 | NEVER LOVE A STRANGER | *Harold Robbins* | 75p |
| T011 798 | A STONE FOR DANNY FISHER | *Harold Robbins* | 60p |
| T015 874 | 79 PARK AVENUE | *Harold Robbins* | 60p |
| T011 461 | THE BETSY | *Harold Robbins* | 75p |
| T010 201 | RICH MAN, POOR MAN | *Irwin Shaw* | 80p |
| T018 148 | THE PLOT | *Irving Wallace* | 90p |
| T009 718 | THE THREE SIRENS | *Irving Wallace* | 75p |
| T013 340 | SUMMER OF THE RED WOLF | *Morris West* | 50p |

**Historical**

| | | | |
|---|---|---|---|
| T013 731 | KNIGHT WITH ARMOUR | *Alfred Duggan* | 40p |
| T013 758 | THE LADY FOR RANSOM | *Alfred Duggan* | 40p |
| T015 297 | COUNT BOHEMOND | *Alfred Duggan* | 50p |
| T010 279 | MASK OF APOLLO | *Mary Renault* | 50p |
| T015 580 | THE CHARIOTEER | *Mary Renault* | 50p |
| T010 988 | BRIDE OF LIBERTY | *Frank Yerby* | 30p |
| T014 045 | TREASURE OF PLEASANT VALLEY | *Frank Yerby* | 35p |
| T015 602 | GILLIAN | *Frank Yerby* | 50p |

**Science Fiction**

| | | | |
|---|---|---|---|
| T014 576 | THE INTERPRETER | *Brian Aldiss* | 30p |
| T015 017 | EQUATOR | *Brian Aldiss* | 30p |
| T014 347 | SPACE RANGER | *Isaac Asimov* | 30p |
| T015 491 | PIRATES OF THE ASTEROIDS | *Isaac Asimov* | 30p |
| T016 951 | THUVIA MAID OF MARS | *Edgar Rice Burroughs* | 30p |
| T016 331 | THE CHESSMEN OF MARS | *Edgar Rice Burroughs* | 40p |

| T011 682 | ESCAPE ON VENUS | *Edgar Rice Burroughs* | 40p |
|---|---|---|---|
| T013 537 | WIZARD OF VENUS | *Edgar Rice Burroughs* | 30p |
| T009 696 | GLORY ROAD | *Robert Heinlein* | 40p |
| T010 856 | THE DAY AFTER TOMORROW | *Robert Heinlein* | 30p |
| T016 900 | STRANGER IN A STRANGE LAND | *Robert Heinlein* | 75p |
| T011 844 | DUNE | *Frank Herbert* | 75p |
| T012 298 | DUNE MESSIAH | *Frank Herbert* | 40p |
| T015 211 | THE GREEN BRAIN | *Frank Herbert* | 30p |

### War

| T013 367 | DEVIL'S GUARD | *Robert Elford* | 50p |
|---|---|---|---|
| T013 324 | THE GOOD SHEPHERD | *C. S. Forester* | 35p |
| T011 755 | TRAWLERS GO TO WAR | *Lund & Ludlam* | 40p |
| T015 505 | THE LAST VOYAGE OF GRAF SPEE | *Michael Powell* | 30p |
| T015 661 | JACKALS OF THE REICH | *Ronald Seth* | 30p |
| T012 263 | FLEET WITHOUT A FRIEND | *John Vader* | 30p |

### Western

| T016 994 | No. 1 EDGE – THE LONER | *George G. Gilman* | 30p |
|---|---|---|---|
| T016 986 | No. 2 EDGE – TEN THOUSAND DOLLARS AMERICAN | *George G. Gilman* | 30p |
| T017 613 | No. 3 EDGE – APACHE DEATH | *George G. Gilman* | 30p |
| T017 001 | No. 4 EDGE – KILLER'S BREED | *George G. Gilman* | 30p |
| T016 536 | No. 5 EDGE – BLOOD ON SILVER | *George G. Gilman* | 30p |
| T017 621 | No. 6 EDGE – THE BLUE, THE GREY AND THE RED | *George G. Gilman* | 30p |
| T014 479 | No. 7 EDGE – CALIFORNIA KILLING | *George G. Gilman* | 30p |
| T015 254 | No. 8 EDGE – SEVEN OUT OF HELL | *George G. Gilman* | 30p |
| T015 475 | No. 9 EDGE – BLOODY SUMMER | *George G. Gilman* | 30p |
| T015 769 | No. 10 EDGE – VENGEANCE IS BLACK | *George G. Gilman* | 30p |

### General

| T011 763 | SEX MANNERS FOR MEN | *Robert Chartham* | 30p |
|---|---|---|---|
| W002 531 | SEX MANNERS FOR ADVANCED LOVERS | *Robert Chartham* | 25p |
| W002 835 | SEX AND THE OVER FORTIES | *Robert Chartham* | 30p |
| T010 732 | THE SENSUOUS COUPLE | *Dr. 'C'* | 25p |

### Mad

| S004 708 | VIVA MAD! | 30p |
|---|---|---|
| S004 676 | MAD'S DON MARTIN COMES ON STRONG | 30p |
| S004 816 | MAD'S DAVE BERG LOOKS AT SICK WORLD | 30p |
| S005 078 | MADVERTISING | 30p |
| S004 987 | MAD SNAPPY ANSWERS TO STUPID QUESTIONS | 30p |

---

NEL P.O. BOX 11, FALMOUTH, TR10 9EN, CORNWALL
  Please send cheque or postal order. Allow 10p to cover postage and packing on one book plus 4p for each additional book.

Name ........................................................................................................

Address........................................................................................................

........................................................................................................

Title ........................................................................................................
(SEPTEMBER)